RETROSPECTIVE ADVENTURES

Retrospective Adventures

by

FORREST REID

FABER AND FABER LIMITED
24 Russell Square
London

First published in May Mcmxli
by Faber and Faber Limited
24 Russell Square London W.C.1
Printed in Great Britain
At the Bowering Press Plymouth

IN MEMORIAM

To S. J. Ireland (King's Liverpool Regiment)
Killed in Action, 12th October 1916

If I should tell you now, the day is breaking
Over these sad drenched fields beside the river
Where once you walked and planned your life and poetry—
Would you not hear me still, would you not come?

Or have you taken with you dream, and poetry—
That none will ever write, since it was yours—
Taken them down into that world of darkness
Where you lie now so quietly, at rest and alone?

All that you had you gave—your life, your youth,
Your youth's ambition—gave all ungrudgingly.
They have taken all, and left you dead, and heedless
Of what may be.

You lie there patiently, sharing a secret glory,
Far from these woods that knew you, these sad drenched
        fields, this sad grey river:
Unknown, unvisited, by a few remembered—
In your last deep sleep—in your cold earthy bed.

                                                        1916,

NOTE

Nine of the following pieces have been taken from a little book, *A Garden by the Sea*, long since out of print. *Minor Fiction in the 'Eighties* appeared in *The Eighteen-Eighties: essays by Fellows of the Royal Society of Literature; Persuasion* as an introduction to the novel of that name in the 'World's Classics' series. The rest are gathered from the files of various periodicals, and I wish to thank editors and publishers alike for permission to reprint them. All have been revised, and in several cases two or three articles have been re-fashioned into one.

F.R.

CONTENTS

11

CONTENTS

MISCELLANEOUS ESSAYS

TALES

BOOKS AND WRITERS

ANDREW LANG AND
LONGMAN'S MAGAZINE

Some time ago, when staying in a country house not far from London, I came upon a set of *Longman's Magazine*. The volumes, fresh and bright as if they had been issued only yesterday, half filled a bookcase on the landing just outside my bedroom door, and every night I turned the pages of one or two of them before going to sleep. It was not much more than a turning of the pages, the little reading I did was of the most desultory kind. Part of the charm lay in the awakening of old memories and associations, for *Longman's* still flourished in the days of my boyhood and youth, when I read it assiduously. Being methodical in such matters, I now worked my way through the entire lot, and never before had I realized how much this was Andrew Lang's magazine. Little wonder that before long he was bombarded with manuscripts intended for the editor—manuscripts which, it must be confessed, he received anything but gladly, for his was not a long-suffering nature. He expresses his annoyance again and again in those monthly causeries—his once famous and now sunken *Ships*—nevertheless, the manuscripts continued to arrive. As a matter of fact the journal during its whole life was edited by Charles J. Longman himself, though the influence of Lang, I think, is visible everywhere, and he was by far the most constant contributor.

15

The first number of *Longman's* appeared in November 1882. Its cover was of a drab green, its shape rather dumpy, and its price sixpence. It was not an illustrated magazine; it was a purely literary venture; and its appearance, aim, and standard remained unaltered till the end. I preferred it then, I still prefer it, to any of its more expensive rivals. Here are some of the contributors to the first volume—F. Anstey, Austin Dobson, J. A. Froude, Edmund Gosse, Thomas Hardy, W. D. Howells, Richard Jefferies, Andrew Lang, Mrs. Oliphant, and Robert Louis Stevenson. It is a goodly list, and in later volumes we find the work of Henry James, Bret Harte, W. H. Hudson, W. E. Norris, Baring-Gould, Margaret L. Woods, E. W. Hornung, 'Q', and Eden Phillpotts.

Everywhere there are indications of Lang's tastes both in literature and out of it. There are articles on fishing, articles on golf and cricket, the poems usually are by poets of his school, the serials by his favourite novelists—Stevenson, Clark Russell, Rider Haggard, Stanley Weyman, E. W. Hornung. Only the name of Rhoda Broughton is missing; but Rhoda clung staunchly to her own publisher, Bentley, and to his magazine, *Temple Bar*.

Yet undoubtedly, for many years, the chief attraction, the one that gave *Longman's* its individual tone, was Lang's monthly contribution, *At the Sign of the Ship*. Journalism these *Ships* were, of course, but it was journalism of an exceedingly rare kind. None of his English contemporaries could have supplied that particular blend of humour, irony, colloquialism and erudition, which was the secret of Lang's charm. True, his work never really reached, and still less was maintained at, the level of the newspaper work of Anatole France and Jules Lemaître. In comparison, it was careless and scrappy, while its content was far less rich. But in the beginning, before the constant strain of over-production made him jaded and indifferent, it came closer in spirit, and even in manner, to *La Vie Littéraire* and *Impressions de Théatre* than anything else. Its learning was as pleasing as its gaiety; he had not yet forced his talent nor begun to harp, for lack of more enticing subjects, on dreary trivialities of history and anthropology.

In the very first *Ship*, dated January 1886, he stated his intention:

> What men collect, what men debate,
>   What Bain has bought, or Christie sold,
> Whatever serves to illustrate
>   The Fashions of the Days of Old,
> How Cambridge pulled, how Oxford bowled,
>   Wild Lore of Races white or black,
> Of these shall many a tale be told
>   In this our Stall of Bric-à-brac!

Which means that he proposes to wander at leisure through the world that attracts him, pausing every now and again to gossip about his discoveries. It may be—and in fact is—a narrowly circumscribed world, with high walls built all round it to exclude everything distasteful, yet in his company it is still extremely pleasant to loiter there. The gossip has style, is irradiated by wit and tinged with poetry, while the touch is light as the winged seeds of dandelion clocks:

'*Water of Time for Passion of the Heart!*'

'It is a beautiful line, certainly. It reads as if it came out of Rossetti, or from a play of Webster's, or of Ford's. It means the draught of many years that lulls grief as surely almost, if not so swiftly, as those fabled Lethean streams where the souls *securos latices et longa oblivia potant*!

' "Water of Time for Passion of the Heart" is but the name of a recipe in an old cookery book: "*A Queen's Delight*, or the Art of Conserving and Candying. Printed by *T. Winter*, for *Nat. Brook*, at the Angel in Gresham College. 1668." The "Time" referred to is only thyme, and the water is a draught to cure a stitch.'

That is typical of the spirit in which Lang composed his divagations. He is playful and bookish; he appears to be improvising; yet there is a wealth of literary allusion and quotation, while the manner has a peculiar grace as he passes easily from angling stories to first editions, from Greek pastoral poetry to the latest thriller. Only we must be prepared for the fact that thrillers (including adventure stories) were nearly the only modern fictions for which he had much use. Rarely, indeed, were the right novels extolled in these *Ships*. Poems had a better chance, both because his taste in poetry was finer, and because his judgement was not here perverted by a determination to discourage realism at any cost. Yet if most of the tales he praised are now dead and forgotten, we can still read and be amused by his reviews of them. His method is seldom critical (or only indirectly so), but its freedom from solemnity, its romantic digressions, its irony and felicity of phrase, are wonderfully persuasive:

' "Where a man has received pleasure there should he show gratitude," says Tecmessa in the *Ajax*. I have received so much enjoyment from a little shilling story, *Kalee's Shrine*, that a small but friendly puff thereof seems the proper expression of a grateful nature.'

And the puffs that followed such airy introductions usually had the effect of selling an edition. Lang's influence was amazingly powerful, even though much of what he wrote was obviously dictated by whim and prejudice. But he never pretended to omniscience, never lectured his readers. What, most agreeably, he *did* imply was that the reader's taste probably resembled the reviewer's, since both were intelligent persons, and that it might be worth his while therefore to have a look at *Kalee's Shrine*, and not to bother about Tolstoy:

'I have not read Professor Boyesen's *The Great Realists and the Empty Story-Tellers*, but here is an inducement to study Tolstoy. After reading *Ivan Ilyitch*, Professor Boyesen (to the horror of academic circles) "actually began to develop the symptoms of the mysterious malady" of one of the characters.'

No doubt, at the time, to those who were practising the art of fiction seriously, this kind of thing must have been intensely irritating. All the more so because Lang could be flippant with impunity. He was never taken to task. It is difficult now to see why, but the fact remains that during his lifetime nobody except W. D. Howells ever ventured to cross swords with him; his gay dismissals of the later Hardy, the later Henry James, of all the Russians and most of the Frenchmen, passed unchallenged and unreproved. I fancy at thirteen my taste in fiction was precisely that of Andrew Lang. The strange thing is that with him it should have remained permanent, the still stranger thing that it should have been accompanied by a rare literary talent and a sensitiveness to poetic beauty. For the sensitiveness is there, is visible in his own work both in prose and verse. But for some reason realism annoyed him, and erotic emotion, except in the romances of his old friend Rhoda Broughton, seems to have moved him chiefly to laughter. There are moments when one feels tempted to say, with Max Beerbohm, that he could only 'enjoy masterpieces at a distance', and that the farther off they were the better: but it would not be the truth. He hailed *Huckleberry Finn* as a masterpiece —which it certainly is—and he was one of the first to appreciate the poetry of Robert Bridges, and, later, of Mr. Walter de la Mare.

Nor would it be true to say that he was a delightful writer about books but not about literature, that his interest was in bibliography and not in criticism. In spite of tiresome limitations, and the impish pleasure he derived from expressing and even exaggerating them, his critical essays on Theocritus, on Edgar Poe, on Gérard de Nerval, reveal an understanding and an imaginative sympathy as delicate as they are illuminating. Only he was afraid of unhappiness, afraid of any tragic spiritual or moral experience when that experience was brought too close to him, when it was not veiled by dreaming and romance. It was because he hated to be told that there is more misery than happiness in life that he wrote as he did of Hardy's later work. He knew perfectly well that *Tess* was a finer book than *King Solomon's Mines* or *A Gentleman of France*; but he would not admit it, its pessimism exasperated him. 'He does but give us of his best' is the faint praise he bestows—a remark that rankled for years before Hardy, in a second preface to the novel, recognized 'the infinite unimportance of both his say and mine'.

It seems odd, but we have the feeling that unless a book happened to be definitely his kind of book, Lang almost preferred it to be completely worthless. Then, if he was in the right mood, he would treat it with a playful good-humour, weaving into it or round it his own fancies, or simply using it as a sort of intellectual spring-board. To whom else, for instance, would the newspaper novels of Xavier de Montépin have suggested an appreciation of Apollonius Rhodius, and who else would have reviewed an artless tale in one of the Christmas numbers after this fashion?

'Mr. Pollock's idea is that someone, in a dream, invented a way of communicating with the people of Mars by means of signals reflected on to the disc of the moon. . . . How was the communication transferred to the pale face of the moon? Mr. Pollock does not tell us how it was done. But I have read in some strange old "volume of forgotten lore" that Pythagoras had a plan which would have done what was necessary. He said that whatever is written in bean juice on this earth reappears on the lunar disc. How long it must be since anyone tried this simple experiment, and wrote a sentence in bean juice! But who is the authority for the opinion of Pythagoras? I fear it is a no more contemporary author than the late Lord Lytton in *The Caxtons*. I can find nothing about this effect of bean juice in Plutarch's essay on *The Face of the Moon*. The ancient folklore of Beans is a most attractive topic to the antiquarian, because it seems wholly out of the question that we should ever understand what it was all about. Why should not Pythagoras let his pupils eat beans? Why had the Athenians a hero called Bean, or Bean-man? Why was it impious to attribute to Demeter, patroness of all other fruits, this discovery of the bean? Why might not beans be tasted by the initiated at the Elusinian mysteries?

'That beans, if hidden under manure, become human beings, is an assertion which Heraclides appears to attribute to Orpheus. This theory, of course, can be brought to the test of practical experiment. And why were beans thrown on tombs for "the salvation of men"? Why was not the Flamen Dialis, at Rome, permitted even so much as to name beans? Who can unriddle all this? It is clear, as Lobeck admits, that there is plenty of religion in beans.'

But when he definitely disliked his author, there was usually a scratch, a faint contempt, behind the banter. The publication of the famous *Journal* of the Goncourts, which created so much discussion elsewhere, was greeted in the *Ship*, not indeed with abuse, but, far more cruelly, with the story of The Mourning Lady in the omnibus:

'She told how she lost her first child; all the omnibus wept. The very conductor concealed his features in his handkerchief. The death of the second child renewed the emotion. Over the demise of the third the omnibus regained its calm. The fourth child was devoured by a crocodile, on the banks of the Nile. Here the whole omnibus laughed; yet that child suffered most.'

Such endearing tales enliven all the earlier *Ships*. They generally come in as illustrations of the subject he is writing about, but not always; now and then they are couched simply in the form of an inquiry:

'Can anybody supply the conclusion to the following scrap of exciting narrative? The writer was walking and being sad, when he met a gentleman with two ladies. As we passed each other, the gentleman said, obviously in the course of a narrative he was relating, "So a month later they went back to the Island, and they found the Doctor and the Slave both dead!"

'I cannot say how anxious I am to know more about the Doctor and the Slave. Who were, in the first place, "They"? Why had they left the Island? What Island did they leave? Why did they return to it? What were the Doctor and the Slave doing there? How came it that they were both dead? Were there any other people on the Island? The whole thing opens up such a charmingly wide field to conjecture. When did it all happen? It may have been in any time and place, from an Island of the Sporades, in Homeric Greece, to one of the Archipelagos at the back of Australia to-day. Probably we shall never learn any more about it; the graves of the Doctor and the Slave will remain unknown, like the grave of Arthur.'

Queries of this sort were as a rule taken seriously, and led to earnest correspondence. Occasionally there were indignant letters of expostulation. One such arrived from a lady —'and not from Scotland'—in righteous denunciation of 'a foolish article, which puts mischief into young people's heads'. The article was merely one of the lighter-hearted *Ships*, in the form of *A Treatise on Practical Jokes*. A sample will show its dangerous quality:

'The principle underlying the Common Hoax is of great antiquity. The joke lies in making a statement at once inconsistent with veracity, and calculated to produce terror or disappointment. The young humorist may practise this form of wit almost as soon as he has learned the use of language. Thus he may tell a younger brother or sister that:

'There is a lion in the garden.

'A giant is coming up the road.

'Either of these jokes may produce a great dread, and cause an infinity of pain, which is highly ridiculous, as there is no real ground for alarm.

'*Disappointment*.

'This may be simply and almost infallibly produced by the assertion that "There is a present waiting for you in the dining-room, Tommy!"

'1. There may be no present.

'2. It may be of an inexpensive and undesirable character, say half a brick, neatly wrapped up in brown paper.

'This also may be practised on older people. Take the case that Captain X is engaged to your sister Jane. You may observe, "Jane is in the parlour". When the Captain finds she is not there you may say, "Sold again!" Much point may be added by locking the parlour door on the outside and running away. When once the principle of this joke is mastered it will be found capable of endless modification.'

But it is the note of good talk, running all through them, which really makes these *Ships* such agreeable reading. It is the talk of a scholar, a collector, a bookman, a fisherman, and a lover of outdoor games. Lang may not have written quite so easily and rapidly as he appears to have done, but he possessed an extraordinary facility, and it was this gift which in the end betrayed him. He exploited it; wrote too much; wrote when he was feeling tired and dull; wrote when he had little to say; wrote unceasingly and everywhere. To this fatigue, this failure of material, the later *Ships*, alas, bear witness! As the years go by they become less brilliant, their charm diminishes, more and more space is given to the reports of missionaries upon primitive folklore, to narratives of prophetic dreams, to dull researches in the by-ways of Scottish history. For a brief period fresh life was obtained by the introduction of longer critical studies—an essay on *Robert Bridges*, an essay on *The New Humour* (which he invented), an essay on *Fiction*, wherein, apropos of love stories, occurs the chilling remark that 'with the flight of time a man's real interest is apt to betake itself in other directions, and an elderly novelist must write about the heart of youth with little more enthusiasm than about the tarts and toffee of boyhood'. It was an odd reflection to come from one who had never really outgrown a taste for still earlier tarts and toffee, but Lang was full of such petulant inconsistencies, such childish generalizations from the mood and prejudice of the moment. It sufficed that he himself had no ear for music, to make him propound the theory that a love for poetry is probably incompatible with an appreciation of 'the sister art'. How this can be reconciled with the fact that Milton, Shelley, and a host of other poets have directly expressed their love for music he does not try to explain.

To *Longman's* he remained constant while it lasted—that is to say, for twenty-three years. Then the end was reached. It was found to be impossible for a purely literary journal published at so low a price to compete with the rapidly increasing number of illustrated magazines, in which the pictures were at least half the attraction. 'Better to withdraw,' the editor writes in the last number, 'than to try to secure a new lease of life in a totally different character though under the old name.'

1938.

MASTER ROMNEY ROBINSON

O n the 23rd of April 1793 was born a poet whose name may now be forgotten, but whose genius for a brief period —say from 1801 till 1806—dazzled the literary world, or at all events that portion of it residing in the north of Ireland. One it continues to dazzle, and the *Juvenile Poems* of Master Romney Robinson, with 'a short account of the author by a Member of the Belfast Literary Society' is a book with which I would not willingly part. The 'short account' is particularly pleasing. Here we get the babblings of Romney's father, all well worth preserving; here we get the verses inspired by and written to the child; and here we get a list of subscribers to his *Poems*, which, though it is printed in double columns, fills twenty-seven pages. The date of the book is 1806, and it was published to enable Romney, then aged thirteen, to proceed to Trinity College, Dublin. Wildly optimistic as this scheme may appear, it nevertheless succeeded. The subscribers were numerous and enthusiastic. The Lord Lieutenant wanted sixty-three copies, the Lord Chief Justice forty-two. The Countess of Massareene was content with twenty-one, and the Bishop of Elphin with twenty; but Bishop Percy of Dromore (Percy of the *Reliques*) required forty, and his wife ten. What on earth did they do with them? It is not surprising that a second edition of the

Poems, this time issued from London, rapidly followed the first, which had been published in Belfast. Both, at any rate, are charming little volumes, and the most charming thing about them is the frontispiece—a portrait of Master Romney Robinson himself.

Now these portraits differ in the two editions, though clearly each is a sketch from the same larger picture by Robinson *père*. I prefer that of the first edition, which is a pen-and-ink drawing, also by old Robinson; the other is merely a steel engraving, but gives a more detailed and elaborate background. The poet is discovered seated under an oak-tree, and he is either looking for acorns, or listening to the song of a hidden bird. Or is it only a poem that is dropping to him from the clouds, for Romney wasn't a bit the kind of boy who would want acorns? Certainly, those delicate, pointed, rosetted slippers he is wearing will be ruined if he tries to climb the tree, to say nothing of his nice white trousers and cambric ruffles. In the first picture he has come out without his lyre or even a book of verses; but in the second he has remembered these things, and they lie there, for the moment neglected, on the grass at his feet.

The chief point to be noted is that the picture epitomizes the whole Romney Robinson myth. That myth, I am afraid, was the creation of a fond and foolish father, backed by a group of elderly sentimentalists. Not that I need talk, for a single glance at the poet convinces me that I too should have subscribed to his book. Poor child, his inspiration did not really descend to him from Heaven, as we see it descending in the picture. One virtue, at least, he can claim for his Muse, that she was completely and invariably 'on the spot'. You had but to suggest a subject and Romney produced his poem—produced it, moreover, in the twinkling of an eye.

Amazing the subjects that *were* suggested. Mr. Coulson of
Lisburn suggested a machine in his damask manufactory,
which happened to have attracted his young friend's attention. 'A very unpromising subject,' sniffs the Member of the
Belfast Literary Society, giving himself airs; but Romney
found it all right. There was no nonsense about Romney:
we can see him striking, perhaps, a preliminary thrum on
his lyre, but after that setting methodically to work. The
more I think of it, the more likeable I find Romney: he *looks*
nice, as I have already said; at any rate he looks, and was,
as different as possible from the morbid little wretch who
might have snubbed Mr. Coulson.

> Four rollers here of polish'd wood we view,
> Two different kinds, the sycamore and yew.
> Above, the screws, of iron made, are seen,
> And massy bars of metal come between;
> They seem to keep the rollers firm and tight,
> Which by continual friction have grown bright.
> Beneath, a horizontal wheel is found,
> Turned by a horse, then the machine goes round.

It does indeed; and what is significant about it is that these
lines are neither better nor worse than Romney's other
poems; I myself, in fact, prefer them to the more ambitious,
the more didactic and patriotic efforts. The same thing happens again and again. Mr. Ritchie takes the boy round the
shipyards, and Romney, with *The Triumph of Commerce*, becomes the first poet to celebrate the Belfast shipping indus-
try, thus anticipating Mr. Richard Rowley. This astonishing
child never stumbles, is never at a loss: the first poem we
have—written at the age of six, and to a Dr. Crawford, who
had cured him of a fever—is as mature as the last. Here is the
opening stanza:

Again on Fancy's wings I fly;
Again I strike the trembling lyre!
Thousands are born and thousands die,
Yet few can feel poetic fire.

Romney feels it, and after all it *is* amazing as the work of a child of six. Let us glance for just a moment at his school record:

Midsummer, 1803. (He was then aged ten.)

Latin.	Overtook a class in Virgil, from whom he
Roman History.	gained the premium.

Christmas, 1803.

Sacred History.

Civil History.	Examined in Homer, and was adjudged the
Greek.	first premium.

Latin.

Midsummer, 1804.

Sacred History.

Civil History.	Overtook the head class, and was ex-
Mythology.	amined with them in the whole of the
Logic.	entrance course of Trinity College,
Greek.	Dublin.

Latin.

Romney's intelligence is, in truth, as remarkable as the lack of intelligence displayed by everybody else mentioned in the *Short Account*. It was not his fault if from his first breath he was dedicated to Apollo and the Nine. Brought up in an atmosphere of wondering admiration, how could he help but be a little priggish? The child had only to glance at his portrait hanging on the wall to see himself decked out in all the trappings of a youthful bard. People old enough to know better addressed flattering verses to him; the word

29

'genius' was for ever sounding in his ears. Listen to the Member of the Belfast Literary Society:

'While yet in his nurse's arms there appeared to be something extraordinary in the tone of the infant's feelings. . . . When his son was about two years old, Mr. Robinson, having drawn two pictures from *The Hermit of Warkworth*, was in the habit of reading aloud some pathetic passages of that beautiful poem. The child used to listen with fixed attention, watch with anxiety the variations of expression in his father's countenance, and shed tears as he observed him affected. Mr. Robinson conceived the attention of the infant an indication of something extraordinary, and delighted to put it to the trial; so that the child would frequently sit with patience listening to *The Hermit of Warkworth*.'

'Six months without the option' I should think might meet Mr. Robinson's case. As for the luckless infant, we may judge of the number of these 'trials' from the fact that before he was three he was able to repeat whole passages of *The Hermit of Warkworth*. What *is* this *Hermit of Warkworth*, anyway? Who wrote it? And how bad is it? These are questions I do not propose personally to investigate. Concerning Romney's original work, 'it is not clearly recollected by Mr. Robinson what were the first poetical lispings of the child; several couplets and stanzas, however, composed by him in his fifth year, are extant'. I myself elsewhere have written a few spurious things for Romney, and even indulged in an imaginary portrait of him, which I can't help feeling is more likely to be true than that of the Idiot of the Belfast Literary Society.

From now on we see him beginning to make friends though never, alas! does another small boy appear upon the scene. His friends are the 'elegant and ingenious "Hafiz

(T. Stott, Esq., of Dromore)', with whom he exchanged
verses; Mr. Cunningham of Dromore House; Bishop Percy;
Dr. Crawford; Mr. Ritchie; Mr. Hayley; the Reverend
Drummond; Dr. Anderson of Edinburgh; and the eccentric
Earl of Massereene, whom he visited at Antrim Castle.

'Lord Massereene made an agreement with him, that at
whatever time either should die, the survivor should write
an elegy on the death of the deceased. This melancholy duty
Romney performed for his lordship not long after.'

Served his lordship right, is my own comment; and if the
same fate had befallen every member of that asinine crew
they would have got little more than their deserts. Even
when he was sent to school at the Belfast Academy, we hear
nothing of Romney's finding companions of his own age. It
is Dr. Bruce, the headmaster, who is the 'friend of young
genius', and to whom he addresses the very last of his
poems, written at the advanced age of nearly thirteen:

> To thee the pleasing, anxious task's assign'd
> To form by just degrees the youthful mind;
> To ope the valued hoards of classic lore,
> Young taste investing with the golden store;
> To clip exub'rant Fancy's soaring wing,
> And from Imprudence bid Experience spring.
>
> Oft have I marked a youth by sloth enchain'd,
> O'er whom dark Ignorance despotic reigned,
> Feel, by thy guardian care, the genial ray
> Beam o'er his sightless mind the living day.

One thing I should like to know, and that is whether
Romney ever showed his verses to his schoolmates. I don't
think so: he was no fool; and 'youths of sightless mind' have
their own unpleasant methods of criticism. A few years

later he himself tried to suppress his book, and, I imagine, by that time was no longer quite so keen on the Belfast Literary Society. Certainly, though he lived to be eighty-nine, he never wrote another poem.

After so marvellous a dawn his subsequent career may seem slightly commonplace. Nevertheless, it was distinguished. He was elected to a fellowship in Trinity College, Dublin; he became Deputy-Professor of Natural Philosophy; he received the College living of Enniskillen; he was appointed Astronomer of Armagh Observatory. To think that I myself might actually 'have seen him plain', and, with luck, even have received a pat on the head from him, for he survived until 1882! But by that time Romney Robinson, the poet, had long been forgotten—and particularly by the Reverend Thomas Romney Robinson, D.D.

1924.

EMILY BRONTË

Shall earth no more inspire thee,
Thou lonely dreamer now?

I

It is, I confess, with a somewhat guilty feeling that I write
the name Brontë at the head of this essay. How often, I wonder, has it been written before? Even Anne, the gentle and
not very exciting Anne, has had a fate which none but
Enoch Soames could envy. The lonely parsonage at Haworth, the slightly macabre drama enacted there, the novels,
the poems, the three strangely different personalities (five,
if we count in the father and the brother), all that there
was to say about them must surely long ago have been
said.

Only, of Emily, perhaps, this will never be quite true.
Her work is so enduringly fresh that each succeeding generation will approach it as it approaches the living world of
Nature, finding in it the same eternal re-birth, the same
mysterious power to draw forth a new wonder and a new
delight. To the story of her life nothing, indeed, is likely to
be added. It was uneventful, except in a spiritual sense; and
the spiritual adventure she herself has recounted in her
writings—in her poems and fragments of poems, and in her
great tragic novel, *Wuthering Heights*. She died at the age of
thirty, her genius ignored or misinterpreted, for Charlotte's
introduction to *Wuthering Heights* reads very oddly to-day.

It is apologetic and explanatory, clearly prompted by the tenderest loyalty; but at the same time it misses everything or nearly everything that matters.

Yet Charlotte defended Emily to the best of her ability, and perhaps can scarcely be blamed for not recognizing that *Wuthering Heights* stands farther above her own novels than *Villette* does above *Agnes Grey*, or *The Tenant of Wildfell Hall*. Her attitude was natural, considering the peculiar accidents of circumstance. She had become famous—spectacularly famous—*Jane Eyre* had been an immense success, and her later novels had increased her reputation, while *Wuthering Heights* had been so complete a failure that it is questionable if any copies were sold except to a few circulating libraries. Such reviews as it got described it as crude, unpleasant, brutal, an immature experiment in Charlotte's own manner; and even now, when it is almost universally praised, I cannot help doubting if its genuine lovers are many. Its strangeness, of course, must impress the least sensitive reader, but a recognition of its beauty is another matter. That beauty is so pagan, so rugged and so wild, despite an element of homeliness in it, that it may easily bewilder or repel rather than charm. And then, *Wuthering Heights* stands on a different plane from all other novels.

To begin with, it is a work of direct and passionate inspiration. There is beauty of phrase, but no sustained, outstanding beauty of style, while most of its admirers will tell you that it is the worst-constructed story in the world. I do not share this opinion, though I think it very likely that its author gave little thought to the problem of construction. The drama was there before her, or, rather, within her, and she wrote it, like all amateurs, simply in the way that came easiest. She was, indeed, so thoroughly in possession

34

of it that she could have begun anywhere; and actually she began at the end.

The story, therefore, like some of Conrad's tales, moves back upon itself, advances, stands still, comes forward with a rush, while the indirect method is employed throughout. But the unity of atmosphere is unbroken. We get the impression, not that the imaginary narrator is building up a carefully symmetrical structure, but that he is absorbed, possessed, by something which has actually happened—something which, for the relief of his own mind, he must tell.

It is this intensely individual and intimate quality that brings the book so close to us. Nor is there, to me at all events, anything amiss with that introductory episode (invariably objected to nevertheless) in which Mr. Lockwood accepts Heathcliff's hospitality for the night. On the contrary, this so-called 'technical blunder' seems to me a felicity. For in it the peculiar note of the tale is sounded clearly and unmistakably, the atmosphere is prepared, the action definitely set on a supernatural or spiritual plane. It is the prelude that prepares us for those later scenes which are haunted by the ghost of Catherine Earnshaw; it foreshadows the ending, when that strange restless phantom, crying in the cry of every gust of wind that moans about the old gaunt house, waxes stronger and stronger, till at last it breaks through the thin, worn barrier of Heathcliff's bodily senses, and lures him to his doom.

Instinctive, unconscious art it may be; but none the less surely great art—great poetry at all events! Not that I wish to claim for the book any miraculous perfection of execution. There are passages in the earlier dialogue—Heathcliff's description to Nelly Dean of the Linton's house, for instance —that draw us up sharply by their impossibility. No boy ever talked in that quasi-literary fashion; least of all, a boy like Heathcliff. But where there is this wealth and power, this tremendous imaginative conviction, this glow of life, even such lapses as these matter little, are felt, only on the turn of the page to be forgotten.

The beauty of *Wuthering Heights* is created by sheer intensity of feeling, by a fire of the creative imagination that sets all ablaze in its own flaming ecstasy. Actually it is a naked book, without ornament. It contains no elaborate descriptions of nature, none of that detailed noting of the colour and mood of a landscape which we find in the work of Thomas Hardy. A line suffices; and it is by a magic of suggestion that the moorland scenery is kept so constantly before us—in rain and storm, in sunshine and frost and snow. For we never appear to be reading of these things; certainly they are never insisted on. On the other hand, the two chief characters are more perfectly in harmony with, more closely woven into, their surroundings than any characters in any tale by Hardy. They are themselves a part of a great pagan hymn to earth; their lives, their minds, their passions, have been moulded by the winds that sweep across the bleak dark moors; we cannot even imagine them in another setting.

This, perhaps, is what gives the book its grandeur. The scene is part of the drama, and through drama and scene we get the sense of immense spiritual forces in conflict. If the tale is gloomy—in places terrible—its gloom is never exaggerated, never morbid. A fantastic humour shines through the darkness; while even a note of tenderness and gaiety is sounded towards the close, in the love story of Hareton and the younger Catherine.

II

Perhaps I am too much inclined to regard *Wuthering Heights* as a personal confession. There are no personal reflections in it, no views, no moralizings. But a single passage will show what I mean. Catherine is describing her dream of heaven to Nelly Dean, who is shocked, and tries to interrupt her. The impetuous Cathy will not be silenced. 'This is nothing,' she cries; 'I was going to say that heaven did not seem to be my home; and I broke my heart with weeping to come back to earth; and the angels were so angry that they flung me out into the middle of the heath on the top of Wuthering Heights; where I woke sobbing for joy.'

Now this speech is entirely in character, but it would be equally so if we found it in one of Emily's own letters: it is Emily's spirit that permeates the whole book. The plot is invented; but both plot and characters are the expression of a desire that could find no outlet in life, and therefore found one in fiction. Behind the story, prompting it, was an ever-present longing, which I think had haunted Emily Brontë from childhood. Cathy *is* Emily, if not the whole of Emily, and Heathcliff, I am convinced, is a wish-fulfilment. The mystic has said that it is through his passions a man reaches God, and certainly a purer, more spiritual passion burns in *Wuthering Heights* than in any other novel I have read. Indeed, one of the virtues of the book is that it is written wholly out of Emily's own experience, contains nothing that she cannot, so to speak, vouch for personally. And since she knew little of physical love except what she must have heard and read about it, there is no physical love in the tale. Heathcliff, whatever deeds he may do, whatever

37

words may be put into his mouth, remains clean as fire; and the story of his life, despite those deeds and words, has a strange and beautiful innocence.

For of course it *is* more Heathcliff's story than Catherine's. It is the story of his love for Catherine, in which the desire of the flesh has no place, so that it remains unaltered by her death. The union of the body means nothing (as poor Isabella Linton discovers), the union of the spirit is all. That union we may take as at last accomplished when Nelly Dean finds Heathcliff in the narrow, panelled bed by the open window, with the rain washing over him.

'His eyes met mine so keen and fierce, I started; and then he seemed to smile. I could not think him dead; but his face and throat were washed with rain; the bedclothes dripped, and he was perfectly still. The lattice, flapping to and fro, had grazed one hand that rested on the sill; no blood trickled from the broken skin, and when I put my fingers to it, I could doubt no more: he was dead and stark.

'I hasped the window; I combed his black long hair from his forehead; I tried to close his eyes: to extinguish, if possible, that frightful, life-like gaze of exultation before anyone else beheld it. They would not shut: they seemed to sneer at my attempts: and his parted lips and sharp white teeth sneered too!'

If Emily Brontë was not a conscious artist, her vision was so clear, her possession of her subject so complete, that she achieved again and again that perfection through economy which is the conscious artist's aim. Consider the account of Heathcliff's last days. It is briefly, even sparsely, told, yet no elaboration could have added to it. It is at this point, too, that for the first time the full secret of the book is revealed, and the warning of the prelude justified. 'She has disturbed me, night and day,' cries Heathcliff, 'through eighteen years—incessantly—remorselessly—till yester-night; and yester-night I was tranquil. I dreamt I was sleeping the last sleep by that sleeper, with my heart stopped and my cheek frozen against hers.'

Nor is it left just there. Near the end a hint is dropped that even this last sleep is troubled. Nelly Dean, while professing scepticism, more than half believes in the 'idle tales' that she cannot resist repeating to Mr. Lockwood:

'Idle tales, you'll say, and so say I. Yet that old man by the kitchen fire affirms he has seen two on 'em, looking out of his chamber window, on every rainy night since his death: and an odd thing happened to me about a month ago. I was going to the Grange one evening—a dark evening, threatening thunder—and just at the turn of the Heights I encountered a little boy with a sheep and two lambs before him; he was crying terribly; and I supposed the lambs were skittish, and would not be guided.

' "What's the matter, my little man?" I asked.

' "There's Heathcliff and a woman, yonder, under t' nab," he blubbered, "un' I darnut pass 'em."

'I saw nothing; but neither the sheep nor he would go on; so I bid him take the road lower down.'

'There's Heathcliff and a woman, yonder, under t' nab.' How exactly right the rough words are!—the touch of genius, the touch of the master-hand.

III

I have no doubt at all that Emily Brontë loved Heathcliff very much as Catherine loved him. Not blindly, recognizing what was evil in him, but recognizing, too, an essential nobility, and accepting him for what he was, because, through all his evil-doing, he never became an exile from the spiritual world, never quite lost his divine birthright. He might be devilish in his revenge, his soul might be warped and marred, but he was, in his fierce loyalty, the symbol of faithfulness and strength. Probably his darker qualities made his single-hearted devotion all the more attractive: they naturally would. And at any rate, according to Emily's doctrine, death at once and for ever wipes out the stains and sins of life: the soul returns, in the end, 'divine, to the Divinity'.

> I know our souls are all divine,
>   I know that when we die
> What seems the vilest, even like thine
> A part of God himself shall shine
>   In perfect purity.

Much of Emily Brontë's faith is contained in those simple lines, so strangely thin when compared with her prose. And I believe that had she lived to create other heroes, she would not have been able to avoid giving them most of Heathcliff's qualities, however modified—and inevitably weakened—by happier impulses, a happier fate. Had she not already written of his childhood (an early, yet recognizable sketch) in the lovely and characteristic poem called *The Two Children*?

> Heavy hangs the rain-drop
>   From the burdened spray;
> Heavy broods the damp mist
>   On uplands far away.

EMILY BRONTË

Heavy looms the dull sky,
   Heavy rolls the sea;
And heavy throbs that young heart
   Beneath that lonely tree.

Never has a blue streak
   Cleft the clouds since morn;
Never has his grim fate
   Smiled since he was born.

Frowning on the infant,
   Shadowing childhood's joy,
Guardian-angel knows not
   That melancholy boy.

Day is passing swiftly
   Its sad and sombre prime;
Boyhood sad is merging
   In sadder manhood's time.

All the flowers are praying
   For sun before they close,
And he prays too—unconscious—
   That sunless human rose.

Blossom—that the west-wind
   Has never wooed to blow,
Scentless are thy petals
   Thy dew is cold as snow!

Soul—where kindred kindness
   No early promise woke,
Barren is thy beauty,
   As weed upon a rock.

Wither—soul and blossom!
You both were vainly given:
Earth reserves no blessing
For the unblest of heaven!

Yes—a wish-fulfilment, I am convinced: a dream play-
mate, a dream love. And with Emily to love at all was to
love for ever. She loved Haworth and its moors. Like
Cathy's, her feelings were as deeply rooted in her native soil
as were the ancient thorn-trees that grew around her home
—so deeply rooted that when in a foreign country she
comes upon a little scanty patch of brown heath, it awakens
in her a passion of homesickness that is the passion of the
lover for his beloved.

It is improbable, I think, that even had she lived on
through middle-age, and gained a wider experience of life,
her work would have altered much. The poems, which are
scattered over a period of many years, reveal nothing of
value that is not in *Wuthering Heights*, and there is little in
Wuthering Heights that may not be found, in germ at least,
in the poems. Her mind was deep, but I should imagine not
particularly acquisitive. Her genius was lyrical—intensive
rather than extensive. She died, very likely believing that
the failure of her novel was final; at all events no fragments
were found after her death to show that she had contem-
plated a second.

But such speculations, though tempting, remain speculations. I think it likely that in *Wuthering Heights* she said all,
or nearly all, she desired to say—in prose at least. If this be
so, I don't think she would have continued to write, would
ever have become, like Charlotte, a professional author.
And I think still less that in actuality she would have found
her 'sunless human rose'. In actuality there was her brother

Branwell and—more fortunately—the bulldogs. Throughout the poems we find plenty of stoicism, an occasional moment of mystical rapture, but hardly a gleam of the natural happiness of youth. She was buried 'beneath the church-aisle stone', and even this burial-place somehow seems to me inappropriate, for what had she to do with churches? One would have liked to picture her as lying under her beloved turf-sods, with the open sky above her grave, just as she saw her own Catherine and Edgar and Heathcliff lying, in the peaceful, exquisite close of *Wuthering Heights*.

'I sought, and soon discovered, the three headstones on the slope next the moor; the middle one grey, and half buried in heath; Edgar Linton's only harmonized by the turf and moss creeping up its foot; Heathcliff's still bare.

'I lingered round them, under that benign sky; watched the moths fluttering among the heath and harebells, listened to the soft wind breathing through the grass, and wondered how anyone could ever imagine unquiet slumbers for the sleepers in that quiet earth.'

1920.

MINOR FICTION
IN THE EIGHTEEN-EIGHTIES

Having promised to write a paper[1] on the minor fiction of the eighteen-eighties, I foresee that my task may prove difficult. I do not wish to concentrate on the scene and the conditions, because in that case I should merely be reproducing in less lively colour the pictures already so brilliantly painted of the 'seventies. The 'seventies and 'eighties practically form a single period; the scene and conditions undergo no striking change prior to the 'nineties; therefore I think my best plan will be to choose certain representative authors and through them try to give as comprehensive a view as may be of a very heterogeneous mass of material.

It is an artless method, but considering the extent of the ground to be covered I can think of no better. To put it mildly, a great many novelists were busy in the 'eighties, so busy that with not a few of them two novels a year appears to have been the normal rate of production, and it is to be remembered that two novels then meant five volumes, more often six. True, I have read a considerable number of these books, but most of them I read long ago, so that they are now but the veriest phantoms, floating in a mist of associations real

[1] Originally published in *The Eighteen-Eighties*: essays by Fellows of The Royal Society of Literature. (Cambridge: The University Press. 1930.)

44

or imaginary, the season and the place—summer or winter, river or seashore or chimney corner—often emerging in far more vivid detail than the author and his work. I do not know why I should find it easier to remember where and when I read this or that book than to remember (beyond a mere general sense of tone and a few detached scenes and characters) its contents, but so it is.

I was brought up in a house full of novels, most of them belonging to the 'seventies and 'eighties, and in my teens I read with an appetite not easily sated. Moreover, I read honestly, that is to say not merely with the eye, but sounding each syllable. I never skipped a word, for instance, of those lengthy descriptions of sunsets provided so liberally and methodically by William Black. Unlike the descriptions of Victor Hugo and Thomas Hardy, between which I found a mysterious affinity (the description in *Far from the Madding Crowd* of the rain washing away the flowers from Fanny Robin's grave still strikes me as pure Hugo), they have left no impression on my mind except that they were rhetorical flourishes. And I fancy this is true, that they really had nothing to do with the story, but were stuck in at regular intervals to pad it out. I never skipped a word of the moralizings provided by novelists with a 'purpose', or a 'problem'; though there was less virtue here, 'problem novels' possessing for me at that time an odd fascination.

It was in 1883 that Olive Schreiner, with *The Story of an African Farm*, produced what must have been among the very earliest of these. I mean of the more modern variety, the 'hill-top' variety as it came to be called, for of course there had been the experiments of Charles Reade and Wilkie Collins. But it was *The Story of an African Farm* which paved the way for the *Yellow Asters*, *David Grieves*, and *Heavenly Twins* of the 'nineties. Miss Schreiner, if she stood a little apart from the band of feminine novelists associated with the New Woman, nevertheless practically invented her. The Woman's Rights novel, the Religious Doubts novel, the Sex novel—seeds of all these were wafted from her farm in Africa to produce a variegated crop of fictions bearing such disconsolate or provocative titles as *A Sunless Heart*, *A Superfluous Woman*, *The Woman Who Did*—works widely discussed at the time, though it would be difficult by any effort of imagination to reanimate them to-day. The interest they excited was violent and brief. They annoyed Andrew Lang; they gained the sympathy if not the admiration of Thomas Hardy; they left Henry James and the small æsthetic camp indifferent. And of them all, *The African Farm* alone to some extent survives, because of the strong emotion behind it. When I say 'survives', I mean survives in the memory of the older generation, for it is not a book to be re-read. If we have read it and cared for it in the days of our youth, it will be wiser to leave it at that. Even in the 'eighties its appeal must have been mainly to youthful readers, with whom the generosity of its spirit would outweigh crudities of form and characterization. To myself the book appealed profoundly, and in an ancient copy lying on the table before me quite a jungle of marked passages remains to show me where I was moved, if not, alas! to show me why. My favourite chapter must have been that containing the allegory of the Hunter and Truth, since this is pencilled from beginning to end, while Lyndall's dissertations on the rights and wrongs of women get not a single mark. I must confess I still prefer the allegory to the dissertations, though what chiefly strikes me now about all these marked passages is that so few of them have any connection with the story. As I view them at present, they are a series of technical errors, expressing merely the author's views, reflections, and aspirations, which apparently had the dubious merit of coinciding with my own. Yet I can see, too, that they would not have been so effective had I simply encountered them in a book of essays or sermons. This in fairness must be granted to Miss Schreiner: her story created the state of mind most likely to prove receptive to her 'message'. The book was not conceived as a work of art, but there was inspiration in it, and a tremendous sincerity. It was an indictment, a sermon, a confession of faith, an appeal for justice, anything you like except a work of art; and as it stands it is an odd mixture of caricature and reality. The caricature may be involuntary, since it is completely devoid of humour; but Bonaparte Blenkins, the villain, is not a real man (he bears, in fact, though sadly degenerated, a distinct resemblance to Mr. Punch), Waldo—my own dear Waldo—is not a real boy, and Lyndall, I am afraid, though she was the author's darling, is not a real girl. What *is* real is Olive Schreiner, and where she identifies herself with her characters the fundamental feelings ring true. The humanity of the book is unmistakable. The author packed between its covers everything she had to say: she was not afraid to let herself go, not afraid to gush; it was all infinitely more personal, infinitely more confidential, than most autobiographies.

I think it was George Meredith who read and accepted the manuscript for Messrs. Chapman & Hall. In this he displayed considerably more commercial acumen than James Payn had shown when he turned down *John Inglesant*, for both books were enormously successful. *The African Farm*, however, unlike *John Inglesant*, reflected the new spirit which had begun to manifest itself among more serious novelists, but which so far had received scant encouragement from their critics. It was before everything a book of revolt, a demand for freedom, though all Olive Schreiner herself was interested in

was the social question. In other quarters the revolt was
based on æsthetic grounds. The novelist felt himself to be
hampered: there were certain subjects he wished to treat,
but was only allowed to treat dishonestly, if at all. There
arose a clamour for what a character in one of Henry James's
stories calls 'the larger latitude'. The ironic little tale in question, *The Death of the Lion*, was perhaps rather cruel, since it
must have been difficult not to associate Guy Walsingham,
the imaginary author of *Obsessions*, with a lady who, also writing under a masculine pseudonym, had attracted a good deal
of attention just then. Both *Keynotes* and *Discords*, though I
have read neither, I suspect to be experiments in 'the larger
latitude'—which phrase, I need scarcely add, means latitude
to write with greater frankness of the relations of the sexes.
It was bitterly opposed—among the most acrimonious of the
opposers being several of our novelists themselves, notably
Mrs. Oliphant, who attacked the later tales of Thomas
Hardy with a virulence that now leaves us gaping. Everybody has heard of the storm created by the publication of
Tess and *Jude*, but much earlier than this, the love scenes in
Two on a Tower had been censured as unpleasantly suggestive,
while *The Return of the Native*—*The Return of the Native* of all
books—had been described in the columns of the *Athenaeum*
as 'betraying the influence' of decadent French fiction (*Madame Bovary*). Earlier still, and still more amazingly, even
Wilkie Collins, with *The Law and the Lady*, had contrived to
offend the innocents. There would be little point in reviving
these ineptitudes were they not the outward and visible
signs of a widespread inward and spiritual prudery. An edi-
torial note which appeared in the *Graphic* of the 30th of
January 1875 reveals the remarkable state of mind that had
been created by this attitude of moral vigilance.

'In last week's instalment of *The Law and the Lady* the

following paragraph, which occurs on page 83, column 2, was printed thus: "He caught my hand in his and covered it with kisses. In the indignation of the moment I cried out for help." In the author's proof the passage stood as follows: "He caught my hand in his, and devoured it with kisses. His lips burnt me like fire. He twisted himself suddenly in the chair, and wound his arm round my waist. In the terror and indignation of the moment, vainly struggling with him, I cried out for help." The editor of this journal suppressed a portion of the paragraph on the ground that the description as originally given was objectionable. Mr. Wilkie Collins having since informed us, through his legal advisers, that, according to the terms of his agreement with the proprietors of the *Graphic*, his proofs are to be published *verbatim* from his MS., the passage in question is here given in its original form.'

One up to Wilkie! we may too hastily think; but this was not to be the last word. The crafty editor perfectly foresaw *his* opportunity, and sure enough, when *The Law and the Lady* had run its course as a serial and was issued in the customary three volumes, the *Graphic*, beneath the title of the work, instead of a review printed an apology to its readers for having offered them a tale the true and undesirable nature of which had only been discovered after its first chapters were in print. Possibly the apology was sincere (one never knows); possibly moral feelings really were wounded; in any case it was inevitable that a point of view so narrow, so *stupid*, should lead to a reaction, and in the 'eighties the backward —or forward— swing of the pendulum had already begun. Quite apart from *The African Farm* and its defence of the 'New Morality', the early novels of George Moore and George Gissing were experiments in naturalism. True, in the case of Gissing there was to be no tampering with the proprieties, and even the naturalism remained far from un-qualified. But George Moore showed a less conciliatory spirit, and in his very first story, *A Modern Lover*, published in the same year as Miss Schreiner's book (1883), through the mouth of Harding the novelist he produced his mani-festo. 'We do not always choose what you call unpleasant subjects, but we try to go to the roots of things; and the basis of life, being material and not spiritual, the analyst inevit-ably finds himself, sooner or later, handling what this senti-mental age calls coarse.'

Gissing, I think, never handled what any age, however sentimental, could call coarse, but he had a passion for the sordid (founded on dislike), and even when this was not inherent in his theme, a kind of flatness in his style produced a drab and dispiriting effect. His reputation has been kept alive more by the fact that his books are still sought after by collectors than by any particular charm or merit they possess. Behind them is neither a lyrical nor a dramatic im-pulse, and we cannot help suspecting that their monoton-ously despondent tone is at least to some extent due to the author's own low vitality. If he never wrote a cheap or an insincere passage, on the other hand, in all those novels of lower middle-class life I cannot recall a beautiful one. And the explanation lies deeper than the choice of subject. In the slum scenes of *The Princess Casamassima* Henry James used material quite as sordid, but there was joy in the making of the book, and a genius that infused its darkest pages with the spirit of life and beauty. To the composition of his novels Gissing brought the knowledge of an earnest and intelligent student of social conditions, but he was not a genuinely creative writer, not what we call a born novelist, and he never really learned the technique of the naturalism he tried to emulate.

'She proceeded to eat a supper scarcely less substantial than that which had appeased her brother's appetite. Start not, dear reader; Alice is only a subordinate heroine.'

'Oh, the gravity of conviction in a white-souled English girl of eighteen! Do you not hear her say these words?'

Alas! it is just such tiresome little apostrophes that prevent us from hearing her. It seems to me extraordinary, in fact, that Gissing's desire to write a realistic novel should have carried him no further than it did, that his experiments should have stopped short with the matter, leaving the manner to look after itself. There were models with which he must have been acquainted. Whether one approved of the subject or not, surely it was plain that the method of *Madame Bovary* had a good deal to do with the sense of reality it produced, and whether one liked that method or not, surely it proved the advantage of possessing *a* method. But whatever other changes were taking place, whatever other activities were astir, except in the work of Henry James and George Moore the technique of fiction in the 'eighties remained unaltered. The author's annoying comments continued to come crashing through the illusion like stones through a sheet of glass. And sometimes these 'asides', these confidences, extended for pages. Only too frequently, indeed, they were there for no other reason than that they did extend for pages, and so helped to fill out the compulsory three volumes. Lengthy discussions (dialogue only by courtesy) fulfilled a similar purpose. Any convention is a drawback, but the three-volume convention was a disaster. Most of the novels of the 'eighties are too long. Even where he does not quite shamelessly resort to padding, we see the author deliberately slackening his pace because he must not reach the end too soon. And the faults we find in the lesser writers are present also in the works of the masters. If there is less genius in the novel of to-day, I think we may at least claim that there is a more scientific technique, and a more faithful reproduction of natural speech. Let me give, in relation to the latter point, an example of what I mean. One of the chief merits of the novels of Rhoda Broughton is the vivacity of the dialogue, but re-read a page of that dialogue, merely changing 'Have not I?' and 'Do not you?' to 'Haven't I?' and 'Don't you?' and note the result: the actual sound of the voices immediately begins to reach us. After making due allowance for the modifications in our speech that time probably has brought about, I think it will hardly be denied that in the modern novel the writing *is* more flexible than it was in the 'eighties, that the novel itself contains less surplusage, that it does, in short, show an advance in craftsmanship. True, the question instantly suggests itself—Does the average novel either of the 'eighties *or* the nineteen-thirties matter? And if not, what is the position? In the 'eighties Henry James, Hardy, Meredith, and Stevenson were all writing, while from America came at least one masterpiece, *Huckleberry Finn*.

The 'eighties are sufficiently removed to enable us to obtain a kind of Pisgah view of them. Looking back across the intervening stretch of half a century we *can*, for our present purpose, see our novels and novelists divided into groups or schools—the realistic, the romantic, the pastoral. But when we come to consider the more outstanding works with an idea of seeking relationships with the past or future our time-scheme presents an oddly broken line. Thus, though it is not fanciful, perhaps, to point to a relationship between W. H. Mallock's *New Republic*, published in 1877, and Mr. Aldous Huxley's *Crome Yellow*, published in 1921, what have we in between? Casting back from *The New Republic* we reach

Headlong Hall and *Nightmare Abbey*, which constitute, I suppose, the fountain-head. Again, Baring-Gould's *Mehalah* has nothing in common with the rural tales of Thomas Hardy, but a great deal in common with *Wuthering Heights*. *John Inglesant* may have derived something from *Esmond*, but the historical romances of Stanley Weyman, 'Q', and Conan Doyle owe far more to the tales of Dumas than to *The Cloister and the Hearth*, while one of the most brilliant books of our decade, Richard Garnett's *Twilight of the Gods*, takes us straight back to *Vathek*. As for the modern mystery story, what has it in common with *The Moonstone* or *No Name*? while still less is it comparable with the tales of the Irish novelist Sheridan Le Fanu, whose work at its best (though only at its best) has a streak of genius running through it, hovers on the edge of a rather dreadful kind of poetry.

Probably the most popular novels of the late 'eighties and early 'nineties were the romances. I do not include *John Inglesant* among them, because, though it was popular and a romance, it was essentially a spiritual confession, a novel of ideas, very nearly as much so as *Marius the Epicurean*, and spirituality is hardly the distinguishing quality of *King Solomon's Mines*, *Dead Man's Rock*, *A Gentleman of France*, or *The White Company*. It was, I venture to say, Andrew Lang who to a large extent created the vogue of the romantic school. For Lang could make a reputation, or at any rate sell an edition, in a way no reviewer can to-day. And he loved these books—loved them so well that they seem to have had the power to blunt his critical faculty, which could be fastidious enough in other directions. The actual writing did not appear to matter so long as there were plenty of fights and adventures. Of course it must have mattered really, but he could close his ears to the most slipshod style if the story was of the kind he fancied. I remember reading a novel called *Bail Up!* dedicated to Lang 'by special permission', which struck me even at the age of fourteen as a little crude. The comic passages—as is usually the case—were particularly excruciating, and Lang, whose own gaiety was so charming, must have loathed them. Still, he *would* have these books, and nobody dared to contradict him. His prestige, his learning, his wit and his irony were too formidable: in the heyday of his influence not a voice was raised in revolt, and even timid disagreements were larded with compliments. He could be generous when it pleased him. He wrote charmingly of Rhoda Broughton, with a graceful, half-affectionate playfulness, which conveyed at the same time a perfect appreciation of her talent. Yet (and it might be in the same article) he would ridicule a tale by Tolstoy without having troubled to read it. He described *Esther Waters* as the unfortunate production of an Irishman without a sense of humour, and dismissed Hardy's *Tess* in tones of magnanimity that must have been infuriating. He infuriated Henry James, though he had praised *Washington Square*, and done Miss Annie P., or Daisy Miller the honour of bringing her into his delightful book of epistolary parodies, *Old Friends*. But it was the early James that Lang liked, the James who, largely on the strength of *Daisy Miller*, actually for a few years achieved popularity. If he disapproved of the subject of a book or the point of view of a writer, no sincerity, no subtlety of treatment could win his praise, while if the subject were to his taste he could tolerate almost any treatment. On the other hand, when both subject *and* form pleased him—then, even in the case of such exotic writers as Poe and Gérard de Nerval, he became the most sensitive and sympathetic of critics. But he was whimsical, Puckish, sometimes not without a hint of cruelty in his wit, and his taste in fiction remained to the end the taste of a schoolboy who is good at games.

Whether we attribute it to 'freakishness', or to an odd insensibility, with the solitary exception of Stevenson, the more important novelists of his generation had very little for which to thank Lang. Even his appreciation of Rhoda Broughton's work we cannot help suspecting to be, in part at least, due to friendship. Elsewhere he shows not the slightest sympathy with her kind of novel. His treatment of it is to play with it like a cat with a mouse, giving delicate but painful taps at the style, plot, and characters, before the final pounce that finishes it off. But for Rhoda Broughton he reserved another method. Miss Broughton did not, in conversation at all events, take her novels very seriously, and this in itself would appeal to Lang. That she must have taken them seriously in one sense, however, that of being profoundly moved by what she was writing at the *time* of writing, is obvious. The emotion behind them must have been genuine since it still lives. She founded her own school and carried it on through the 'seventies and 'eighties—the school that is, for me at least, permanently associated with Bentley's Favourite Novels, fat dark-green books, the contents of which had usually first been serialized in *Temple Bar*. I once planned to read them all, and I think must have come pretty near to succeeding. In the Bentley tradition, after *Not Wisely but too Well* and *Cometh Up as a Flower*, Rhoda had it very much her own way till the late 'eighties, when Miss Corelli was admitted to the fold, and promptly upset everything, capturing the public by the irresistible baits of melodrama, and an occultism that smacked of the Egyptian Hall.

With *Belinda*, published in 1883 (evidently my *annus mirabilis*), Rhoda Broughton, I think, reached the highest point of her attainment. She had been writing then for seventeen years, and without losing any of her early power had acquired more restraint. The love scenes in *Belinda* have all the old zest, but it is now under firmer control, and her wit and humour are more abundantly in evidence here than in any other of the tales. The interest of *Belinda*, as indeed of all the novels of her first period, is frankly and exclusively erotic; but the passion does come through; there are no young women in fiction more genuinely in love than Rhoda Broughton's. What they experience, I admit, is largely an infatuation of the senses, and only a physical infatuation, I suppose, could work the physical havoc which brings more than one of these heroines to an early grave. The heroes are of tougher fibre; *they* survive all right—superb animals, glorious in strength if ugly of feature. This worship of brawn no doubt is carried to a point where to the weakling it may become just the least bit trying. The male whose interests are intellectual is so exclusively used as a foil to some Herculean numskull. We see him wrapped in overcoats and mufflers, an umbrella tucked under his arm, and galoshes on his large flat feet. There is something ruthless in the way the physical infirmities of Belinda's husband, Professor Forth, are kept before us. They acquire in the end almost a moral quality, become a part of the general despicableness of his character—its meanness, selfishness, joylessness, and narrow-mindedness. For not only is the intellectual male usually depicted as unsound in wind and limb, but he is also denied any compensating graciousness of manner, and, above all, his loves are feeble as his muscles. Not for him splendid, reckless passions, and it is by the capacity for experiencing an overwhelming passion that man in these novels is judged. True, in the tales of her second period, Rhoda worked gradually away from this point of view (her sense of humour was so strong that this was inevitable once the emotional impulse had begun to die down), but in the earlier, and to my mind distinctly better novels, the hero, whatever the hue of his moral character, whether he have the black reputation of Colonel Stamer (in *Not Wisely but too Well*), or the innocent record of 'a non-reading, hard-rowing, foot-balling, cricketing' youth like David Rivers, Belinda's lover —the hero, whatever his moral virtues or vices may be, *must* be endowed with two transcendent physical qualities, a superb body, and a capacity for fierce and devouring passion.

Rhoda Broughton's outspokenness concerning such things, if perfectly comprehensible, is none the less unusual—was unusual, that is to say, at the time when she wrote. We can imagine the effect certain of her love scenes must have produced on readers of the 'eighties, accustomed to heroines of an angelic modesty and decorum. The books were read and adored, but they were also banned and banished as being 'coarse and unmaidenly'. They were not actually wicked— wickedness was reserved for Ouida, and naturally there were no 'brown, painted harlots' in Miss Broughton's pic-tures of county society; but she was all the more dangerous because her characters were human. 'I began my career as Zola,' she remarked in her old age to Mr. Percy Lubbock. 'I finish it as Miss Yonge. It's not I that have changed, it's my fellow-countrymen.'

Her outstanding qualities were energy, humour, and a generous emotional sincerity. She had little sense of style, and her habit of writing in the historic present (which she abandoned, I think, only after the publication of *Alas!* in 1890) is not without its inconveniences. Nevertheless, her books had the warmth of life in them, and their popularity is not surprising. Moreover, considering the narrow range of subject, the variety we find in these, for the most part tragic, love dramas is remarkable. It arises from the fact that the love motive is felt so intensely that fresh incidents and situations have never to be sought for, but spring up spontaneously in the writer's imagination. Nothing quite like these novels had been done before, though only too much was done afterwards, one of the most popular imitations, *Comin' thro' the Rye*, on its first anonymous appearance actually having been attributed to Rhoda. The irrepressible F. C. Burnand parodied her in *Punch*, and this burlesque novel—*Gone Wrong*, by Miss Rhody Dendron—later appeared in book form, with a cover design by Linley Sambourne. To *Punch*, also, Du Maurier contributed portraits of 'splendid ugly men'. But these were jests of honour, tributes to her success, the novels are not in the least absurd, and the reader to-day, should he return to them, will laugh and be sad in the right places.

A searching comment on her own early fictions she herself supplied when an old woman (she died in 1920). Such, at any rate, I take her last story, *A Fool in Her Folly*, to be. In this posthumous tale it seems to me she deliberately showed the other side of the medal. Surely there have crept some memories of the past into her half-satiric, half-sympathetic portrait of Charlotte. It is just such a novel as *Not Wisely but too Well* that Charlotte, in her enthusiastic innocence, has produced, and the manuscript of which so shocks her parents that they burn it and she has to write it all over again from memory. *Love* is the title of Charlotte's work; a volcanic love her theme; her hero a dark, passion-scarred man. This hero, when half-way through the second version of her novel, Charlotte meets in the flesh. But note the difference in Miss Broughton's new presentment of the type. Bill Drinkwater is Colonel Stamer of *Not Wisely but too Well* reduced to reality. His failings are no longer veiled in a romantic glamour, but particularized. He was expelled from Eton, a similar result followed when he was sent to an Army tutor in Yorkshire, and his later career has been marked by a trail of unsavoury episodes. Upon Charlotte, however, the true significance of these vulgar little affairs is quite lost. She is as blind to it as was the youthful Rhoda herself. She bathes her lover in the transforming light of imagination— and through his passion for *her*, sees him achieving redemption. Alas, this time the black sheep is really black: so far from ennobling him by her affection, poor Charlotte, having kept a tryst with him at a lonely shanty on the downs, narrowly escapes a much worse misfortune than the disillusionment in which her grand passion ends. The Miss Broughton who wrote this book is certainly not the Miss Broughton who wrote *Joan*, *Nancy*, and *Red as a Rose is She*.

Yet 'Rhoda', says Mr. Percy Lubbock, 'to the end of her life, wore an air of the eighteen-seventies; myself I have seen her, a generation later, with a trailing gown and a parasol and a croquet-mallet, contriving to wield all three at once with effect' (an impossibility, I'm afraid, since to wield a croquet-mallet, even *in*effectively, requires two hands); 'and though it was difficult to think that she was the creator of her gushing Joans and Nancies and Belindas, she evidently came to us from their time and place; and if she hadn't written her novels she had lived in them, in that high-coloured England of big houses and big meals and big families.' Certainly, the big houses and big meals and big families form part of the charm of the novels. The very appearance of these works, with their delightful steel-engraved frontispieces, carries us back to a more leisurely, mellower age. Myself, as Mr. Lubbock would say, I can recall it, or the aftermath of it—not dimly, but brokenly—in such isolated pictures as impress themselves, usually quite inexplicably, on a child's mind. For that age died slowly, and more slowly, I dare say, in Ireland than in England. There are no crinolines in my pictures (nor for that matter in Rhoda's), but there are crinolettes and parasols and spotted veils and small toque-like hats and lengthy if not trailing gowns—all, in my memory, still inextricably bound up with earliest visions of feminine loveliness; and it was thus that Miss Broughton's heroines were apparelled. I confess I admire them, and regret the world they lived in. If I could, I would sweep away nearly every invention of the intervening years—motor-cars, aeroplanes, wireless, movies, talkies, and gramophones. Most of these are intrusions on privacy, on the liberty of individual choice, since, if they are to exist at all, everybody must put up with them. I have an affection also for big houses, and anybody who has been brought up in one must know that big families are the best. Miss Broughton's is the 'county' world, and I like that too. Probably there are London scenes in her books, but I do not remember them; for me the novels have a countrified and familiar aspect, over which I would gladly linger. But if I am to cover my ground I must pass to other books and other scenes, and the London scene will do as well as any—sophisticated, worldly, amusing—as we find it in the strangely underestimated work of W. E. Norris.

The career of Norris began thirteen years later than that of Rhoda Broughton; he was really of our decade, his first novel, *Mademoiselle de Mersac*, having been published in 1880, after running as a serial in the *Cornhill*, where it was illustrated by George Du Maurier. There were no novels by Norris in our house, and I have forgotten how I procured *Miss Shafto*, *A Bachelor's Blunder*, *Major and Minor*, *Thirlby Hall*, and the rest. But I know *why* I procured them. It was because they were in Bentley's list: never can a publisher have inspired greater faith. Here there can be no doubt about origins: whatever value we may set on the achievement it is plain that Norris got his idea of the novel from Thackeray. His fiction is the fiction of a man of the world, well-bred, detached, not taking himself or his work overseriously (one of the causes of his undoing), deploring any emphatic display of emotion, amused, at times mildly cynical, but always kindly. He tells a story, of course, but it is as little startling as he can make it, and there is only just enough *of* it to hold together an easygoing comedy of manners. Norris does not always end his fable with a wedding, but tragedy is as little in his line as mystery or melodrama. What he chiefly relies on, and what is the main source of our enjoyment, is his lightness of touch, which is particularly happy in the drawing of those idle, clever, young good-for-nothings, who constitute by far the most amusing portraits in his gallery. We cannot call them villains, still less can we call them heroes, these young gentlemen of expensive tastes and slender if any means, whose engaging imperturbability and deplorable morals enliven the pages of Norris's best novels, and who, we cannot help suspecting, were regarded by their creator with considerable affection. They live by their wits and on their friends—sometimes, alas! their friends of the opposite sex. Moreover, they are utterly selfish; their intelligence, their wit, and their graces of person and manner being employed solely to gain their own ends. In spite of this, the charm they exercise upon long-suffering relatives is completely convincing, for the simple reason that we feel it ourselves. They have a playful, ironic humour which passes easily into insolence when nothing is to be gained by politeness. On the other hand, they never indulge in self-pity, never whine when misfortune overtakes them, never, above all, lose their composure, even in the most trying circumstances. They take risks and abide by their luck. They are not in the end allowed to triumph, but when detected and exposed they have a delightful gift of leaving the virtuous both looking and feeling extremely foolish. Philip, in *No New Thing*, whose fortunes we follow from early boyhood till his marriage with Signora Tommasini, the great operatic contralto, —fat, *passée*, good-natured, nearly old enough to be his grandmother, but with heaps of money—is an excellent example of what Norris could do in this line. His career may be little more edifying than that of George Moore's 'modern lover', but then he is so much more tolerable as a man, and so infinitely more amusing as a companion. We *feel* his attractiveness, whereas we have to accept Lewis Seymour's on the author's word, since it depends, apparently, entirely on his good looks.

Unfortunately, Norris wrote with an always dangerous, and eventually disastrous, facility. The gift was there, but he exploited it, and though he never lost his grace of manner, the earlier liveliness failed under the strain of over-production, and his lack of imagination became more and more evident as his material ran out. The later novels are frankly pot-boilers, composed mechanically to a formula, the fable scarcely varying from tale to tale. *The Rogue, Matrimony, Adrian Vidal, No New Thing*—he wrote, I dare say, a score of novels as good or nearly as good as these, and perhaps another score that do not fall immeasurably below them; but the few I have mentioned contain everything that will be found in the rest. Yet I have a feeling that the best books of Norris may, like those of Trollope, one day be revived. I have re-read them myself quite recently with undiminished pleasure, for, thanks to the purity of his style, they have not dated in the least. They are, I suppose, what used to be called 'society novels', and, though there are rural scenes, deal with a world where titles are plentiful and even a bachelor cannot live comfortably under two or three thousand a year. For the more familiar picture of English middle-class life we may turn to F. Anstey's two serious novels, *The Giant's Robe* and *The Pariah*.

Or rather to one of them, for, though *The Giant's Robe* has some delightful humour and a tragic and exciting plot, it is of the later book I really wish to speak, tragic and enthralling also, but with a tragedy more subtle and a plot less in evidence. Anstey himself was far too modest about his writings. If I may be pardoned for introducing a personal note, he was aware that I collected his books and it pleased him, nevertheless he maintained that nobody else read anything of his except *Vice Versâ*. In a letter now before me he says:

'I was going to write to you in any case, but somebody sent me your *Mercury* article yesterday and I wanted to thank you—as I do now—for your extraordinarily kind and generous mention of my work, and particularly of *The Pariah*.

'As you imply, that unfortunate book had no luck. On the day of its publication there was a long notice in *The Times*, with scarcely a good word in the whole of it.

'It, *The Pariah*, was immensely long, dull, with no character or incident—a suggestion in it of Miss Charlotte Yonge (this I'm afraid I thought a little unkind). Finally, I was recommended to give up attempting to write third-rate fiction (another nasty one) and go back to the light work by which I was best known.

'As a rule, I suppose, even an unfavourable long notice in *The Times* acts as an advertisement of a book, but I doubt whether this one did *The Pariah* any good.

63

'I found that a few of my friends, and those whose opinion I valued, thought well of the book. The majority of the reading public gave it a miss. I think there was a cheap edition, but the book—like, for that matter, most of my performances—has been long out of print. Two or three of them still survive and still sell about a hundred copies a year between them. There is no demand for mid-Victorian humour nowadays. Bright young people have their own humorists, and, I don't mind owning, jolly good ones—I want no better myself than Wodehouse, for example.

'I am glad *you* have Burnand's copy of *The Pariah*. I remember going to see him shortly after I had sent it. He was then living at the Boltons and just recovering from an illness. Arthur à Beckett was in F.C.B.'s bedroom and the latter staged a little scene for my reception.

'When I came in I found Arthur reading aloud *The Pariah* to F.C.B. who was slumbering peacefully.

'However, as a matter of fact, he liked the book a good deal better than I expected.

'The writing of it—off and on—took me about three years, and though it held me, was a great strain.

'So, though unfavourable criticism has now depressed me for long, I was not at all sorry to have an excuse for returning to work which was more congenial.

'*The Brass Bottle* had some success. I dare say it sold about ten thousand copies—but none in America, where one critic informed me that a much cheerier fellow than I had written the same story centuries ago in *The Arabian Nights*. As you say in your article, the success of *Vice Versâ* has always handicapped the stories that followed it. I tried various veins to avoid comparisons—and that only disappointed the Public more. They liked to know what they were getting—and they never did, so they left off getting.

'Still, I enjoyed whatever I wrote and it was a good time while it lasted, so I don't complain.

'Again with heartiest thanks and kindest regards,

'Yours most sincerely,

'ANSTEY GUTHRIE.'

Thus the malicious critic has power to wound. *The Pariah* is not third-rate; it is an admirable novel, standing far above the average fiction of both its day and ours, far too good to be forgotten. The portrait of Allen Chadwick, the loutish, undersized, uneducated, uncomely, cockney youth, who wakes up one day to find himself a rich man's son, is a delicate and beautiful study, to some extent anticipating that of Kipps. But all the circumstances of the story are different, and Allen's temperament is both less adaptable and more sensitive. Transplanted into an environment where he is disliked and looked down upon; blundering, shy, by no means clever—the innate kindness and generosity of his nature are belied at every turn by his unfortunate speech, manner, and appearance. Hectored and bullied by a coarse-grained father who desires to make a gentleman of him while not understanding very clearly what a gentleman is, and to this end has married an aristocratic but impecunious widow who (with an eye to the advancement of her own brood) is careful, beneath a veil of apparent sympathy, to keep her stepson's shortcomings well to the fore; despised and disliked by his stepbrothers and sisters, Allen in the end is turned adrift, the cuckoo tactics succeed, the pariah is eliminated. The tragedy is quiet, with from the first a kind of hopelessness in it; and for all its pathos there is never a hint of sentimentality. I do not know that the novel attracted any particular attention. It was not what was expected, and therefore probably aroused disappointment.

E

Anstey had the bad luck to write in his first story a book which was ever afterwards to be associated with his name, so that no matter what new ground he broke up, to the public he remained and still remains the author of *Vice Versâ*. I can think of no other explanation for the neglect of his later books. After all, *Tourmalin's Time Cheques* is quite as original and very nearly as amusing as *Vice Versâ*. So are *Under the Rose*, *The Travelling Companions*, and all that series of stories in scene and dialogue beginning with *Voces Populi* and ending with *Lyre and Lancet*.

With the exceptions of *The New Arabian Nights* and *The Twilight of the Gods*, the only experiments in the fantastic I can recall belonging to the 'eighties are Anstey's. *Vice Versâ*, *The Tinted Venus*, *A Fallen Idol*, *Tourmalin's Time Cheques* —these endearing tales, in which the quaintness of the situations is exquisitely opposed to the realism of the talk and characterization, act upon one's spirits like sunshine upon a barometer. They are true flowers of the comic genius, and each is, into the bargain, the work of a born story-teller. Observation, invention, a delightful sense of human absurdity, and a gift for writing dialogue with a mimetic skill that creates the very illusion of the human voice—all these qualities have kept them as fresh to-day as when they were first published.

And so the extremely slender thread, with a few knots tied in it, each representing a group of novels, by which I have sought to guide myself through a far too intricate subject, brings me at last to that particularly home-grown product, the pastoral novel. Here, close to the soil, we breathe the very smell of England, and here, in the works of Thomas Hardy, we find the English genius, a little earthy perhaps, but spontaneous, strong, triumphant, in its supreme gift of poetry. And in the work of those less famous writers with whom alone I am concerned, there is an equally strong local flavour. There are flashes of poetry in the novels of Richard Jefferies—*Greene Ferne Farm*, *Amaryllis at the Fair*, *The Dewy Morn*—though all three are failures. Jefferies, in truth, apart from his power of description, was but poorly equipped as a novelist. He had little gift for creating character, little power of imagination (hence the failure of *Wood Magic*), a conventional point of view, and a technique more artless even than that of most of his contemporaries. He wrote one masterpiece, *Bevis*, but *Bevis* is a book about boys, a dream of his own boyhood, and everything in it springs from memory, from a love of Nature, and an inexhaustible joy and patience in noting the details of the natural scene. And even *Bevis* he did his best in the last chapters to spoil. Luckily that was impossible, we can safely ignore those chapters, for anybody with the slightest feeling for the novel form must see that the book really ends when Bevis and Mark return from New Formosa. It was published in 1882, in the customary three volumes, and failed. Later it was mutilated and the abridged version published in one volume, with pictures, in the hope of attracting a juvenile audience—and failed again. Finally it was re-issued in the present century as Jefferies wrote it, and this third appeal was at least moderately successful. It seems to me the best novel about boys ever written, with the possible exception of *Huckleberry Finn*; in fact, in its own line, which is not that of *Huck*, I believe it to be unsurpassable. At the same time I am much less certain that it is the best book *for* boys. In my own boyhood I thought it dull. Yet Bevis is a real boy, and apart from his taste for killing things lived exactly the kind of life I liked most. For some queer reason it was the human, the personal appeal I found wanting. Bevis was too detached and self-centred. Therefore I never cared for him in the way I cared for George Manville Fenn's heroes. Unlike them, he refused to be woven into my own imaginings; the book left me cold, and I doubt if at that time I finished it.

But I have read it half a dozen times since. It was the only story Jefferies ever wrote into which he was able to put his whole heart, and this in itself indicates his limitations as a novelist. He knew far more about Bevis and Mark and Pan the spaniel than about his mature heroes and heroines, and was far closer to them. They were a part of Nature, and it was Nature that he loved and understood. He was far more interested in the building of the raft, the exploration of the lake, the lessons in swimming and sailing, even in Pan's private exploits, than in the conventional love business of his grown-up fictions.

Greene Ferne Farm (1880) is the best of these. It is a short novel, less than three hundred pages of big print. It contains a few beautiful passages of descriptive writing, and two or three fairly good chapters; but the individual note of Jefferies, the note that is carried right through *Bevis*, sounds only intermittently.

'Mr. Ruck, very big and burly, was shaped something like one of his own mangolds turned upside down: that is to say, as the glance ran over his figure, beginning at the head, it had to take in a swelling outline as it proceeded lower. He was clad in a snowy-white smock-frock, breeches and gaiters, and glossy beaver hat.

'This costume had a hieroglyphic meaning. The snowy smock-frock intimated that he had risen from lowly estate, and was proud of the fact. The breeches and gaiters gave him an air of respectable antiquity in itself equivalent to a certain standing. Finally the beaver hat—which everybody in the parish knew cost a guinea, and nothing less—bespoke the thousand pounds at the bank to which he so frequently alluded.'

And again:

' "Hur be a upstanding girl, that Margaret Estcourt. A' got a thousand pound under the will."

' "And the Greene Ferne Farm when the widder goes."

' "Five hundred acres freehold, and them housen in to town."

' "A' be a featish-looking girl, you."

' "So be May Fisher; but a' bean't such a queen as t'other. Margaret walks as if the parish belonged to her."

' "If a' did, her would sell un, and buy a new bonnet. . . ."

'The sound of singing came from the open door under the tower hard by.

' "Dall'd if it beant 'I will arise'."

' " 'S'pose us had better go in." ' '

In such passages can we not hear the echo of another voice, that of the author of *Under the Greenwood Tree*? Those chapters, too, in which Margaret and Geoffrey, the un-declared lovers, are lost on the downs at night, might have been conceived by Hardy, though here it is Jefferies who is writing. They find shelter in an ancient tomb or dolmen, and possibly it is this that recalls the scene, written more than ten years later, in which Angel Clare and Tess flee from justice across Salisbury Plain. True, no cloud of doom hangs over Jefferies' lovers, no ironical President of the Immortals makes sport of them; it is only that both scenes impress upon us the same sense of a vast lonely space and of immemorial time in contrast with the pitiful fragility of human life. We are face to face with earth and sky and night, conscious of an immense silence through which the small mysterious voices of Nature reach anxious, questioning ears.

And in the simplicity of treatment there is a kind of grave instinctive poetry, a beauty, Greek in spirit if not in form, and utterly alien from and beyond the reach of 'fine writing'.

Still, when all is said, *Greene Ferne Farm* remains an amateurish effort, and in the same year, 1880, there had appeared a much more remarkable novel of rural life. Baring-Gould's half-forgotten tale, *Mehalah*, if not a great book is at least a memorable one. It would be memorable if for nothing else than that the author of it is, I should think, Emily Brontë's only disciple. In its subject, in its principal characters, in its conception of love as a kind of spiritual or demoniac obsession, in its violence, in its wild and lonely setting, *Mehalah* inevitably reminds us of *Wuthering Heights*. The likeness, indeed, if it forms part of the book's fascination, is also its misfortune. *Mehalah* is powerfully written; set it among any group of novels of the better class and it will stand out as a bold, striking, and picturesque work; the one comparison it *cannot* survive is the comparison it forces us to draw.

For it is not, as *Wuthering Heights* is, born of the spirit. It has everything else, everything but just this unanalysable quality which cannot be imitated, the bright naked flame. *Mehalah* is good prose fiction, but *Wuthering Heights* belongs to the world of great poetry—is of no school, betrays no influences; were it the only novel in existence it could hardly be a thing more unique and isolated.

On its own plane, however, *Mehalah* is worthy to survive. The time is 1780 or thereabouts, the scene the glittering, desolate Essex salt-marshes, the subject a passionate and un-requited love. How far Elijah Rebow, consciously or un-consciously, may have been derived from Heathcliff does not matter. He never appears to us as a dark, fallen angel (and how far *that* aspect depended on the fact that Emily Brontë was in love with her hero it would be useless to seek, though one can guess that under a certain type of examination he would emerge as the projection of a repression). Rebow, if he was suggested by Heathcliff, nevertheless is *not* Heathcliff: much less is Mehalah Catherine Earnshaw; and the author's realization of his characters remains throughout clear and consistent. Rebow is as violent and ruthless as Heathcliff, as constant in his love, while the passion that consumes him is as absorbing and as clean as Heathcliff's; spiritualized, one might think, by its very intensity. He rants at times, but so does Heathcliff. Both are ready to commit any action that may bring them nearer to their heart's desire; both are revengeful, implacable, and in most directions unscrupulous. And Mehalah seems to Rebow his ideal mate, as Cathy is Heathcliff's. But a sharp divergence here is given to the march of the drama, for Mehalah hates and defies Rebow and loves the worthless, easy-going George. To get the girl into his power Rebow sticks at nothing. He betrays her lover to the press-gang, robs her and her widowed mother, plots against them, buys up their impoverished farm, burns the house down over their heads, and finally, by lying, scheming, and violence, gets them beneath his own roof at Red Hall. This gaunt red-brick house, standing bare and bleak and lonely above the level of the marsh, without a tree to shelter it, and where, in the cellars under the stone floor, Rebow keeps his maniac brother chained like a wild beast—this house is in itself a Brontë conception. The whole theme of the book might have scared off anybody but a Brontë, and by what miracle it escapes melodrama I do not know. That it does escape it, however, I think is unquestionable. The story unrolls itself against a background of water and sky. The smell of the sea is in it, the brown salt weed drying on the flats, the sound of oars and of boats being launched and beached, the cry of wild duck and curlew, now and then the report of a gun: and, though it is not a tale of smugglers and we are not told of a single cargo that is run, smuggling somehow is going on all round us.

There are faults, glaring enough—passages of false rhetoric, passages of stilted dialogue, antiquarian and other tiresome digressions—Mrs. de Wit's allusions to her son's 'galliwanting' become trying, the characters sometimes say the wrong thing, or the right thing in the wrong way; but in the great dramatic moments the style becomes strangely clarified, and so living and moving is the whole conception that faults are no sooner perceived than they are forgotten. What is the secret of the emotional force that strikes through such a book as *Mehalah* and holds us, for it is rarely to be found in modern fiction? Is it that the novelist of to-day cares less for his characters, regards them more in the light of 'copy'—cares less for everything?

Mehalah was a rather odd book for a parson to have written, even though he did not intend to sign it. Where rustic religion is concerned, the tone if not cynical is completely disillusioned.

'Mrs. de Wit was a moralist, and when nearly drunk religious. . . .

' "I always make a point to believe the worst. I'm a religious person, and them as sets up to be religious always does that." '

'The "dearly beloveds" met in the Lord's house every Lord's day to acknowledge their "erring and straying like lost sheep" and make appointments for erring and straying again.'

There is not the slightest attempt to point a moral, or to

preach. The attitude towards women is to say the least un-
flattering, while such an episode as that of the curate's children and the bat is in the spirit if not in the manner of
Mr. T. F. Powys.

'At that moment a rush, a roar, an avalanche down the
narrow stairs, steep as a ladder. In a heap came the whole
fourteen, the oldest foremost, the youngest in the rear.

' "We've got him, we're going to drown him."

' "What is it?" feebly enquired the father, putting his
hands to his ears.

' "We'll hold him to the fire and pop his little eyes."

' "No, they're too small."

' "Into the water-butt with him!" '

Just one more book I should like to mention, not because
it is characteristic of our period—for really it would be
more in place in a paper on the 'nineties—but because it
has never, I think, met with anything like the appreciation
it deserves. And after all it *was* published in the 'eighties, in
1887, appearing first anonymously in *Temple Bar*, and then
in a single slender dark-blue volume. (I am ending up, you
see, fittingly if quite unintentionally, with yet another
Bentley book: 'that wise old publisher', as Miss Corelli
called him, when he accepted *A Romance of Two Worlds*
against the advice of several members of the firm.) *A Village
Tragedy*, by Margaret L. Woods, is a realistic pastoral novel,
but it is a work of infinite delicacy, written in a simple lucid
prose that in itself is a joy, rare then and rare to-day. The
tragic plot is as simple as the writing, the characters lowly—
the hero being almost inarticulate—but, in spite of its
gloomy shadows, there is a beauty in this love tale that
approaches the idyllic. Beauty and sadness alike spring in
some measure from the youth of the lovers, their pathetic
inexperience if not innocency, for Annie and Jesse are really

little more than children when they are thrown into each other's arms—Annie the farm drudge, and Jesse the workhouse boy, now working on the farm too. The disaster is not of their making; it is the result of the cruelty, prurience, and stupidity of their elders; for there has been nothing but friendship between them when the girl in the middle of the night is dragged out of bed and thrust out of doors by her suspicious and half-drunken aunt and mistress. She seeks shelter, naturally enough, in the boy's cottage, but it is an unfortunate step, and her aunt sees to it that it shall be irretrievable. It may be objected that in the misinformation that prevents Annie and Jesse from getting married, in Jesse's long illness, and in the railway accident which kills him just when at last there seems to be a chance of happiness—it may be objected that in such a sequence of accidents, all unfortunate, there is a hint of the arbitrary; and it cannot be denied that the dice have been heavily loaded against Annie and Jesse, though no more heavily than in many a novel of Hardy's. Still, the little book remains of a rare distinction, and takes rank amongst our finest pastoral novels.

Like *Mehalah*, it is among those that ought, if out of print, to be reprinted. *A Village Tragedy*, *The Pariah*, *Mehalah*, *No New Thing*—if I were re-issuing a selection of novels of the 'eighties I should begin with these four. But I should not end there; there are others—at least a score—whose ghosts would haunt me reproachfully if I did. Fifty years! A man considers himself to be only middle-aged at fifty, yet for a book it is far beyond the allotted span. The thought might well awaken a mood of chastened melancholy in the most confident author. Luckily, youth is untroubled with such thoughts, or I dare say nobody would think it worth while to begin to write, which would be a pity. It is when we see the books we ourselves have once so enjoyed—or perhaps even written—dropping into oblivion, that a spirit of tenderness towards the past is aroused. Let us cultivate it, without neglecting the present. It *may* one day—who knows? —breathe some faint friendly whisper among our own dry bones.

1930.

SOME REFLECTIONS ON
A MIDSUMMER NIGHT'S DREAM

It is many years since I saw a play by Shakespeare, and I remember little of the adventure except that I did not enjoy it, and that Sir Frank Benson was unnecessarily hideous and wonderfully agile as Caliban. Therefore, when I learned of Mr. Doran's approaching visit to Belfast, I decided that I must go to see another Shakespeare play, and after prolonged study of the programme chose *A Midsummer Night's Dream*. Unfortunately, in the meantime, I have re-read the thing. I knew it might be unwise, but I risked it. And now I am very much afraid I shall not see Mr. Doran after all. I have had my private performance, and it has left me with no desire for a public one. The two, I feel certain, would clash, and the earlier has left on my mind a remarkably pleasant impression.

To begin with, it took place in the open air. Secondly, it was lighted by the moon. I had no idea there was so much moonshine in anything as there is in this very young and rather broad comedy. It is a good comedy; it is beautiful; and the prose and verse, the fooling and the magic and the lovers' vows, melt into one another as easily and naturally as 'a tune into a tune'. Only, am I wrong to think that its dramatic value is slight in comparison with its lyrical charm—that Helena, Hermia, Demetrius, Lysander, Hippolyta, Theseus, are mere mouthpieces for the poetry? Certainly, the intrigue seems to me as artificial as possible. How the wooers fare in their wooing matters not a straw. Their loves are light as thistledown, without a trace of affection in them, or anything more lasting than a brief summer appetence. Love, for them, is a toy, a plaything, at most a fever of the blood, 'momentary as a sound', coming and going at a fairy's call, having its source in the juice of a flower squeezed into the sleeper's eyes. And because we are in dreamland it does not matter, does not strike a wrong note as it does in *Tristan and Isolde*. Yet to see in it all, as Brandes sees in it, 'a great symbol', 'the germs of a whole philosophy of life', to see in Theseus, as Dowden sees in him, 'Shakespeare's early ideal of a heroic warrior and man of action', is, I confess, beyond me. I am unconvinced. Theseus is no more than a puppet serving his purpose in a tale that bears exactly the same relation to life as do the tales of *Ma Mère L'Oye*. If it comes to that, he is a good deal *less* actual than Puss in Boots, and, except in Bottom and his companions, there is scarcely an attempt at human characterization throughout the play, such a little touch of nature as Hermia's 'I am not yet so low, but that my nails can reach unto thine eyes', standing out merely because of its rarity. No; what matters is the poetry, which is everywhere, and which becomes most wonderful just where it is most fantastic, as in Puck's song, 'Now the hungry lion roars'.

There are lines one lingers over, 'following darkness like a dream', following them on strange journeys through the day and night, drugged by their murmuring beauty. And this I strongly suspect to be wrong from a dramatic point of view. In fact, I remember Yeats telling me it to be so, while I was standing beside him, watching one of Synge's plays. There was a moment when that play, *The Well of the Saints*, became purely lyrical, and though it appealed to me, Yeats shook his head.

Now in my private performance such moments did not matter, because when they were reached the whole thing simply came to a stop, leaving me to taste the coolness of 'faint primrose beds', or watch the elves dancing 'to the whistling wind'. That was one reason why I enjoyed it. I had time to dwell on the contrast between the fairy-poetry, delicate as the green lamp of a glow-worm, and the quaint realism of the descriptive passages: the hounds

> With ears that sweep away the morning dew,
> Crook-knee'd, and dew-lapp'd like Thessalian bulls;

the 'bank whereon the wild thyme blows', and all the rustic scenes.

Why not accept the thing as it is? Why search for dubious under-meanings? The village clowns of *A Midsummer Night's Dream* are the only creatures of flesh and blood in it. These so-called Athenian craftsmen, rehearsing and acting their foolish drama, are really very like the peasants in an early novel by Thomas Hardy, and serve much the same comic purpose, while remaining none the less a part of the poetry. For, despite their clumsiness and homely speech, they are more in harmony with the world of Puck and Titania than the courtiers are, and help to make that world convincing, as if endowing it with a share of their own solidity. Puck, the rustic fairy, the 'lob of spirits', stands in much the same relation to Oberon and his train as the human rustics do to Theseus and his court. In Puck, as in Bottom, there is all the zest and rudeness of life.

> And sometimes lurk I in a gossip's bowl,
> In very likeness of a toasted crab;
> And, when she drinks, against her lips I bob,

And on her withered dew-lap pour the ale.
The wisest aunt, telling the saddest tale,
Sometimes for three-foot stool mistaketh me;
Then slip I from her bum, down topples she,
And 'tailor' cries, and falls into a cough.

That's the stuff to mark; not nonsense about 'Shakespeare's early ideal of a warrior and man of action'.

And it is the moon who is the presiding spirit. She shines over the whole drama; her influence is felt by all the actors in it. Time is measured from moon to moon. She is the 'old moon' that wanes, 'the watery moon' who 'looks with a watery eye'. She is 'like to a silver bow new bent in heaven', and she is Phoebe, who beholds 'her silver visage in the watery glass'. Singing 'by moonlight' under her window, Lysander has won the love of Hermia, and Hermia, if she refuse Demetrius, is to be a nun, shut in a cloister, 'a barren sister' all her days, 'chanting faint hymns to the cold fruitless moon'.

Puck is 'swifter than the moonë's sphere'. Oberon and Titania can fly round the world 'swifter than the wandering moon'. While Titania and Oberon quarrel over possession of the Indian boy,

The moon, the governess of floods,
Pale in her anger, washes all the air.

Oberon has seen Cupid 'flying between the cold moon and the earth'. When Bottom is weary, the fairies must 'fan the moonbeams from his sleeping eyes'. The artisans rehearse their play by moonlight:

Doth the moon shine that night we play our play?
A calendar, a calendar! Look in the almanac; find out moonshine, find out moonshine.

79

And in the play itself, the 'tedious brief scene of young Pyramus and his love Thisbe',

> This man, with lanthorn, dog, and bush of thorn,
>   Presenteth moonshine: for, if you will know,
> By moonshine did these lovers think no scorn
>   To meet at Ninus' tomb.

Can you really imagine that after bathing in all this lunary magic I shall be so foolish as to place myself at the mercy of a limelight man? No. 'This green plot shall be our stage, this hawthorn brake our tiring-house.'

1924.

HENRY JAMES[1]

In one of his prefaces, writing of that curious group of tales which includes *The Figure in the Carpet*, *The Next Time* and *The Death of the Lion*—tales dealing with 'some felt embarrassment, some extreme predicament, of the artist enamoured of perfection'—Henry James says that he was asked 'Where on earth, where round about us at this hour, he had found his Neil Paradays, his Hugh Verekers'? 'I was reminded,' he adds, 'that these eminent cases fell to the ground unless I could give chapter and verse for the eminence. I was reduced to confessing I couldn't.' The unnamed questioner can hardly be congratulated on his tact, since chapter and verse, one might have supposed, James had given sufficiently in the writing of the tales themselves; and he now gives it again in the two volumes of his letters, carefully and admirably edited by Mr. Percy Lubbock. Reticent, elusive, impersonal in all but manner, as most of these letters are, it might indeed be said that everything else he gives is, in comparison, superficial—the mere ebullition of charming, sympathetic, but not particularly intimate talk. Henry James had a gift for friendship—up to a point: but the things he did not mention were, one somehow feels, numerous, and exactly those that would have

[1] *The Letters of Henry James*. Edited by Percy Lubbock. 2 vols. 1920.

been most revealing. In his fictions he 'went behind' as few
of his characters as possible, and, reading his letters, we
very soon become aware that he does not intend to go
behind himself either. We rejoice in their humour, in their
felicity of phrase; we marvel when he lets himself go,
expands, like some full-blown rose, in the payment of a
compliment or the acknowledgement of a gift; but we rejoice
how much more in that single fragment which was not
addressed to anybody, and feel that Mr. Lubbock acted
wisely when he printed it here. It was written at Rye, a
few years before the novelist's death, when he was planning
a tale later on abandoned, and in it we seem to get, if only
for a single midnight hour, the spontaneous, the natural
Henry James.

'I take up this again after an interruption. . . . I needn't
expatiate on this—on the sharp consciousness of this hour
of the dimly-dawning New Year, I mean; I simply make an
appeal to all the powers and forces and divinities to whom
I've ever been loyal and who haven't failed me yet—after
all: never, never yet! . . . Let me fumble it gently and
patiently out—with fever and fidget laid to rest—as in all
the old enchanted months! It only looms, it only shines and
shimmers, *too* beautiful and too interesting; it only hangs
there too rich and too full and with too much to give and to
pay; it only presents itself too admirably and too vividly,
too straight and square and vivid, as a little organic and
effective Action. . . .

'Thus just these first little wavings of the oh so tremu-
lously passionate little old wand (now!) make for me, I feel,
a sort of promise of richness and beauty and variety; a sort
of portent of the happy presence of the elements. The good
days of last August and even my broken September and my
better October come back to me with their gage of divine

possibilities, and I welcome these to my arms, I press them
with unutterable tenderness. I seem to emerge from these
recent bad days—the fruit of blind accident—and the pros-
pect clears and flushes, and my poor blest old Genius pats
me so admirably and lovingly on the back that I turn, I
screw round, and bend my lips to passionately, in my gratitude, kiss its hands.'

There is something charming and touching about these
lines. They evoke the lonely hour, the lonely room, and the
lonely writer. Their emotion reaches us, and we read them
with a strangely-mingled pride and joy and sadness and
affection. We know they were not intended for any eyes
but his own, yet they seem to be addressed to us as nothing
else in these pages is addressed to us, carrying with them a
deeper and completer intimacy and sincerity.

In the letters themselves he writes less of his work than
might have been expected. We gather, as I have said, what
it meant to him (and it meant nearly everything), but we
gather it for the most part from scattered hints, little notes
of explanation, and, later on, too often of discouragement.
He is a novelist before he has written a line of his first novel.
Through all his earlier wanderings, when he is sending home
dutiful accounts of places and people, glimpses of the European Scene, he is really accumulating material, learning how
to use it, searching for the exact corner of highly-civilized
life that will best repay the cultivation he may bring to it.
Nothing is left to chance; nothing can deflect him from his
path. With a youthful gravity, with a curiously *un*youthful
discretion, he proceeds step by step, gathering impressions,
but never unduly impressed (by persons at all events), self-
effacing, supremely intelligent, quietly sure of himself, of
his vocation, his talent. There is a wisdom, a decorum, in
his attitude, all the more remarkable because these qualities

do not in the least diminish the impression we receive of freshness and ingenuousness. An almost boyish freshness, indeed, he preserved far beyond the period when it is apt to fade, and in surroundings where it might very quickly and easily have perished. One would have expected a sensitive young American, passionately interested in literature, to have been a good deal dazzled, if not overawed, by the giants of the *Diner Magny*, yet in 1876 we find him writing to his father: 'I had also the other day a very pleasant call upon Flaubert, whom I like personally more and more each time I see him. But I think I easily—more than easily—see all round him intellectually.' One may be pardoned, perhaps, for not quite sharing this confidence, and the liking certainly turned later to *dis*like—a dislike so pronounced, indeed, that it invalidates most of his criticism of Flaubert's work. Flaubert, we cannot help suspecting, must have said or done *something* to offend, and, if so, one has the further suspicion that it was never forgotten, never forgiven.

At this time Henry James had already planned what he desired to do, and in *Roderick Hudson* had begun to do it. Two years later he writes to his brother William, who had commented severely on the 'thinness' of *The Europeans*:

'I think you take these things too rigidly and unimaginatively—too much as if an artistic experiment were a piece of conduct to which one's life were somehow committed. . . . I have a constant impulse to try experiments of form, in which I wish to not run the risk of wasting or gratuitously using big situations.'

The 'big situations' were to come in good time, but William James was never to be an appreciative reader. He could not understand that delight in 'experiments of form' which was to produce more and more elaborate masterpieces, until manner and technique came at last to overshadow everything else. Nobody, for that matter, seems to have understood, or, if they did, to have cared, and an ever increasing discouragement is reflected in the letters of the middle years. When he sends *The Tragic Muse* to Stevenson he writes: 'I can't (spiritually) afford *not* to put it under the eye of the sole and single Anglo-Saxon capable of perceiving how well it is written.' It was a forlorn hope, we feel, for Stevenson had never really been an enthusiastic admirer. Had he not said that he *hated The Portrait of a Lady*? One naturally has one's preferences; I myself plump for *The Spoils of Poynton*; nevertheless, if one hates *The Portrait of a Lady*, one is hardly likely to love *The Tragic Muse*.

This surely exaggerated sense of failure first began to haunt him after the publication of *The Bostonians* in 1886, and led to those wasted years when he took to writing for the theatre. He must, I imagine, have written nearly a dozen plays in all, and I think only three of these were ever produced, and not more than five or six printed, though *The High Bid* (*Covering End*), *The Other House* and *The Outcry* were re-written as fiction.

The decade between 1890 and 1900 marks the summit of Henry James's achievement. It was in those wonderful years that he produced such things as *The Pupil*, *The Middle Years*, *The Altar of the Dead*, *The Spoils of Poynton*, *What Maisie Knew*, *The Awkward Age*, *The Turn of the Screw*, *The Great Good Place*. The celebrated 'manner' was now perfected, had a delightful suavity, a rich poetry, an exquisite expressiveness. As I think of the work of these years I somehow think of the scene in the story called *Nona Vincent* (not one of his most famous), where the tired playwright drops into a chair in his lonely lodgings, and the vision of Nona comes to him. This scene could not have been written, as it exists, ten years earlier—the instrument was not then sufficiently per-

fected—and had it been written ten years later it would not
have been the same; the softness, the ease—qualities essential to the successful interpretation of such a mood—would
have been drowned in a brilliant virtuosity. The technique
has now become part of the story, and the style has not yet
become the involved jargon of the last phase. Consider, in
this relation, *What Maisie Knew*. Told directly, it would have
been merely a sordid little drama of the divorce court; but
told as James tells it, through the clear, fresh, uncompre-
hending mind of the child, it is lifted on to another and
infinitely higher plane without losing a shred of its reality.
Only, a moral beauty now irradiates it, and nothing could be
more admirable than the way in which out of that unsavoury
world of treacheries and vulgarities there emerges the
triumphant figure of Mrs. Wix, the 'straighteners' grimly
set, as she carries her young charge towards a future in
which, if poverty and struggle loom large, at any rate there
shall be no more horrors of the kind that makes mere *clean-
ness* seem the highest crown of life.

Again, in *The Awkward Age*, does not the secret of its success lie in the careful preparation of the ground? The leading
theme is Mrs. Brookenham's jealousy of her daughter Nanda.
Any other novelist would have made the description of this
passion his trump card, and devoted pages to analysing it:
Henry James does not even tell us of its existence. We discover it for ourselves, gradually—from words let drop, little
things that happen—this being the only one of his novels in
which he goes behind none of his characters, but keeps
throughout to a nakedly dramatic form. It may appear an unnecessarily difficult way of doing things—a problem set up
simply for the pleasure of solving it—but it is not really so.
The effect, when we *do* make our discovery, is infinitely
more profound, more thrilling, because of the suspicions

that have been slowly, half unconsciously accumulating in our minds, without receiving the author's direct confirmation. It is entirely due to this gradual revelation that the scene of the French novel, in which Mrs. Brook—to keep her lover Vanderbank—sacrifices Nanda, sacrifices herself, sacrifices Vanderbank too—and all uselessly, all in vain—it is because of this, that a scene which in an ordinary novel would strike us as comparatively trivial becomes so tremendous, bringing everything to the ground in one ruinous crash from which there can be no recovery.

These novels and tales of Henry James's maturity are unique not only in English but in European literature. There is nothing that bears even a remote resemblance to them, and it is unlikely that there ever will be. They could not, for several reasons, be popular, but on the other hand their author was never a neglected writer, therefore his attitude in regard to the obtuseness of reviewers and the indifference of the general public may seem a little unreasonable. After all, the only kind of success he did *not* achieve was the kind that in *The Next Time* and the other literary tales is regarded as vulgar. Henry James, however, hankered after popularity —popularity as it is understood by novelists who understand nothing else—and I remember my astonishment when, in the first letter I ever received from him, he expressed, though not overtly, this desire. Certainly he made no slightest compromise to achieve it. Or did he? Henrietta Stackpole, in *The Portrait of a Lady*, was perhaps his idea of a compromise, and it would be amusing, if it were not pathetic, to find him referring to a masterpiece like *The Turn of the Screw* as a pot-boiler.

What he utterly failed to grasp was that in the increasing difficulty of his style, far more than in any subtlety of technique or choice of subject, lay the real stumbling-block over which in the end even his most ardent disciples tripped. That style, it must be admitted, was in its last phase a hindrance rather than a help to illusion—successful only in such things as *The Jolly Corner*—things essentially exotic, and depending for their effectiveness on the elaboration of a ghostly atmosphere, to which indeed it marvellously lent itself. But for anything else it was a bad style, and when carried into the dialogue absolutely fatal to credulity. Struggling with the bewildering intricacy of *The Golden Bowl*, one even begins to doubt—which of course is stupid—the whole theory of conscious art. '*Les plaisirs que l'art procure ne doivent jamais coûter la moindre fatigue*', and after all, books like *Wuthering Heights*, or *Jude the Obscure*, or *La Rôtisserie de la Reine Pédauque* (to mention three of my own favourite novels) are written with the utmost simplicity. Yet place *Wuthering Heights* beside that mature and masterly performance, *The Wings of the Dove*, and note what happens. It is not the work of the beginner, the amateur, that suffers. Viewed side by side, *The Wings of the Dove* seems an elaborate work of art fashioned in a studio by the cunning hand of man, but *Wuthering Heights* is a radiant thing that has been breathed into wild and imperishable life by the breath of the Divine Spirit.

Have I wandered from the letters? I'm afraid so. I read them in the hope that I should find therein a revelation of Henry James, but are they, any more than the autobiographies, truly revealing? I don't know quite what I expected, but I think I should have known had I found it. I read attentively; I was in the presence; the veil now and then trembled as before a withdrawal; but it was not withdrawn; I know now it never will be; it is still through a veil that, seated on the other side of a ghostly chess-board, I see 'the faint figure of an antagonist, good-humouredly but a little eerily secure—an antagonist who leans back in his chair with his hands in his pockets and a smile on his fine clear face'.

I have read through more than once all the novels and tales of Henry James. I formed from them and from his other work a picture of their author; but if I have found nothing in the *Letters* to falsify that picture, on the other hand I have found nothing to help it out. On the contrary, in certain of his fictions, in a story like *The Altar of the Dead*, say, we are with him in a way we never are in his correspondence. Perhaps he kept a journal, but there is no hint of such a thing, and one remembers that he didn't care much for the celebrated *Journal* of the Goncourts. So we must content ourselves with that solitary fragment from which I have quoted at the beginning of this essay.

1914—1920.

W. D. HOWELLS

I

In an essay on modern fiction Mr. Howells has said: 'The moving accident is not its trade; and it prefers to avoid all manner of dire catastrophe. . . . What is unpretentious and what is true is always beautiful and good, and nothing else is so.' Elsewhere, throughout his numerous critical writings, he has repeated this judgement again and again. His delight in realism and his intolerance of romanticism crop up, indeed, at every point. The only excuse for a novel's existence is that it shall give you a faithful picture of life: the mere plot—he has little interest in that, almost a contempt for it. 'In one manner or other the stories were all told long ago. . . . Neither arts, nor letters, nor sciences, except as they tend to make the race better and kinder, are to be regarded as serious interests, and they cannot do this except from and through the truth.'

Dogmatic generalizations are seldom convincing, and though we may accept this one in so far as it condemns the spurious and insincere, a difficulty is immediately created by the precise meaning we happen to attach to the word 'truth'. For many readers *Wuthering Heights*, while aiming less at superficial plausibility, will seem in another and more intimate sense truer than Jane Austen's delightful fictions, or than such deliberately unromantic chronicles as *The Lady of the Aroostook* and *April Hopes*. The 'truth' of the two last tales (they are both by Mr. Howells) is, in fact, largely a matter of photographic accuracy; that is to say, it is the truth of conscientious reporting, the truth of the eye and the ear; and one might add that in most of his works Mr. Howells is content with an outward fidelity. His realism is seldom the imaginative realism of Flaubert, of Tourguéneff, of Conrad or of Tolstoy. He has said that 'whatever is true is beautiful', but he ignores Bacon's most apposite warning, 'There is no excellent beauty that hath not some strangeness in the proportion.' Now there is very little, too little, 'strangeness' in Mr. Howell's novels: hence, I think, the effect of flatness which so many of them produce. Even his style, admirable in its purity, is more remarkable for neatness than for beauty. Like the substance of most of his fictions, it is rarely touched by imagination, is essentially prosaic; there is hardly a metaphor, hardly an image, to be found in all his forty or fifty volumes.

Certainly, if the truest picture of life is to be obtained by an exhaustive presentment of the commonplace (painted not with the bitterness and exasperation of a Huysmans, but with a mildness that at times approaches the naïve) such things as *April Hopes*, as *The Lady of the Aroostook*, would take rank as masterpieces. Yet one is loath so to place them. Life is never quite so simple as this. We are inclined to suspect that had the observer been gifted with a more penetrating insight the result would have been different; to suspect that if he had delved farther below the surface he would have found there *was* something there. Or is this thinness, this flatness, deliberate? for he can be subtle enough, and even profound, when his subject is worthy of him. Unfortunately subjects, like soils, vary considerably in the degree of their richness, and from the fields Mr. Howells has for the most part elected to cultivate one can hardly expect a very dense harvest. Only, why choose such barren tracts? Why, at any rate, choose them so frequently? Is it part of the theory, his particular theory, of realism? *The Lady of the Aroostook* is a kind of apotheosis of the trivial, yet it is characteristic of the great majority of his fictions, is a typical Howells novel, and if it did not fall immeasurably below his really fine work criticism would have little further to add.

Let me, for a moment, examine the story more closely. The situation (that of an unsophisticated village maiden finding herself the only female on board a small steamer sailing from America to Europe) may be piquant and amusing, but is scarcely in itself sufficient to fill out a couple of volumes. One of the passengers falls in love with her, and by the time they reach Europe a marriage is arranged. Positively, that is all. The lovers themselves are the least distinguished persons imaginable, their love-making is anything but impassioned. The only thing in the book not completely obvious is the reason why Mr. Howells should have bestowed upon his heroine the hideous name of Lydia Blood. And yet the tale is so diffuse that, after it has run on for a couple of hundred pages, there seems to be no reason on earth why it should not run on forever. The author, in fact, relies unblushingly on its love passages to hold our attention. This, in spite of a rebuke to novelists, in his *Criticism and Fiction*, for devoting themselves so exclusively to the treatment of a single passion, 'and that one not the most important in life'. In practice, no other novelist of his talent has shown himself so absorbed in a love-story for its own sake. He is an unconscionable matchmaker, and if, by a miracle, his lovers are not in the end united, is quite capable of introducing a fresh candidate for the lady's hand. Even *The Undiscovered Country*, which opens so promisingly, after the first few vivid and striking scenes presenting a group of grotesque spiritualists and professional mediums who congregate in a dingy house in Boston to pursue their supernatural investigations, develops disappointingly into an ordinary love-story, differing from its companions, where it differs at all, only in its less usual setting.

It is clear, I think, that the desire to give a perfectly accurate picture of average everyday life is responsible for the unimaginative effect that so much of Howells' work produces. The world he sets himself to describe has no particularly high interests, and for that very reason has been chosen as representing the world in which most people live. The theory of realism is pushed to the point where it excludes all that is exceptional—the exceptionally good, the exceptionally bad, the exceptionally clever, the exceptionally dramatic. But the drawback to this highly conscientious view is, that to write a very moving book about absolutely commonplace people in absolutely commonplace circumstances is impossible. No doubt, outwardly at least, the heroine of *Washington Square* is commonplace, and even dull; but then Henry James has invented for her a situation, an emotional conflict, that brings out all her latent qualities of loyalty and honesty. Mr. Howells in most cases prefers to leave the situation as humdrum as the people.

Of course, we become much more conscious of this if we read a number of the novels in succession than if we read only now and again, at judicious intervals, an isolated tale. A too continuous reading leaves an impression of something irritatingly trivial in the lives of these young men and women. Their spiritual experiences seem to be so exclusively connected with the mild fluctuations of their affections, and these sentimental divagations are apt to move so slowly that the whole thing becomes wearisome, and the reader listens for the tinkle of inevitable wedding-bells with a growing impatience, even if he does not actually 'skip'. It may be questioned, moreover, if within its own strongly-marked limits Mr. Howells' work *is* consistently realistic. A strain of conventionality runs through it, which, from this point of view, must constitute a vitiating element. It springs, I know, from a desire not to disappoint, not to hurt our feelings; but the happy ending, for example, when it occurs so frequently as it does here, is not conducive to an appearance of perfect sincerity even in the most optimistic of observers. He says of modern fiction that 'the moving accident is not its trade', yet more than one of his own fables is brought to a pleasant conclusion simply by the introduction of such an accident. Indeed, the weakness of his invention is shown less by a poverty of incident than by the accidental nature of those incidents which do occur. In *The Undiscovered Country* it is very feeble, surely, when Ford sets out on his travels, to bring him to the precise spot whither Egeria had wandered with her father; and it is still feebler to allow the same hero, who has been presented to us all through the book as a struggling journalist, to make, in the end, some mysterious discovery, 'an ingenious combination, known to all house-keepers', the profits from which place the newly-wedded lovers in easy circumstances for the rest of their lives. If these things are not accidental, it is difficult to know what is; and, in *A Woman's Reason*, poor Fenton's adventures might have been borrowed from a popular melodrama. Can we, in fact, accept as serious realism work which is so obviously designed to please, and which, into the bargain, ignores everything in life that may not be spoken of in the schoolroom or printed in the popular magazine?

II

And one might leave it at that were it not for those four admirable novels upon which the reputation of Howells ultimately must rest. They, however, contain the ripe fruit of so delicate and charming a talent that one is inclined to wish their author had written nothing else. Certainly, in comparison, nothing else he has written very much counts.

It was in 1885 that he published the first of these books, *The Rise of Silas Lapham*. It marked an epoch in his work, and far more than fulfilled the promise of the earlier tales. *Silas Lapham* comes so near to being a masterpiece that the hopes of Howells' admirers must have risen very high indeed. It illustrates all the strength and very little of the weakness of his theory of fiction: it illustrates, incidentally, the value of that mysterious quality, charm. There is something extremely personal, natural, and unassuming about the book. It is full of humour and observation, and of the happiest little touches which throw a glamour of art over a somewhat drab and prosaic material. The opening device, for instance, of having Lapham interviewed by a journalist for the *Solid Men of Boston* series, is so felicitous as a means of letting the reader into his confidence that one wonders it has never been imitated. No scene of comedy is droller than that describing the flutter aroused in the democratic Lapham household by the arrival of the invitation to the aristocratic Coreys' party. The various members of the Lapham family are all magnificently there, vividly alive, and the whole novel, with its quiet distinction, has a fine, homely flavour, difficult to describe, but very easy to enjoy. Nothing more 'national', more of the soil that produced it, than *Silas Lapham*, probably ever was written.

As a family chronicle it is surpassed in Mr. Howells' work only by his masterpiece, *The Kentons*, which came seventeen years later. And the two books have much in common. The atmosphere of both is light comedy, with a sprinkling, a summer shower or two, of tears. The interest of both lies in the faithful picture of a family whose tranquillity is disturbed by the advent of a suitor for one of the daughters. In both, the parents are simple, unsophisticated people, and the children very lovable. And both show at its highest that rare and inimitable quality of Mr. Howells, his personal charm. In *The Kentons*, indeed, this charm is so great that it becomes a spiritual beauty, a kind of sympathetic medium through which the whole book is seen. It is hard to imagine anybody *not* liking *The Kentons*. The story is slender in the extreme, but we want no more: the touch is so delicate and masterly, the tone so good-humoured, the portraits are produced so easily, by so effortless and graceful an art, the book is so filled with the spirit of youth, that we turn the last page with a sigh of regret. And the execution is as flawless as the conception. As in *Silas Lapham*, the people are more important than the story, but they are exactly the kind of people to make such a story possible, to fit exquisitely into its scheme, so that story and characters are inseparable. The stage is neither overcrowded nor too sparsely peopled. There are Judge Kenton and his wife; Bitteridge, the villain of the piece; Bitteridge's mother; the Kenton girls, Lottie and Ellen; Lottie's admirer, the English boy, Mr. Poggis, aged sixteen, with his perpetual air of surprise, and his perpetual conversation consisting chiefly of 'Well, rather!' 'Oh, I say!' and Boyne Kenton, that most delightful of all delightful youngsters. They are travelling in Europe, and the scene where Boyne comes into his sister Ellen's bedroom at night, and, sitting down on her bed in his dressing-gown, tries to confide in her his half-grasped thoughts and emotions, emotions really inexpressible, for he has fallen in love with the youthful Queen of Holland—this scene—on the face of it so whimsical and homely, so, in one sense, absurd—has an exquisite naturalness and tenderness that wrap it in a kind of poetry and make it one of the most touching things in literature. It is good, amazingly good, any writer might be proud to sign those pages, but no other writer could have written them, for they are in the highest degree individual. In them we have Mr. Howells at his best. What it comes to, I suppose, is that they are profoundly felt, and that the feeling has the quality, the beauty, of complete understanding.

The Kentons, then, is a delicious thing, but its very perfection of good humour reveals our author's limitations. It is the *kindest* story in the world. In *The Minister's Charge* (1885), the novel which immediately followed *Silas Lapham*, a broader and more dramatic note is struck, but the book as a whole has not the perfection of *The Kentons*, fails as a work of art because an essentially tragic theme is forced at the end to a happy conclusion. *The Minister's Charge* is the story of a boy who comes up from a country village to Boston to make his fortune, and finds the struggle a hard one. Certainly the portrait of Lemuel Barker (the boy in question) is one of Mr. Howells' finest achievements. It is drawn with a beautiful understanding of youth, and a sympathy that could not be surpassed. Excessively serious and conscientious, though by no means priggish, Lemuel has a strength and nobility of character, the gradual emergence of which, under trial, is really the subject of the tale. It is a good subject, and in Mr. Howells' hands becomes increasingly powerful and dramatic. As a love-story, too, it is the most moving he has written. Lemuel falls in love with

a shop girl—a silly, attractive, clinging little thing, whose
fragile charm we feel even through her pathetic vulgarity.
The whole situation is eminently of the stuff of tragedy.
For, as Lemuel develops, he becomes awakened to the
intellectual and spiritual limitations of his sweetheart—a
disillusionment that is rendered even more complete
when he meets with a girl who might really have been
his mate, and falls in love with her, and she with him.
But he is no Shelley. He remains, with a characteristic
Quixotism, loyal to Statira, whose whole nature is absorbed
in her passion for this beautiful and strange young man who
had told her he loved her. Then the inevitable happens: it
is only the inexperience of youth that makes Lemuel think
he can conceal a waning affection: Statira quickly notices
the change, suspects the truth, and under the burden of
misery falls ill. Her lungs, always delicate, become affected:
she is nursed by a devoted friend, 'Manda Greer, but grows
worse. One day, after a quarrel with Lemuel, for which
'Manda Greer is partly to blame, she has an attack of
haemorrhage, seems on the point of death. A reconciliation
follows, and, filled with remorse, Lemuel determines to
marry Statira at once. To do this he has to sacrifice his
career, and take a position as conductor on one of the
street cars, where, on the very first day, he meets with an
accident. The situation is poignant in the extreme; one can
imagine what the author of *Jude* would have made of it; but
alas, it is too poignant for Mr. Howells, who in the few
pages that remain does what he can to alleviate it. We can
almost see him struggling between his conscience as an
artist and his creed of optimism. In that struggle the book
goes to the wall. 'Let it go, then,' we can imagine Mr
Howells saying. 'There are other things more important.
'Neither arts, nor letters, nor sciences, except as they tend

to make the race better, etc. . . .' But how, in this case, *is* happiness to be achieved? Obviously, only by some sort of juggling with the truth. So when Lemuel comes out of hospital and goes back to the country to become a school-teacher, still with the intention of making a home for Statira, to our amazement Statira herself, who up to this point had been presented as living on and for her passion alone, shows herself suddenly anxious to break off the engagement, and go away with 'Manda Greer. In this last chapter she becomes quite a different person—pert, vain, and selfish. There is no self-sacrifice implied; she who was dying of love is suddenly heart-whole, and practically declares that she will have nothing more to do with Lemuel, leaving the reader the easy task of drawing his own conclusion, of following the author's hints, and uniting Lemuel with the other girl. For all this it is hard to forgive Mr. Howells. One of the best things in the book was the skill with which he had made us sympathize from the beginning with *both* Lemuel and Statira, and see the problem from both points of view. Statira was flighty and silly, but she was warm-hearted and true, with something childish and taking in her ways. That Mr. Howells should deliberately destroy this effect, produced with much subtlety, and undermine the impressiveness of his whole work by striking so false a note at the end, is tragic. Yet it is impossible to deny that the novel up to the last two chapters is a fine one.

That is the pity of it. That is where his theory of naturalism breaks down. He loves his art, but he does not love it well enough, does not, certainly, love it so much as he hates what is painful or unhappy. The next book, *Indian Summer* (1886) is, with the exception of *The Kentons*, the most perfectly finished and rounded of his novels. The action passes in Europe, and it is the story of a middle-aged man who, from a chivalrous reluctance to hurt her feelings, allows a young girl to imagine he is in love with her, when really he loves an older lady, her guardian. In the end the girl discovers somebody she prefers to her elderly lover, and so leaves the way open for Colville to marry the guardian. The theme, with a different arrangement, might have attracted Tourguéneff, but it must be confessed that, as Mr. Howells treats it, it leaves us disappointed. The book exists for the portrait of Colville, with his whimsical humour, his gentleness, melancholy and drollery. There is in Colville a natural goodness and unselfishness, and, despite his superficial cynicism, a sweetness and boyishness which make of him a charming figure, a kind of complement to the delightful Penelope Lapham, though Mr. Howells is now and then inclined to allow the burden of his years to hang too heavily upon him, so that, with the child Effie Bowen, we should almost put his age at seventy-five rather than forty-one. As the title of the book indicates, the story is cast in an autumnal key, and at times a ghostly feeling of the past is indeed brought up before us very beautifully and skilfully. Tourguéneff would have made of it a poem, but Mr. Howells, possibly through a weaker sense of the value of tone, just fails to do so. And again we are inclined to lay the blame at the door of that fatal theory of the 'moral purpose'. The Tourguéneff book might have been a shade morbid, the autumnal quality would have been more insistent, the story would have ended on a note of disillusionment, and that would be contrary to the theory that it is one's duty to encourage—to encourage even elderly lovers.

'Neither arts, nor letters, nor sciences, except as they tend to make the race better and kinder, are to be regarded as serious interests,' and there can be no doubt that Mr. Howells' best novels, even some that are not quite his best, fulfil these conditions. They are so kindly themselves, so wise and so humorous, so human and unpretentious, that while reading them we are thankful to bask in their sunshine. We forget the existence of evil, for it is never present even in his least agreeable characters. The faults of the books are never faults of taste, of slovenly writing, of unintelligence; and it seems almost ungrateful to demand more from them than they offer, and to feel dissatisfied because a talent, at its best so delightful, so delicate and individual, should lack one or two qualities which might have raised it to a higher rank.

1919.

HUGH LOFTING
AND THE NURSERY SHELF

With our first plunge into the sea of fiction we accepted some very queer things. Its literary quality was not what endeared a story to us. In those far-off days one had never heard of literary qualities. We liked perhaps the tune of a poem, but the less emphatic rhythms of prose were too subtle to be grasped; and at any rate the books on the nursery shelf possessed none. Yet the fact remains that certain of these were read once only, others again and again, so that something more than a mere curiosity as to what was going to happen in the story must have been involved. What was that 'something more'? I myself, for example, knew a fair amount of the prose and all of the verse in the two *Alices* by heart, but later on, in my teens, I had an even greater though a different kind of affection for several of the tales of George Manville Fenn.

Sympathy, I now see, explained the attraction of the Fenn stories. In them there were usually two characters between whom existed a relation that strongly appealed to me, and the adventures, in my imagination, thus acquired an emotional quality which might have surprised the author. On the other hand, a story designed to touch the emotions, a deliberately pathetic story such as *Misunderstood*, left me not only dry-eyed but coldly hostile. Nor was this just one's

tiresomeness. *Misunderstood*—read aloud by a grown-up sister
—did not exactly bore me, but its two small heroes,
Humphrey and Miles, produced a sense of irritation not un-
mixed with scepticism. I knew they were 'dear little boys'
—their every word and action proclaimed it—but this in
itself put me off. I distrusted 'dear little boys'; I felt that in
actual life they did not exist; the sentimental humour with
which they were presented did not amuse me; I disliked the
pathos, and I particularly disliked the references to a dead
mother. This antipathy never reached the point of positive
loathing inspired by *Little Lord Fauntleroy*; it consisted rather
in an uneasiness, a feeling that I was being made to listen to
what ought not to be talked about—to what no real boy
ever *would* talk about. In short, I disliked the *kind* of sentiment, which was not my kind. Older persons must have
found my taste difficult to gauge. At any rate, I could tell of
one tragic Christmas when I received no fewer than three
books by that dreariest of impostors, G. A. Henty, and of
the disgraceful scene that followed. At thirteen one *does*
look a gift-horse in the mouth, or at least I did.

In the days I refer to, children's books were seldom
attractive. Their authors turned them out methodically, but
there can have been little 'joy in the making'; they were
hack-work. Boys' books were different, because so many tales
actually written for grown-ups—tales like *The Wreck of the
'Grosvenor'*, or *King Solomon's Mines*—could easily be squeezed
into this category, and, as everybody knows, *Treasure Island*
actually was written for a boys' magazine. But on the
nursery shelf few treasures were to be found. Even now
there are not many, and, with the exception of the *Alices*,
most of those that exist came too late to beguile my own
childhood. I feel certain, for instance, that I should have
loved *The Three Mulla Mulgars*, and *A Little Boy Lost*; and one

might add to these the best books of E. Nesbit. *The Wind in the Willows* I shall not add; its sniggering sophistication rules it out; I would much rather include *The Water Babies*, though *The Water Babies* is a thing hopelessly spoiled, really only half a story, the rest being a tract dedicated to the Victorian parent. And so we reach the subject of the present paper, the tales of Mr. Hugh Lofting.

When *Alice's Adventures in Wonderland* first appeared it must have been a hard book to describe, and it is the same with Mr. Lofting's *Dolittle* volumes. They are not like anything that had been done before; they are made for reading aloud, and there should be a cat and a dog asleep on the hearthrug, and the reader should be elderly, with spectacles, and, in spite of her enwrapt audience, not unmindful of the clock on the nursery chimney-piece. At any rate, whether read aloud or in silence, they give one the comfortable feeling of listening to the spoken word. Mr. Lofting's stories are not fairy-stories, they are not adventure-stories, they are not matter-of-fact stories, they are not animal-stories (at least of any hitherto known type), but are a blend of all four, with the animals predominating, and the fairy element absent—except, indeed, that the animals talk. Perhaps the nearest thing to them is *Puss in Boots*, and it is not very near. Still, if Mr. Lofting has hankerings after immortality, he may take pleasure in the thought that *Puss in Boots* is no gift of yesterday. *Le Maistre Chat*, by Charles Perrault, was published in 1697. What a first edition to discover! Even the British Museum does not possess a copy, for no books disappear so rapidly as do children's favourites. Doctor Isaac Watts reminds us in a well-known poem that their little hands were made to tear off bindings, and their little paint-brushes to embellish illustrations. However, though half a dozen avenues suddenly open out before me, I

fields. Adventures follow, and still further adventures in *The Voyages of Doctor Dolittle*. The scheme of this second book is different. There is a little boy in it, who comes as the Doctor's assistant, and the story partakes more of the nature of a wonder-book—with a floating island, a journey along the bed of the sea, and other marvels. This is Polynesia's book. In it she takes the upper hand and keeps everybody right—which is what she likes. 'Shall I sing *Home, Sweet Home*?' asks poor Prince Bumpo, humbly wishing to please. 'No,' answers Polynesia. 'Then he'd never go back. Your voice needs a rest.' The reply is characteristic, for the centuries have not sweetened Polynesia's temper.

When I read the first *Dolittle* book I supposed this would be all, but I was reckoning without Mr. Lofting's inventiveness, the vein was very far indeed from running out. In the third tale a circus is started, the Doctor's African trip having left him in debt, and a circus appearing an easy way of raising money. Certainly, all the members of his gifted family are well equipped for such a profession, but at first he thinks it more prudent to join forces with a Mr. Blossom, an old hand at the game, though Mr. Blossom's is the kind of circus he likes least—a travelling circus, and not a very splendid specimen at that. Mr. Blossom's animals are dirty and unhappy, but in spite of difficulties and the opposition of the human members of the troupe, the Doctor soon begins to work wonders, while his own animals have an unprecedented success. Polynesia now retires into the background; the new heroine is Sophie from Alaska.

Sophie is a performing seal, and Sophie has received bad news from home and wants to get back to Alaska as quickly as possible. The Doctor is worried. Much the simplest plan, of course, would be to buy her from Mr. Blossom, had there been money to do so. But the Doctor's capital is precisely

£2 5s. 9d., which is not nearly enough: therefore the only thing is to help Sophie to escape. The plan has to be carefully engineered, but all the other animals, and with them the faithful Matthew Mugg, are eager to give advice and assistance. Jip, the dog, as usual is particularly full of bright ideas; nevertheless, if Sophie is ever to reach Alaska it is plain that she must go by sea, and the nearest sea, the Bristol Channel, is a hundred miles away. Were there any rivers or canals it would not be so hard to manage, but to get to the nearest river Sophie has to cross forty miles of open country, and how she is to travel incognito along the high roads (or for that matter the low roads) is a problem. To begin with, she is so big! A bonnet, a cloak, and a thick veil may do something, and one need take only the night coaches; still, it will be difficult even in the semi-darkness for Sophie to pass as a lady friend of the Doctor's. Having no legs is a drawback; indeed, everything about poor Sophie suddenly appears to be a drawback—including her superb sealskin coat, which the Doctor's cheap fifteen-shilling coat never quite hides, and which keeps on attracting the attention and envy of her female fellow-passengers. They accept her at first as an interesting, but very soon regard her as a most mysterious, invalid; nor does Sophie's tendency to slip off the seat on to the floor help matters. The Doctor arranges her in a corner, but she flops dreadfully. Besides, the veil makes her want to sneeze, and when she does sneeze she nearly lifts the roof off. Coaching has to be abandoned.

The chief feature of the next book, *The Caravan*, is the production of the canary opera. For this there is an all-bird cast, and the orchestral instruments are a sewing-machine, a razor and strop, a chain, and a cobbler's last and hammer. These were selected by the birds themselves, who also composed the music; the Doctor, of course, acting as conductor and producer. The sewing-machine is a particular favourite, because of its stimulating effect upon the voice. For the truth of this at least, I can vouch. Instantly it called up a scene from the past, and I saw my nurse Emma seated at her sewing-machine, while Dicky, the canary, from the sunlit nursery window let out his full voice in a swelling rapture that soared high above Emma's accompaniment. It also, I may add, recalled a memorable performance of *La Bohème* at Covent Garden, with Bonci, the great Italian tenor, triumphing again and again over an orchestra that had got out of control.

To me one of the many charms of these *Dolittle* books is that, without neglecting old favourites, each brings into the foreground a new set of animals. Hence their variety. In *Doctor Dolittle's Zoo* the rats and mice are the heroes, and the yarns they spin at their club are as good as anything in the earlier tales. We get the stories of the Hotel Rat, of the Prison Rat, of the Volcano Rat, of the Museum Mouse, of the Stable Mouse; we even get a detective story for Kling, a new type of character, a dog detective, who solves in fine style the mystery of Moorsden Manor.

Mr. Lofting's tales, to my mind, are incomparably the best books for children that have been given to the world since the two *Alices*. There is not a false note in the whole five volumes (a sixth, I believe, has appeared in America, for though Mr. Lofting comes of a north of Ireland family, America is his country). He is a happy man, a public benefactor: I should think his books must have done more to establish an excellent understanding between their youthful readers and the furred and feathered communities than all the teaching that was ever taught and all the preaching that was ever preached.

1923—1927.

W. H. HUDSON[1]

I. A Naturalist's Boyhood

To say that *A Little Boy Lost* and *Far Away and Long Ago* are the most delightful of all Mr. Hudson's books is, of course, merely to express an individual preference. Another reader will prefer *A Shepherd's Life*, a lover of romance will vote for *The Purple Land*, a lover of birds for one of the books about birds. But actually I had a further and a better reason for bracketing together my own two particular favourites. They ought to be *read* together. Though one is a highly imaginative, and sometimes fantastic tale written for youngsters, and the other an autobiography, they are in a very real sense complementary, each throwing a different yet almost equally revealing light upon Mr. Hudson's childhood. Now that we have the autobiography we can see how essentially true, despite its fantasy, was the earlier book. We can trace in what really happened the origin of many of the episodes in the invented story—those beautiful episodes, for instance, of the spoonbill, of the spotted snake, of the children of the Mirage, even of the Lady of the Hills. And these differ only from corresponding episodes in the autobiography in that they are shown to us through the veils of dreamland. Mr. Hudson as a child was very like the Martin of his tale, and one might go further and say that in the tale we get even

[1] *Far Away and Long Ago*. By W. H. Hudson. 1918.
The Book of a Naturalist. By W. H. Hudson. 1920.
W. H. Hudson: A Portrait. By Morley Roberts. 1924.

closer to that child's spirit than we do in the autobiography, which is characterized by a note of reticence, and is certainly of all autobiographies one remembers the least egotistical.

Far Away and Long Ago, then, is a book which, if it should ever come their way, ought to please young as well as older readers, because Mr. Hudson's was exactly the kind of life they must often have imagined for themselves. They will think he was extremely fortunate, and they will be right. Shut in a town, he would have been a little boy lost indeed. Out in that wild free country, everything around him contributed to the growth of his mind and spirit, ministered to the development of his simple tranquil genius.

The book is full of queer people as well as of birds and beasts. It plunges us into a world that is fresh and lovely, a world wherein wild picturesque things happen, wherein the oddest persons appear and disappear. To read it is to feel the wonder and charm of a quite new experience, to live, on those broad open plains of La Plata, through a boyhood which seems temporarily to be ours, though it was really only Mr. Hudson's. We are surrounded by the glory of the earth, by life and the love of life; and Mr. Hudson's art has the magic quality of unsealing our eyes, and indeed of opening all our senses, to that vivifying glory. There is a marvellous passage in the chapter called 'Boyhood's End' wherein the whole adventure is summed up, but which is too long to be quoted in full:

'What, then, did I want?—what did I ask to have? If the question had been put to me then, and if I had been capable of expressing what was in me, I should have replied: I want only to keep what I have; to rise each morning and look out on the sky and the grassy dew-wet earth from day to day, from year to year. To watch every June and July for spring, to feel the same old sweet surprise and delight at the appearance of each familiar flower, every new-born insect, every bird returned once more from the north. . . . To climb trees and put my hand down in the deep hot nest and feel the hot eggs. . . . To lie on a grassy bank with the blue water between me and the beds of tall bulrushes, listening to the mysterious sounds of the wind. . . . To ride at noon on the hottest days, when the whole earth is a-glitter with illusory water, and see the cattle and horses in thousands, covering the plain at their watering-places; to visit some haunt of large birds at that still, hot hour and see storks, ibises, grey herons, egrets of a dazzling whiteness, and rose-coloured spoonbills and flamingoes, standing in the shallow water in which their motionless forms are reflected. To lie on my back on the rust-brown grass in January and gaze up at the wide hot whitey-blue sky, peopled with millions and myriads of glistening balls of thistle-down, ever, ever floating by; to gaze and gaze until they are to me living things and I, in an ecstasy, am with them, floating in that immense shining void!'

That is the true spirit of animism, and if I, a town-bred, stay-at-home child, brought up in surroundings so infinitely commonplace when compared with Mr. Hudson's, could share its rapture, small wonder that I regard him as having been an uncommonly lucky little boy!

Here is another and more objective picture, a portrait of Doña Mercedes, chosen from an extensive gallery because of the dogs in it:

'She was the biggest and fattest woman in our neighbourhood . . . not a lady by birth, not an educated person. . . . She sat always in a large cane easy-chair, outdoors or in, invariably with four hairless dogs in her company, one on her broad lap, another on a lambskin rug at her feet, and one on

rugs at each side. The three on the floor were patiently waiting for their respective turns to occupy the broad warm lap
when the time came to remove the last favoured one from
that position.'

Of course, the autobiography is primarily the story of a
worshipper of Nature. The small boy in whose company we
wander over the plains and linger by the pools and swamps—
this little tree-worshipper and bird-worshipper—has from
the age of six, when we first make his acquaintance, the
same absorbing loves, follows eagerly the same pursuits, that
are to be his in youth and manhood. 'My feathered friends,'
he says, 'were so much to me that I am constantly tempted
to make this sketch of my early years a book about birds.'
Luckily for us he resisted the temptation. When he is writing about other animals (there is a beautiful chapter called
'A Serpent Mystery'), or about human beings, his work, to
me at least, is so much more interesting that I half resent
and wholly deplore that lifelong devotion to birds. In the
autobiography they are not given undue prominence; the
other creatures get a full share of attention, and there is a
constant variety. If one had to find a fault, it would be that
our little boy is too much inclined to efface *himself*, there
being so many wonderful outside things he wishes to show
us. True, we see him closely, and get to know him as intimately as he desires; but none the less we feel that there is a
secret he is withholding from us—perhaps a secret impossible to share. He is, even in his confidences, a most reserved
little boy; one who goes his own way and thinks his own
thoughts. We may divine part of his secret, perhaps, through
Mr. Hudson's spiritual interpretation of Nature, which at
times reminds us of Wordsworth's, and is always more that
of a poet than of a man of science. For even when he is writing of flowers and trees and insects there runs through

Hudson's work an undertone of dreaming, of mysticism. It became an overtone in *A Little Boy Lost*; hence that book's special charm. And always the prose is simple, clear, and harmonious. This beautiful style, I am convinced, came to Mr. Hudson as naturally and easily as breathing: I should be much surprised if, like Robert Louis Stevenson, he had ever played the sedulous ape to anyone. It is not difficult to recognize an acquired style, and while it may be—in the rare case of a Charles Lamb—very delightful, yet I must confess that the older I grow the higher value I set on simplicity.

II. *The Poet as Naturalist*

Mr. Hudson is a benevolent magician. His innocent spells 'give delight, and hurt not', but they are remarkably potent. I began his *Book of a Naturalist* on a dark winter day, when the rain had blurred the windows, while out of doors a dismal umbrella'd and waterproofed world passed hurriedly to and fro along the streaming footpaths; and straightway I found myself in the windless quiet of a summer pine-wood—expectant, attentive, watching swarms of little red ants ascending and descending the smooth trunk of a tree, bent on a secret task. Time and place and season changed as I reached other chapters (choosing at haphazard, for it matters not a straw in what order they are taken), but always the feeling of enchantment and adventure remained: I was happy and in good company, and desired no more.

For me these Hudson books (with a few exceptions) are a perpetual delight. I can read the best of them again and again, yet I am no naturalist, am a lover of lawns and gardens (which he will tell you is a bad sign), and find the most beautiful scenery in the world insufficient unless I 'have one with me wandering'. Of course, I should like to see with my bodily eyes all the wonderful things Mr. Hudson sees, but I lack the patience and a pair of field-glasses. Possibly, too, I lack the noiseless and practised tread. I think there must be something in this; otherwise why, when I walk in a wood, should I count myself lucky if I catch so much as the whisk of a squirrel's tail? Mr. Hudson would say that it is because I am usually accompanied by one or two 'canine pests', who rush on ahead, bent on their own impetuous investigations. But I like 'canine pests', so when I wish to get into really close touch with the wild creatures I fall back on Mr. Hudson—always Mr. Hudson.

This raises a pertinent question. Why is it that I can read the Hudson books, absorbed, captivated, charmed, when most other books about Nature, those of Richard Jefferies, for example, pall on me so quickly? 'But the Dwarf answered: No; something human is dearer to me than the wealth of all the world,' and it is this mysterious 'something human', I think, which holds my interest and makes Mr. Hudson's books (quite apart from their style) so much more enticing than those of Jefferies and his followers.

I should even go so far as to say that this 'something human' has a direct effect on the style. The prose of Jefferies —except in *Bevis*, where he is very human indeed—irritates me in much the same way as does the verse of Swinburne. I have always a feeling that he is writing a great deal about very little, that he could go on for ever, and that he *will* go on until the appointed space has been filled. Those verbose overcharged descriptions are evocative only in a vague and cloudy way; they are detailed, yet produce an impression of emotional gush, and the essential, the creative word is lost in an undisciplined lavishness that almost borders on vulgarity. It is never so with Mr. Hudson. He knows the value of restraint, of selection. Though the contemplation of Nature arouses in him an emotion as strong as any to be found in the most rapturous pages of Jefferies, it is an emotion under control, and there is a mind behind it. He calls himself a sentimentalist, but not a hint of sentimentality is visible in his work. He never indulges even in that anthropomorphism which has made the work of several modern naturalists popular. His animals have individuality; they are, we might even say, Hudsonized; but if by any chance they did begin to talk, it certainly would not be to express the ideas or aspirations of mankind.

What then, it may be asked, is the human note I have alluded to as constituting the particular charm of these studies? It might better have been called an autobiographical note, for Mr. Hudson seems more in sympathy with his furred and feathered friends—ever so much more indeed—than he is with humanity. Towards mankind he maintains an attitude of detachment as complete as that of his Little Boy Lost—his small restless traveller, who will form no ties, strike no roots, but will wander from place to place as the roving instinct in his blood prompts him—lonely as a cloud.

There is a reason for this, and he gives it. 'We are not *in* Nature,' he tells us, and that is that. *We* may not be, but *he* most assuredly is. Hence, perhaps, here and there, certain insensibilities, certain bleaknesses, the more disconcerting for their unexpectedness. The chapter on 'The Great Dog Superstition', for instance, gave me, I confess, very much the shock one might receive were a man suddenly to begin abusing his mother. I am sorry Mr. Hudson thought it worth while to reprint this essay. Not that his dislike of dogs will alter in the slightest degree any sensible person's opinion of them; but for quite another reason. Better far to have let it lie where it had lain for so many years, buried in an old number of *Macmillan's Magazine*. For it is not a good essay, not worthy of its author. I am willing to accept all that is said in praise of lemurs, chinchillas, etc., but the vilification of dogs—those 'skulking creatures' of 'disgusting instincts', and 'smelling abominably of carrion and carnage'—strikes me as at best a peevish performance. The contemptuous remarks about dog-lovers one does not mind. 'Canopholists' these are termed, 'people weak in their intellectuals, and as a rule unveracious'. But the quarrel with the dog himself seems to me stupid, based, as it appears largely to be, on that animal's preference for certain smells which do not appeal to Mr. Hudson. Why shouldn't the dog have his favourite smells? Yet this preference, together with his relationship to the jackal, lead Mr. Hudson to deny any moral virtue whatever to such doggish deeds of his as 'pulling a drowning man out of the water, or scratching him out of a snowdrift'. Even his 'affection for his master—the desire to be constantly with and to be noticed and caressed by him, the impatience at his absence and grief at his loss, and the courage to defend him and his house and his belongings from strangers' is 'a very small and a very low thing'; 'it exists in a great many, probably in a large majority, of mammalian brains'. Why this should make it small and low I have not been able to grasp, but then, from the whole essay little emerges except that Mr. Hudson apparently prefers the qualities characterizing hyenas, monkeys, cats, and harvest mice.

It is true he has tacked on a half-apologetic and wholly perfunctory note at the end of his chapter, but the apology is unconvincing. He reprints the chapter 'just for fun', he says, yet the fun is distinctly an afterthought, and not very infectious. 'We may say,' he tells us elsewhere, 'that unless

the soul goes out to meet what we see we do not see it;
nothing do we see, not a beetle, not a blade of grass.' And
we feel that he, who writes so charmingly of toads and lambs
and rats and pigs, has not seen dogs. He has not seen them,
because on them alone he turns an unsympathetic eye, and
observes them with a mind that is coldly inimical. He sees
everything else he describes in his book, which makes us but
regret the more this unfortunate essay, since it stands out as
the only barren spot in a world of natural magic and poetry.
How eagerly one turns from it to the beautiful chapters on
serpents, to the still more beautiful chapter on moths! and
when he is writing of what he loves how excellent does that
writing become! As he himself says, in this moth chapter:

'It is what we feel that matters. I might have been standing in some wilderness never trodden by human foot, myself
an unhuman solitary, and merely by willing it I had drawn
those beautiful beings of the dark to me, charming them as
with a flowery fragrance from their secret hiding places in
a dim world of leaves to gather upon and cover me over
with their downy, trembling, mottled grey and rich yellow
velvet wings.'

And again, of a crimson underwing moth, who had flown
into his sitting-room and remained there two days and two
nights:

'It was early September, with mild sunny days and misty
or wet nights, and in the evening, when the room was very
warm, we would throw the windows and doors open, thinking of the delicious relief it would be for our prisoner to
pass out of that superheated atmosphere, that painful brightness, into his own wide, wet world, its darkness and silence
and fragrance, and a mysterious signal wafted to him from
a distance out of clouds of whispering leaves, from one
there waiting for him.'

There, in those beautiful descriptions, which are more than descriptions, is the real Hudson, the creator of a lovely, innocent, passionate world wherein we 'walk by flowery places . . . or at some late hour by moonlight . . . with the delight, the sense of wonder in all life, which is akin to, if not one with, the mythical faculty, and if experienced in a high degree is a sense of the supernatural in all natural things'.

III. W. H. Hudson: a Portrait

'The real Hudson', I have said; but what *was* 'the real Hudson'? I opened Mr. Morley Roberts' book about his friend with the liveliest hopes of finding out, or rather of finding support for my own impression: I closed it with mingled feelings of perplexity and disappointment. There is a passage near the end which perhaps explains, or helps to explain, why Mr. Roberts' 'portrait', for all its sympathy and sincerity, left me unsatisfied. 'Hudson,' he says, 'knew well he was difficult to understand. Perhaps the only piece of common vanity in him centred about this. He was not going to let people comprehend him. I have seen a letter in which he actually said that no one could or should.' And, as a matter of fact, the Hudson Mr. Roberts shows us is not the Hudson, nor even like the Hudson, I myself had pictured. Yet still I am unconvinced. The author of *Far Away and Long Ago* lived to be an old man—he was eighty-one when he died, not seventy-five, as he allowed it to be thought (another little peculiarity, if really deliberate), and Mr. Roberts knew him only in the second half of his life. Moreover, the most detailed portion of the biography is that dealing with the final period of all, when ill-health had made of Hudson a distinctly difficult companion, irritable, unreasonable, contradictious.

No doubt there was always a queer streak in him, as there obviously was in his lost little boy. That little boy, for all his charm, showed in certain relations a vein of callousness which was rather more than the careless, natural callousness of childhood. He had a capacity for forgetting people as soon as they had served his purpose; he hardly gave a thought to the mother he had left behind; and he abandoned his second mother, the Lady of the Hills, with an equal blitheness the moment her store of wonders was exhausted. Hudson, one now sees, to some, perhaps to a large, extent shared this capacity. 'He has,' Mr. Roberts notes in his diary, 'the most extraordinary power of instant detachment, and frequently, after being really affectionate, when I say good-bye and shake hands, he'll say "good-bye" without turning towards me as I go, a thing I couldn't do unless I was actually angry with anybody.' And again: 'He often says cutting things, and at times I have wondered whether he meant to do so or not. One great friend of his said to me that he liked to hurt his friends.'

Even Hudson's attitude where animals are concerned, though nearly always it reveals a profound sympathy, now and again draws us up with an unexpected jar. There is that regrettable paper on dogs, which Mr. Roberts speaks of as having been suppressed, but which, on the contrary, was revived in one of his best books with every symptom of pleasure; and what would the members of the S.P.C.A. make of the following scrap of dialogue?

'He went on to talk at large and rather contemptuously of what he called super-humanitarians.

'H, Why I know a lot of people who would feel just as if

a knife went through them if they saw a boy pulling a fly's legs off!

'R. Isn't that natural?

'H. No, it's absurd.

'R. Why, I'd like to have the boy whipped, and whipped hard, if I saw him doing it.

'H. Such a feeling is ridiculous and morbid.'

Yet, personally, I very much doubt if this expresses Hudson's real feeling towards either flies or boys—means, indeed, anything more than that he was in one of those disputatious moods to which he became increasingly prone. Still, the moods are not endearing, and one lays down Mr. Roberts' book with the very definite feeling that Hudson must have put the best of himself into his writings. One knew, of course, he was no crank, no sentimentalist, and could even chat amicably with the snarers of his beloved birds; nevertheless this conversation quoted by Mr. Roberts does not fit in with the passionate indignation aroused by the sight of cruelty which is expressed here and there in Hudson's own writings. He was, to be sure, more in touch with birds and beasts, insects and reptiles, than with humans; which is why he wrote better about them. On the other hand, he understood and interpreted certain types of humanity finely—the shepherds of the Wiltshire Downs, for example—while as an interpreter of Nature he was unique, and not merely, not even principally, because of the beauty of his style, but because of the sympathetic quality of his imagination and temperament.

He had the imagination of a poet. There is a description in *A Shepherd's Life* of an old woman picking the brown dead moss from the lettering on the headstones in a country churchyard, which, in its homely yet intense beauty and gravity, produces precisely the *kind* of effect that the best pastoral poems of Wordsworth produce. As for *A Little Boy Lost*, it is steeped from beginning to end in the poetry of earth. Birds, beasts, flowers, the clouds, the sea, the mist, the sunshine, the little boy—all are alive with the same life, breathe 'that sense of something in nature which to the enlightened or civilized man is not there . . . that sense or apprehension of an intelligence like our own, but more powerful, in all visible things.' And this apprehension, this pantheistic sense of communion with the soul in Nature, was probably the strongest emotion Hudson ever felt.

I dare say it is chiefly because there is so little of this side of the man in Mr. Roberts' portrait that it disappointed me. Evidently there were things in his life of which Hudson rarely or never spoke, and I cannot help believing that these were just the things which might have supplied the missing key to his strange personality. If he *did* deliberately try to be incomprehensible (which is in itself, to me, incomprehensible), can we put much faith in the impression he produced upon his friend—intimate friendship obviously being ruled out at once? 'On the surface Hudson and his books are not a bit like each other,' Mr. Roberts declares, and one may take it that his determination never to allow those who knew him to penetrate below the surface was successful. But in that case the real Hudson *was* the Hudson of the books. Mr. Roberts, I expect, is still too close to it quite to realize the effect his study at times produces. We do not want an idealization, but still less do we want to spy on a sick eagle in his cage, and somehow that is what, in those closing chapters, we are doing. To get an impression of the eagle in the strength and joy of his youth we must turn back to his own pages. At all events, we shall get it nowhere else, and I close these desultory remarks with the words of

W. H. HUDSON

Hudson's younger brother, said wistfully at parting, when
the naturalist was setting sail for England, where he was to
spend the remainder of his life: 'Of all the people I have
ever known you are the only one I do not know.'

1918—1924.

THE POET'S BESTIARY[1]

'A Book of Notes and Queries'—that might be the sub-
title of Mr. Norman Douglas's *Birds and Beasts of the Greek
Anthology*; and for this reason I confess to having found it a
little disappointing. I hasten to add that its charm, learning,
and humour are entirely characteristic, and indeed I might
be at a loss to describe quite what sort of book it was that I
expected. Something less scientific, perhaps, and more in
the nature of a book for lovers of animals and lovers of
poetry. But this is to quarrel with a writer because he has
not chosen the subject we should have liked him to choose.
Mr. Douglas is not primarily concerned with how the
Greeks regarded animals: on the contrary, he necessarily
dismisses that aspect when he rules out from his survey all
the domestic creatures, and with them many of the most
beautiful poems. Here, for instance, is one that can find
no place:

'The labouring ox, outworn with years and toil, Alcon,
gratefully remembering his past works, did not lead to the
slaughter-house; and now, wandering through the deep
meadow grass, he rejoices with lowings over freedom from
the plough.'

The avowed and simple purpose of Mr. Douglas's book is

[1] *Birds and Beasts of the Greek Anthology*. By Norman Douglas. 1928.

merely to identify all the wild animals that are mentioned in the *Anthology*, and he finds 'some hundred and fifty-three of them', the references amounting to 'close upon six hundred'. Consequently, the sentimental view is ignored. Sentimental views of any kind, in fact, are not much in Mr. Norman Douglas's line: still the Greeks *had* this feeling of fellowship with birds and beasts; certain of their philosophic theories were founded upon it, and their poets write of animals with much the same grave tenderness as they write of children. Now and then, indeed, animals and children are unconsciously grouped together, as in the famous lines of Sappho:

'Evening, you who gather all that bright morning scattered; you bring the sheep and the goat, the child back to his mother.'

And the animals may be extremely small:

'Here beside the threshing-floor, O toiling ant, I raise a memorial to you in this dry clod of earth, that the furrow and corn of Demeter may charm you still as you lie within your rustic tomb.'

Mr. Douglas quotes the latter poem, because, I suppose, ants are wild creatures, but quotes it in a version that for me robs it of the quality of which I speak:

> Here by this threshing-floor, ant of much toil,
> A mound I build thee of the thirsty soil,
> That, even in death, Demeter's furrowed grain
> Thee, housed in the ploughed glebe, may yet sustain.

In fact, nearly always he prefers a verse translation.

No longer, my decoy wild partridge, from thy throat
Rings through the umbrageous wood that resonant clear note,
Luring thy pencilled mates that feed beneath the glade;
For thy last journey thou to Acheron hast made.

The only impression created by such involved and irritating jingles is that the Greeks wrote doggerel, which is not the truth. Mr. Douglas might very well have made his own translations, as Anatole France always did.

Having expressed these grumbles, however, I must admit that it would be more to the point to consider the actual content and qualities of a book which is only indirectly connected with poetry, in so far that the material has been supplied by poets. The quainter that material the better Mr. Douglas is pleased. 'Exigencies of versification are responsible for some little botanical and zoological confusion in nearly all poetry,' he says, 'and one really cannot expect these charming people to be meticulous about such trifles; they have enough to do avoiding hiatuses and minding their quantities.' But not all the confusion is due to care for quantities. Some of the scientific guesses strike us to-day as distinctly wild, though doubtless in the poet's mind they may have had an origin more or less plausible. 'Archelaus tells us that serpents are generated out of the spinal cord of a corpse.' 'It is a pity,' Mr. Douglas adds, 'he has left us no larger treatise on Natural History, to judge by the few samples of his learning which are preserved in the Anthology.' Archelaus, however, was no exception, and the reader turning to the fifteenth book of Ovid's *Metamorphoses* will find equally daring views attributed to Pythagoras, that genuine animal lover. And in less abstruse matters than the generation of serpents—matters of direct observation—often the Greeks were right. They 'never shared our notion as to the stupidity of the goose', Mr. Douglas tells us, 'which is not only a most affectionate bird, but an unusually intelligent one as well'. It is also, I can vouch, an excellent guardian of property—and when I say this I am not thinking of the geese who saved Rome, but of a rather painful personal experience. I can remember encountering, when a very small boy, a gander upon whom temporarily had fallen the duties of watch-dog. These he carried out with a conscientiousness and zeal that made even the most innocent approach to his master's house a difficult and dangerous undertaking. Since I was obliged to *try* to approach it, I was reduced to tears; but the heart of the gander remained un-softened, and the more copiously I wept the louder he hissed.

The list of fishes enumerated in the *Anthology* is rela-tively short: there are only twenty-two of them. But then fishes are chiefly beloved of the angler, and, as Mr. Douglas points out, 'it would be difficult to write a lament on the death of a favourite herring'. For all that, the Greeks *had* a favourite fish—the dolphin. For some obscure reason they were extremely fond of dolphins, attributing to them the most surprising virtues, such as a sense of justice, a taste for music, and an affection for mankind. Mr. Douglas ignores the sense of justice, is doubtful about the taste for music, and definitely rejects the affection. 'The dolphin cares no more about us than does the haddock,' he roundly declares —a statement which I can't help feeling very likely may be true. 'A sympathy for man, equally charming and equally fanciful, was attributed to other creatures as well; to the nightingale, for instance, or to the swallow.' That this sympathy does, nevertheless, exist in certain non-human species, we know. Most persons when working in a garden have received friendly advances from a robin (who will even perch on the spade with which we are digging), and W. H. Hudson has reported examples of a similar friendli-ness in pumas and in snakes. Nobody supposes it to be an entirely unselfish sympathy (though the puma's would appear to be), but the marvel (considering our sporting instincts) is that any should exist at all. Indeed, if it comes to that, what *human* sympathy is entirely unselfish? and how precarious it would be if it were!

How comes it that the butterfly is not mentioned once in the *Anthology*, and the moth only once, by Meleager? The cicada, on the other hand, is supposed to share the dolphin's interest in humanity, and therefore becomes the subject of some delightful poems. 'The Greeks loved the cicada,' says Mr. Douglas. 'They loved it; and they ate it. Aristotle says that early in the season the males are the most savoury; afterwards the females; and that the larva of the cicada tastes best before it has burst its covering. A disgusting banquet.' I agree; but then the eating of eels, of the legs of frogs, of living oysters, also strikes me as disgusting. There is no hard and fast rule in such matters: they are questions of taste. To return to reminiscence, I well remember, with another boy, digging up a quantity of large red earthworms. We put them in a pot to use as bait, but the luscious sight of them, all glistening and squirming, made my companion's mouth water. He said he *knew* they would be delicious—though whether eaten raw, or cooked, I was careful not to inquire. At any rate, Mr. Douglas could have added that our nature poets love lambs; and eat them—not sharing the scruples of Pythagoras and Mr. Bernard Shaw. As for the æsthetic aspect, there is perhaps little to choose between the larva of the cicada and a lively piece of cheese, or even a putrefying grouse.

I know I am quite wrong, quite unscientific, but I have to confess that to me the cicada and the grasshopper are one and the same creature. That comes, probably, from having created in boyhood an imaginary Greece on the banks of my native river. There the grasshopper flourished and raised his pleasant din. I never caught one, but Greek boys did, and kept them in little woven cages as pets. Here is a poem by Nikios of Miletos (unquoted by Mr. Douglas) which has a bearing on the practice—from the grasshopper's point of view:

'No longer rolling in the cool tree-shadows can I send forth a happy sound from my quick-fanning wings; for I have fallen into the cruel hands of a boy, who seized me secretly, as I sat under the green leaves.'

Culinary matters, as we have seen, are not neglected in this most original treatise, and Mr. Douglas, if he is not tempted by cicadas, gives us one or two recipes for the cooking of his own favourite fauna. It is all extremely personal and amusing. Its scientific value I am not qualified to discuss, but *Birds and Beasts* belongs to that rare and delightful class of companionable books—books one slips into one's pocket when going out for a stroll through the fields or the woods.

1928.

ARTHUR RIMBAUD[1]

In all literature there is no more enigmatic figure than that
of Arthur Rimbaud; and, I feel inclined to add, none less
agreeable. He had his virtues—they number, I think, two—
courage and sincerity—for the rest, he was selfish, cold-
hearted, ungrateful; while his normal mood seems to have
been one of cynical disdain for everybody and everything.
And this singularly unpleasant egotist was a genius—narrow,
bitter, but intensely vital. His work has exercised an enormous influence on modern French poetry, and it was all
written before he had reached the age of nineteen. In his
own country several biographical and critical volumes have
been devoted to him, among them Marcel Coulon's admirable *Problème de Rimbaud*, but Mr. Edgell Rickword's *Rimbaud: the Boy and the Poet* is the first attempt, I think, to tell
at full length his story in English.

In point of fact, in English it is a rather difficult story to
tell—that is, if one is to tell it without reservation—and,
though Mr. Rickword has written an interesting book, and
a good book on the side of its literary criticism, he has not,
on the side concerning 'Rimbaud, the boy', to my mind
written a convincing one. The principal episode, the extraordinary and unfortunate drama which arose out of the

---

[1] *Rimbaud: the Boy and the Poet.* By Edgell Rickword. 1924.

friendship with Verlaine, is left in comparative obscurity; yet it is just this episode that, psychologically, is so important, because it had such far-reaching effects on the lives of both poets. It altered, for a time at least, the content of Verlaine's poetry; it altered, quite possibly, the whole course of Rimbaud's future career. Marcel Coulon rightly makes it the centre of his work, and his interpretation—bold, subtle, and penetrating—probably comes very near to the truth.

From the beginning, it must be remembered that we are dealing with an abnormal case. Genius is rare, but the precocity of Rimbaud's talent is something rarer still, is in fact unparalleled. The work of a youthful Blake or Chatterton is as nothing when compared with the work of this boy, who at the age of fifteen was already a mature and original poet. The originality is unqualified. It would have been repugnant to Rimbaud's nature to imitate anything that had been done before, therefore all his poems are experiments and discoveries. He invented his own technique, chose his own subject-matter, and the first bundle of manuscripts he sent to Verlaine contained most of the poems upon which his fame rests to-day. Mr. Arthur Symons says that Rimbaud's mind was the mind of the man of action, not that of the artist, but I confess I cannot follow this; to me it seems one might as well say that Villon's was not the mind of the artist. Moreover, he never repeated himself; all his poetry was written before he was eighteen; all his prose before he was nineteen; after that he conceived a violent hatred for literature, referred to his own work as 'absurde! ridicule! degoûtant!' and was furious when he learned that Verlaine had revived it. He became a traveller, a 'négociant', whose one object appears to have been the making of money. He died in 1891 at the age of thirty-seven, his life having already passed into a kind of legend.

And this extraordinary revulsion was, I fancy, at least partly connected with the Verlaine affair. At all events, it is a possible explanation, where hitherto we had been offered none. Concerning his boyhood there is plenty of material—the apocryphal, as usual, being mingled with the true. 'Il était aimé de ses camarades' is a statement Mr. Rickword may accept, but it leaves me incredulous. Rimbaud was liked by Delahaye; later there was Verlaine's infatuation (which counts for nothing); but that the bulk of his school-fellows can ever have felt the slightest affection for him frankly I do not believe. He did not want affection; it bored him; the secret of his superiority, he boasts, is that he is 'sans coeur'; and I do not think it would be an exaggeration to say that his nature was completely anti-social. Unfortunately, our direct information comes chiefly from two sources, both prejudiced—from those who (with some reason) regarded him as Verlaine's evil genius, and from those who, after his death, were anxious to whitewash his reputation. In addition, of course, we possess the testimony of the work itself, sincere to the point of brutality, and always in the highest degree personal. In fact, according to M. Coulon, the light which that work throws on his youth was the main reason why Rimbaud came to reject it.

Now for the facts. He was sixteen when he first ran away from his mother's house at Charleville, in the Ardennes. He remained in Paris a fortnight before being brought home by his schoolmaster. A few days later he ran away again, and, during the temporary absence of their owner, established himself, without permission, in André Gill's rooms. This need not surprise us. To Verlaine's 'enfant aux délicatesses mystérieuses' little peculiarities of that kind would appear perfectly natural: he would think nothing of taking pos-session of anybody's rooms, and making himself comfortable therein until such time as he might be discovered by the proprietor. The astonished Gill discovered him, gave him ten francs, and packed him off.

But Rimbaud was pertinacious. Five months later he again visited Paris, and again had to return home, this time penniless and on foot. It was now that he sent the manuscript of his poems to Verlaine, appealing for help. Nor was the appeal ignored. Without knowing anything of his correspondent, merely with the astonishing poems before him, Verlaine, who was an infinitely simpler and more impulsive person than Rimbaud, replied with enthusiasm. 'Venez, chère grande âme, on vous attend, on vous désire;' and Rimbaud, borrowing the money to pay for his railway ticket, set out once more.

Nevertheless, when the 'chère grande âme' arrived, the older poet was considerably taken aback to find himself confronted by a sulky-looking schoolboy with an amazing accent and enormous hands and feet. At this period he himself had been married for about a year, and his wife was a girl of seventeen. Moreover, he had no house of his own, but was living with his father-in-law—a circumstance he appears to have forgotten when sending his invitation. As it turned out, except by Verlaine himself, the 'enfant aux délicatesses mystérieuses' was *not* expected, was *not* desired. Upon the other members of the household he created a most unfavourable impression. They found him morose, scornful, silent—accepting food and shelter as his right, but expressing not the slightest gratitude for either. His behaviour to Verlaine's literary friends—who had been induced to subscribe towards his expenses—was equally sullen and contemptuous; and when the good-natured Théodore de Banville offered him a free lodging in a room at the top of his house, the boy's dirty habits speedily brought this arrangement also to an end. Madame de Banville and Madame Hugo at first took an interest in the uncouth young provincial, but all that the interest inspired was an extremely typical poem —*Les Chercheuses de Poux*. It may seem an odd return for kindness, but such was Rimbaud's nature: it delighted him to imagine these two ladies killing his vermin, combing his thick hair with delicate fingers and cracking the little lice between their nails. For the 'enfant aux délicatesses mystérieuses' was an anti-feminist. To be sure, he had had his precocious experiences of love, but he does not attempt to deceive either himself or us as to their nature. The poem he wrote about his little country sweethearts reveals an intensity of feeling few love poems possess, but that feeling can scarcely be described as affectionate. Here is a stanza:

> O mes petites amoureuses,
>   Que je vous hais!
> Plaquez de touffes douloureuses
>   Vos têtons laids!

Inevitably the idiosyncrasies of his protégé began to have their effect on Verlaine's own popularity, for he dragged Rimbaud with him everywhere, and under the influence of alcohol the boy's natural quarrelsomeness was apt to turn from aggressive rudeness to physical violence. According to Lepelletier—who, I admit, detested him—he had at this time 'l'air d'un échappé d'une maison de correction'. It is only fair to add that where Lepelletier saw a reformatory boy, Verlaine saw the angel of his *Crimen Amoris*—

> Or le plus beau de tous ces mauvais anges
> Avait seize ans. . . .

—and in his *Poètes Maudits* refers to Rimbaud's 'visage parfaitement ovale d'ange en exil'. It was from the beginning an obsession, and 'pauvre Lelian', whose entire life was merely a sequence of emotional impulses, good, bad, and indifferent, never dreamed of resisting it: the young wife was abandoned, and the 'pitoyable frère' and the 'enfant aux délicatesses mystérieuses' departed together.

There followed the year of vagabondage, which ended in the lamentable Brussels affair—the revolver shot, Verlaine's arrest and imprisonment, and Rimbaud's return to the strictly pious home at Charleville. Conflicting lights are thrown upon this episode—by those who witnessed parts of it, by Verlaine's poems and letters, by Rimbaud's prose fantasy, *Une Saison en Enfer*. Verlaine had sacrificed everything—his friends, his wife, his unborn child, his reputation, and finally his liberty. I do not defend the sacrifice; on the contrary, it was deplorable, utterly weak and selfish; but Rimbaud, having nothing to lose, sacrificed nothing; with him the whole wretched business was no more than another experiment, another revolt against society. He was a genius; he wrote the *Bateau Ivre*, and other amazing things; nevertheless his conduct from first to last was precisely that of the 'young delinquent', without a moral sense, without a conscience, without scruples, and without affection. For one thing at least seems certain, that he never cared a straw for Verlaine. He received the news of the latter's remorse and conversion with cynical scepticism, and his treatment of the poems sent to him from prison was equally in character. 'Je ne commente pas les dernières grossièretés du Loyala,' he writes to Delahaye— among the 'grossièretés' being the famous 'O mon Dieu vous m'avez blessé d'amour', the manuscript of which was rescued by Isabelle Rimbaud from the water-closet to which her brother had consigned it.

He himself, at the age of nineteen, abandoned literature.

An appalling aridity of spirit seems now to have descended upon him, and an aridity of heart had always been his. His two good qualities doubtless remained and were carried with him into his new life, that of a man of action—of commercial activity at any rate—from which the veil has never really been lifted. It was lived far away in the East, where few echoes from the past could reach him.

1924.

PERSUASION

Jane Austen's novels fall into two groups, the first containing *Pride and Prejudice*, *Sense and Sensibility*, and *Northanger Abbey*; the second containing *Mansfield Park*, *Emma*, and *Persuasion*. Separating these periods of activity were a few years apparently unproductive; and in each group we find a masterpiece—in the first *Pride and Prejudice*, in the second *Emma*. *Persuasion* cannot, I think, quite be classed with these, but it has the peculiar interest of being her last completed tale, and gives us, in Anne Elliot, the most lovable of her heroines. Nor is there, even in its less felicitous moments, anything to suggest declining powers. The story never drags, as *Mansfield Park* occasionally drags, its comedy shows no sign of flagging spirits, and its love passages are more intimate and tender than any others Jane Austen wrote.

The book was begun in the summer or autumn of 1815, and at the commencement of 1816 symptoms of the mysterious disease to which Miss Austen was eventually to succumb had already declared themselves. Mysterious—because we do not know what that malady was, beyond the vague description of it as a kind of wasting-away, or decline. She had seemed to be in perfect health when in 1815 she had gone to London, for the publication of *Emma*. Early in

1816 there had been family worries connected with her brother Henry, who in March was declared bankrupt, but these, though they must have caused anxiety, quite fail to account for the physical weakness which from now on gained upon her. In May 1816 she and her sister Cassandra spent three weeks at Cheltenham, and she was then far from well. As the year advanced she grew worse, though still she has nothing more definite to complain of than 'a want of strength', and as late as January 1817 we find her writing optimistically of an improvement. At all events, the feebleness of her body did not affect her mind, and on the 18th of July 1816 the first draft of *Persuasion* was completed. In August she revised it. The penultimate chapter failed to satisfy her; she thought it, as her nephew Mr. J. E. Austen Leigh tells us in his *Memoir*, 'tame and flat, and was desirous of producing something better. This weighed upon her mind; the more so probably on account of the weak state of her health; so that one night she retired to rest in very low spirits. But such depression was little in accordance with her nature, and was soon shaken off. The next morning she awoke to more cheerful views and brighter inspirations: the sense of power revived; and imagination resumed its course. She cancelled the condemned chapter, and wrote two others, entirely different, in its stead.'

This last statement requires some modification. As it stands it is misleading, for much of the conclusion of the cancelled chapter was retained in the revised draft. On the other hand, all that is most important is new—the scene of the Musgroves' visit to Bath, and of Anne's reconciliation with her lover. In the original version the reconciliation takes place in Admiral Croft's lodgings and is much less ingeniously contrived. The Admiral, under the impression that Anne has engaged herself to his cousin Mr. Elliot, deputes Captain Wentworth to tell her that he will have his lease of Kellynch Hall cancelled so that she and her husband may occupy the house. This is not very satisfactory, since, quite apart from the Admiral's own share in it, it is most unlikely that Wentworth would have consented to perform such a task. The incident in fact strikes us as a rather clumsy piece of machinery, though with the actual reconciliation there is no fault to be found.

' "No, Sir," said Anne, "there is no message. You are mis-in—— The Admiral is misinformed. I do justice to the kindness of his intentions, but he is quite mistaken. There is no truth in any such report."

'He was a moment silent. She turned her eyes towards him for the first time since his re-entering the room. His colour was varying, and he was looking at her with all the power and keenness which she believed that no other eyes than his possessed.

' "No truth in any such report?" he repeated. "No truth in any *part* of it?"

' "None."

'He had been standing by a chair, enjoying the relief of leaning on it, or of playing with it. He now sat down, drew it a little nearer to her, and looked with an expression which had something more than penetration in it—something softer. Her countenance did not discourage. It was a silent but very powerful dialogue; on his side supplication, on hers acceptance. Still a little nearer, and a hand taken and pressed; and "Anne, my own dear Anne!" bursting forth in all the fullness of exquisite feeling—and all suspense and indecision were over. They were reunited.'

This certainly is not a poor scene, but the scene substituted for it is better and is brought about with far more plausibility. Readers curious to compare the two versions may easily do so, for the cancelled chapter has been printed both as a separate book and in the *Memoir*.

Jane Austen had never been in a hurry to publish. In this her wisdom was as admirable as her restraint. After her tales were finished she liked to keep them by her in manuscript for a later revision when she should have had time to forget them a little, and the ardours of creation were cooled. The dates on the title-pages of her novels, which follow one another fairly closely, by no means coincide with the dates of composition. Writing to Fanny Knight on the 13th of March 1817 she says, 'I have a something ready for publication, which may perhaps appear about a twelve-month hence. It is short—about the length of *Catherine*.' And she is doubtful whether Fanny will care for it: 'You may perhaps like the heroine, as she is almost too good for me.'

This 'something' is of course *Persuasion*, and *Catherine* is *Northanger Abbey*, which was issued with it though written long before. *Northanger Abbey* had indeed undergone more than one transformation. As *Susan* it was first sold to Messrs. Crosby of London for £10, but never published by them. The manuscript was bought back for the sum given for it, and in 1816, when finally preparing it for the press, Jane supplied the following note. 'This little work was finished in 1803, and intended for immediate publication. It was disposed of to a bookseller, it was even advertised, and why the business proceeded no further, the author has never been able to learn.'

As it turned out, she was *never* to see it published. At the end of the first draft of *Persuasion* she had written—'Finis, July 18, 1816', and exactly a year later, on the morning of the 18th of July 1817, she died at Winchester, whither she had journeyed to receive medical treatment from a Mr.

Lyford, a physician of considerable repute. Both *Northanger Abbey* and *Persuasion* were issued posthumously in 1818 by John Murray, as a single work in four volumes, at the price of 24s., and prefaced by a brief biographical notice of the author.

In 1821 *Persuasion* was translated into French as *La Famille Elliot, ou l'ancienne Inclination*, which strikes us as an odd and singularly old-fashioned title in comparison with Jane's. *Persuasion* is modern—as modern as *Chance*, *Suspense*, or *Victory*. If an alteration seemed desirable, it would have been better simply to have called the book *Anne Elliot*, for it is not a family chronicle, it is Anne's story all through. The other Elliots, Sir Walter, Mary, and Elizabeth (Jane was fond of repeating her Christian names), are very minor characters, we learn nothing more about them than might be gathered from contemporary gossip or from a casual encounter in the Octagon Room at Bath. They are done from the outside, but with an ironical humour that brings them instantly to life. One might add, I think, that where minor characters are concerned there is nothing nearly so vitalizing as this mode of presentment, and Jane was a dab at it. She creates Admiral Croft in a single remark: 'And very nice young ladies they both are; I hardly know one from the other;' and the elder Mrs. Musgrove in her mere silence concerning 'Bermuda or Bahama':

' "But I never went beyond the Streights, and never was in the West Indies. We do not call Bermuda or Bahama, you know, the West Indies."

'Mrs. Musgrove had not a word to say in dissent; she could not accuse herself of having ever called them anything in the whole course of her life.'

This playfulness, this vividly personal note, is by far the most attractive quality in Jane Austen's work; her instinct as to where and when to use it practically never fails her. In her novels I recall only one instance where it seems out of place, and that is in relation to this same Mrs. Musgrove, whose stoutness, I know not why, is supposed to make the expression of maternal grief absurd. But even here we must remember that the good lady's affection for her son only came into existence after his demise; during his career as a schoolboy and young sailor he had been by no means particularly loved. Still, there is just a hint of callousness in the passage, a failure of sympathy, of imagination, and we find in Jane's letters a similar lapse when she writes, 'Mrs. Hall, of Sherborne, was brought to bed yesterday of a dead child, some weeks before she expected, owing to a fright. I suppose she happened unawares to look at her husband.'

But it is possible, and I myself think probable, that *Persuasion* would have been subjected to further touches of revision had its author lived, and in spite of the fact that she had already started on a new novel, the fragment now called *Sanditon*. For *Persuasion*, as we possess it, does not show the perfect mastery of *Emma*. In much of it we have Jane Austen at her best, but as a whole it is uneven. Of her limitations nobody was more aware than Jane herself. She knew what she *could* do, and was utterly determined not to attempt what she couldn't. She left behind her a delightful plan of a novel which was to embody all the suggestions of her friends, and we can see from it what value she placed on outside opinion. Like Wordsworth and Mr. W. D. Howells, she distrusted 'the moving accident': even the very attenuated specimen of it she gives us in the scene of Louisa Musgrove's fall from the steps at Lyme (the main incident in *Persuasion*) suffices to prove its uncongeniality. It is the worst thing in the book. Its dramatic emotion is fatally pumped up, and we breathe a sigh of relief when, after an interlude of swooning ladies, and passionately agitated gentlemen 'staggering against the wall for support', the true Jane returns with the workmen and the boatmen. *They*—excellent fellows—are collected 'to enjoy the sight of a dead young lady, nay, two dead young ladies, for it proved twice as fine as the first report'.

Jane revealed no gift for treating an adventure (even one so domestic as poor Louisa's), she had no gift for poetry, no sense of mystery, no knowledge of the heights and depths of passion, and if she had a more than superficial feeling for nature she kept it severely under restraint. There is not a lyrical moment in all her novels, she rarely attempts a landscape, and the passage in which she gives a description of Lyme has been absurdly overpraised. 'It has been copied', says Francis Warre Cornish, 'into every Dorsetshire guide-book, and has not lost beauty and freshness', but to an impartial eye it reveals neither more nor less sensitiveness than one is accustomed to expect from guide-books.

And all this she knew, and being among the most delicate and conscientious of artists, she worked accordingly—on her 'little bit (two inches wide) of ivory'—with results more clear and cool and quietly brilliant than any we shall find elsewhere till we reach certain little masterpieces by the author of *The Reverberator* and *Washington Square*. Not the later Henry James; with the problems that interested *him* she would have had nothing whatever to do. 'Let other pens dwell on guilt and misery,' she writes in the last chapter of *Mansfield Park*; 'I quit such odious subjects as soon as I can.' And in truth the sinner is as remote from her world as the saint. *Her* subject is an eternal courtship, and her novels are as filled with love-twitterings as the woods in spring. Mothers and daughters alike have no thought but for young bachelors. The entire action is concerned with the vicissitudes attendant on getting engaged to be married, and as soon as Elizabeth Bennet becomes Mrs. Darcy, or Emma Woodhouse Mrs. Knightley, or Anne Elliot Mrs. Wentworth, their potentiality as heroines ceases, in any *new* fiction they might figure in they would infallibly be thrust into the background.

And of all these love tales none is so tenderly intimate as *Persuasion*. Anne Elliot has neither Emma's strength of character nor Emma's brilliance, but she has a sweetness and gentleness that never become insipid: she has charm. Moreover, she really is in love; we feel it in every thought she thinks and every word she utters. Wentworth is less realized, but is sufficiently there to justify Anne's affection, a gallant fellow, rather serious, and regarded with a naïve veneration which one trusts he deserves. Anne alone is presented from the inside; her simple heart is revealed to us; she is a creation touching and beautiful, all delicacy and fragrance. And in her simplicity she must have been more difficult to do than either Elizabeth or Emma. She is so far from showy. She never says witty things; she is intelligent, but not strikingly clever; she has passed her first youth; she is self-effacing and, as Lady Russell says, her 'spirits are not high'. But she is extremely lovable. All Anne's share in the story is perfectly handled, and leaves behind it a beautiful impression of affection, unselfishness, and fidelity.

The comedy is reserved for the minor characters, and it is good, even if here and there there may be a tendency to over-emphasis. This slight exaggeration is visible in the portrait of Mary, whose 'sore throats, you know, were always worse than anybody's', though her letter to Anne is one of the joys of the book. We see it also in Sir Walter. Both suggest the older comedy of humours. Their foibles are too constantly in evidence, their speeches too invariably in character, for truth. Yet who would sacrifice such things as Sir Walter's complaint about the number of plain women in Bath? 'Once, as he had stood in a shop in Bond Street, he had counted eighty-seven go by, one after another, without there being a tolerable face among them.' The elder Mrs. Musgrove is really a more living creation than either her daughter-in-law or Sir Walter. Both Jane and Anne, I feel, underestimate her, as they certainly overestimate the colour-less Lady Russell. Mrs. Musgrove is worth a hundred Lady Russells: she is a singularly pleasant person, the soul of good-natured motherliness, as she sits among the children she has brought 'to improve the noise at Uppercross'.

Of the villains of the piece we get but sketches. Neither Mr. Elliot nor Mrs. Clay is much in Jane's line, for they are not sympathetic, nor can she extract entertainment from them. Mr. Elliot, it is true, before the penultimate chapter was scrapped had a rather more important part to play in the plot than he has now, and Mrs. Clay possesses distinct possibilities which have not been worked out. Still, neither is among Jane's happier conceptions.

This, then, is *Persuasion*—a novel with the slightest of plots and only one fully-drawn character. Nevertheless, Jane Austen has made of it a thing that moves us alternately to laughter and affection. The delicate love reveries of Anne Elliot possess a perennial freshness; the colour has not faded nor the salt lost its savour. There is no strangeness in *Persuasion*, and there are no surprises: we feel perfectly assured that it *will* 'end like an old play', that the evil-doers will be confounded and Jack will have Jill. But there is a mind in it—tenderness, humour, irony, the charm of a delightful personality—and above all there is life.

1930.

STELLA BENSON

I met Stella Benson only once. That meeting was arranged by Mr. Ellis Roberts, in whose flat it took place, and though half a dozen other guests were there, we were left pretty much to ourselves. Stella, I found, was a little deaf, but nothing to speak of. Still, in the general buzz of voices it helped to isolate us in our corner, and our conversation might have isolated us also, for it was not in the least literary; we talked only of animals—I of my dogs, and Stella of more exotic pets. We resumed this talk after lunch, and when we said good-bye it was—on my part at least—with every intention and expectation of meeting again. She scribbled her address for me on a card, but I was returning to Ireland next day, and before I again visited London I had learned of her death.

An hour or two of even the friendliest conversation is perhaps little to go upon, yet a good deal depends on whether a previous sympathy has existed or not, and in my case it certainly had. Stella Benson's books had strongly appealed to me, and I found her very like them, and particularly like this passage, which I take from a travel book, *The Little World* :

'I did not feel financially justified in eating the hotel's Christmas dinner. So I bought some biscuits and a bar of chocolate and went out to the Golden Gate beach. There was a cold swift mist leaping to shore over the tall barrier of the wintry breaking waves. The sun was thickly wrapped away in dark red-grey clouds and the sands looked pink and more ethereal than the sky. Three dogs were very kind to me, teaching me to throw sticks into the sea in the San Francisco way. They and I sat wagging our tails in a cold but cheerful row, sharing biscuits (which they called crackers) and chocolate, and remembering other Christmases. A seagull joined us and proved to be a biscuit-maniac. It ate till it could hardly bend its neck.'

To this I must add a description of an elephant race.

'At the sound of the pistol shot, they moved forward with serene dignity, not even the babel of shrieks and curses from the amateurs on their backs could induce them to fall out of line. In a perfect row they started; in a perfect row they proceeded very slowly along the track, pensively waving their trunks to keep one another in step; in a perfect row they breasted the tape at the other end. And then they all sighed happily, satisfied to feel that they had done their duty. It was the most impressive race I ever saw.'

Hardly surprising that I brought out in return all my ancient bulldog stories, comfortably sure that, however perennial at home, they could not have reached China, though actually, as I discovered, *Apostate had* reached her there.

Stella Benson was a conscious artist. In this she resembled Katherine Mansfield, but Katherine confined herself to the short story, whereas Stella preferred a larger, though still not a very large canvas. Her first three novels were experiments and only partly successful. They were interesting and original, but their cleverness was too apparent; they were even smart. Then, with *The Poor Man* (1922), she seemed suddenly to find everything for which she had been searching, and produced a masterpiece.

The Poor Man is a convincing, at times a painfully convincing book. This is because we all carry Edward, the hero, within us, little germs of Edward, the potentiality to become Edward, and gradually, while we read, begin to suspect that we may be a good deal more like Edward than we had previously realized. For Edward himself did not know how much he was Edward. He partly knew, and once or twice exasperated people told him, but he never wholly knew, and he forgot—forgot quite often—otherwise he could not have gone on living.

Stella Benson never forgets. She may strike us perhaps, for that very reason, sometimes as a little cruel: yet not really cruel, only remorselessly just. She never patronizes, she never condemns; on the other hand, she never pities, never excuses. And Edward needs to be pitied—we feel that nearly as much as he does himself. He draws, before the end of the book, so uncomfortably close to us that we begin to defend ourselves; to say, 'No, I should never have done that: I couldn't have done it in *any* circumstances. Thank God, I am not in the least like Edward.' Adding, rather ominously, 'Though for that matter the poor devil never gets a chance. Emily might at least——' But Emily doesn't. Why should she? How could she? What could anybody do? And when Edward becomes utterly abject we feel less indignation than shame.

For this is a study of weakness. Edward is not vicious, is not brutal: he probably, for instance, was a quite nice little boy. And though hopelessly inefficient, he is not at all stupid, is rather refined. Also he is anything but aggressive, anything but conceited. He is not quarrelsome; he would be the last person in the world to take pleasure in deliberate cruelty: he is only weak—a poor thing—the poor man: it begins and ends with that.

'Blessed are the poor in spirit.' It was never one of my favourite texts, and Edward has not persuaded me to change my mind. As I say, it is with a sense of almost personal shame that we watch him cadging—cadging for loans, cadging for affection; watch him selling what belongs to others; watch him trying to curry favour with the schoolboys he is supposed to be teaching, by secretly drinking with them, by ignoring their insults; watch him sink to his lowest action, when he decamps with the money of a boy of thirteen, who has been left alone in an hotel in Peking.

And all these things Edward does without really wanting to do them. He wants to be decent; he wants people to like him; he even wants to work—only there is nothing he can do. And then, unfortunately, he drinks. It would, indeed, be strange if he didn't, for drinking helps him to forget. As a matter of fact, we, outside the book, do not dislike him: our contempt is too much mingled with understanding. And this is Stella Benson's triumph. It is only because we know him better than his friends do, know every wandering thought and emotion that stirs in him, that we do not detest Edward. I should think no character in fiction has ever been more completely realized, more faithfully presented, than this 'poor man'.

The technique of the book is original. We are told nothing of Edward's past, except that he was shell-shocked, and experienced three air-raids in London; we are told nothing of his people; we are simply plunged into his life from the moment when we find him sitting in Rhoda Romero's room in San Francisco—an unwelcome guest. The effect is peculiar: it is as if by some power we had been made invisible, and suddenly transported into this room, among all these people who are talking more or less intimately. We are not intimate with them; we are intimate only with Edward, because we are prisoners in Edward's body and Edward's mind, and from this on are held there till the spell is abruptly broken on that desolating last page. Edward is an Englishman, and how he came to be in Rhoda Romero's room in San Francisco, how he came to know her and her friends (in his usual capacity of hanger-on) we never learn, simply because Edward never chances to think of these things. We do not even learn Emily's surname till near the end of the book. Edward himself, you see, only learns it then, though his infatuation for her is the one active force in his existence. Characteristically he follows her to China without realizing that she is called anything but Emily: it is only when he is searching an hotel register in Hong-Kong that it strikes him she must have a second name. Nevertheless, he finds her in the end—not in Hong-Kong, nor in Peking, but in Shanghai—and finds at the same time that, like everybody else, she does not want him. 'Can't you leave me alone? I can't bear you. I couldn't bear to touch you—you poor sickly thing.' And so the curtain is rung down.

I should place *The Poor Man* among the very finest of modern novels. It is a thing accomplished without the waste of a word. Stella Benson's style has not the prolonged musical cadence that is most pleasing to my ear; it is impressionistic, concentrating on the phrase rather than the paragraph; but it has colour, precision, individuality. There are pages, such as those describing Edward's nocturnal wanderings through Peking, which are richly poetic. I had marked half a dozen passages to illustrate this, but shall quote one of a quite different kind, because it is a perfect example of Stella Benson's method of presenting in a few lines a character and a scene. Edward has thought frequently of buying a light suit, and, pathetically, of the pleasing impression this suit will make upon Emily when he finds her. With this purpose he approaches Stone Ponting, the small, good-natured American boy he ultimately robs:

' "Let me borrow from you," suggested Edward, turning scarlet in a way that proved his honesty to himself. "It'll be a purely business transaction. I'll pay you two per cent per month. I want a thin suit of clothes."

' "Sure, go ahead," said Stone.

'Edward bought a cream-coloured ready-made suit and saw in the mirror that he looked like an unsuccessful dentist. He walked hurriedly out of the store to escape this dreadful ghost.

' "You look like thirty cents," said Stone.'

From *The Poor Man* on, we get Stella Benson at her best, writing in the way Whistler painted, placing each sentence as he placed a flick of colour, so that it produces its exactly calculated effect. *Pipers and a Dancer* (1924), the next book, is a slighter tale, and one less moving to me personally, but it has the same perfection of execution. It is light, it is delicate, and it pierces through every rag of disguise with which we try to cloak our human nature. Even more than *The Poor Man* it may seem a rather cruel story. But the persons in it, if unheroic, are really very average specimens; it is only that they are stripped naked spiritually, and the naked soul is more shocking than the naked body. After all, most of us who are sensitive are not less self-conscious than Ipsie Wilson, and few of us are so amiable as her American lover, Rodd. Even the overwhelming Pauline has her good qualities, and the gushing Sophie Hinds has hers. It is true we feel no affection for any of them; what is attractive is simply the light of Stella Benson's humour and imagination as it plays upon their tragi-comedy, infusing it with an ironic beauty.

And how wonderfully evocative the writing, how rich in colour and in imagery!

'The voices scratched viciously across the smooth morning air. . . . Heming and his Chinese boy, grinning with anger, were leaning towards each other almost in an attitude of passionate love.'

Or this:

'As they all walked towards the ferry, Ipsie, in a ring of kind faces all at a rather higher level than her own, felt herself physically and spiritually to be a "sweet little thing". Pauline imposed this feeling on her, and Ipsie was not cynical enough to throw it off easily. Ipsie's face assumed a pert childish look, she began to think of sweet little things she might say about Hong-Kong in order to make them all laugh affectionately again. Ipsie could feel this sweetness coming on remorselessly like an attack of indigestion.'

There are tiny vignettes of China, each calling up a background, vivid, decorative, charming as a Japanese drawing, infinitely more effective than the slabs of descriptive writing dear to the ordinary novelist.

'On the little beaches the low tinkling waves broke as sweetly as they break upon the sand-castles of fat-behinded babies in bathing-drawers at Ramsgate.'

And when we reach the last page we see how beautifully proportioned the whole thing is, with all the clumsy redundancy of the ordinary novel omitted, so that the finished work appeals as definitely to our sense of form as a bronze statuette. No writer has ever employed a greater economy, and yet is not everything essential here? When Ipsie Wilson arrived at Hong-Kong 'the edge of the dock was trimmed with a sort of dull lace of other people's friends'. Always Stella Benson's writing has this closely-packed, concrete quality, is not merely a statement of fact, but produces its picture or its story. Even the psychology is dramatized. 'Rodd never seemed to know that Ipsie was an artist though she had told him so several times in the deprecatory voice her Showman had taught her.' How much, on one side, of disappointed egotism, of secret irritation, and on the other, of lazy good-tempered stupidity, is conveyed by that single sentence! It foreshadows the whole future relationship of this odd pair of lovers; it evokes Ipsie, and it evokes Rodd, and it evokes their love-making; while at the same time it evokes the amused intelligence that lies behind them, that has conceived them, in whose clear light they can hide so little.

This Ipsie Wilson—Dear Little Sister Ipsie, Good Sport Ipsie, Wee Sweetheart Ipsie (they are her own self-dramatizations)—this Ipsie Wilson, the artist, who draws things for *Paint*, comes out to China to marry Jacob Heming, an electrical engineer. The same boat brings a pleasant young American, Rodd Innes, who is to succeed to Jacob's position. But also awaiting Ipsie's arrival are Jacob's sister Pauline ('Pauline's voice came rolling like a banner in front of her heavily hurrying figure. "I missed the ferry. Oh, how could I run such a risk of leaving my new little sister lonely in a strange land!" ') and Pauline's devoted friend Mrs. Sophie Hinds, an American writer with a message, 'an artist to her finger tips', and Captain Norman, another friend. They are the pipers; Ipsie is the dancer. Each piper plays his own foolish tune, and for each she dances in character—is the figure his music demands, insists upon. To do her justice, she herself stares at the figure in a sort of helpless fascination, far from admiringly. Only Rodd is conscious that there must be a real Ipsie somewhere; but his consciousness is limited to this, and to a desire to take her away from Jacob. To Pauline she is Dear Little Sister Ipsie, to Jacob she is his own Wee Mary, to Captain Norman, who ventures to embrace her on that understanding, she is Good Sport Ipsie, to Rodd she is simply an unknowable but inexplicably attractive person he wants to rescue from the voracious crew. Unfortunately he is not a very good rescuer: hence the drama. And the scene is China, a vast, strange, sinister land, which seems to isolate this small group of aliens from all the rest of the world, to hold them together so that they cannot escape from one another.

In *Good-bye, Stranger* (1926) the scene again is China, but the story is a kind of modern fairy-tale, in substance subtle, and in form exquisite. It is a delightful story—rich in humour, in character, in imagination—and it is as individual as a poem by Donne. The people, this time, are chosen after her own heart, and are therefore endearingly odd. Or is the quaintness simply due to the method of presentment? Daley, for example, is simplicity itself—an extremely nice girl, not a bit clever; we meet plenty of Daleys in real life. But then, in real life we do not hear the queer little remarks their dogs make to them, and know nothing at all of the queer thoughts and impulses and emotions they are careful to hide just because they *are* queer. Stella Benson knows, understands, and tells us. She knows also about changelings. Daley's husband is a changeling. Her real husband has been in fairyland for seven years, and only comes back in the last chapter at the call of Sibelius's *Valse Triste* played on Daley's Victrola. That Victrola is a symbol—a tragic symbol, though it makes us laugh.

Old Mrs. Cotton, Daley's mother-in-law, is well aware of the symbol—of fairyland, of the two magics—old Mrs. Cotton belongs entirely to Stella Benson's world. So do the missionaries and Lena. Milady and Edna belong more to ours. The tale recounts two days in the lives of these people, and it is as if we had lived with them from childhood. They are the two days in which the story of Daley and her husband reaches a crisis—an absorbing story—whimsical, comic, tragic, the creation of a rare and fastidious talent.

Stella Benson died at the height of her powers. Her last novel, *Mundos*, was never finished, but the last novel she published, *Tobit Transplanted* (1931), shows that her work was gaining in body and breadth without losing its early delicacy. *Tobit* is generally considered to be her masterpiece: I myself prefer *The Poor Man*. At any rate, among other work not so good, she left four novels and one travel-book that are unique and delightful.

1924—1940.

THE HOST OF THE AIR[1]

The Irish people believe in the supernatural. 'If by an impossible miracle,' Lady Gregory says, 'every trace and memory of Christianity could be swept out of the world, it would not shake or destroy this belief.' It is absolute, uncompromising; we may deplore it, or sympathize with it, but it is there, a living factor in everyday life, possessing all the narrow obstinacy that characterizes such a faith when deeply felt. Lady Gregory's *Visions and Beliefs in the West of Ireland* is the Bible of this faith. Its contents have been taken down word for word from the lips of witnesses, all, or nearly all of them unlettered; and the very artlessness and seeming pointlessness of most of the communications lend to them a kind of authenticity, for here obviously there is no particular will to believe, just as, except in one or two echoes from the traditional folk-tales, there is no evidence of the creative imagination having been at work. The cumulative effect of this bewildering mass of evidence is at least sufficient to arouse conjecture. Even those of us who are naturally sceptical may feel inclined to ask, 'What, then, *does* lie behind it?'

Something, to my mind, a good deal more primitive than

[1] *Visions and Beliefs in the West of Ireland*. Collected and arranged by Lady Gregory, with Two Essays and Notes by W. B. Yeats. 2 vols. 1920.

the animism of the Greeks, and at the same time more trivial. 'Evitez le fond des bois et leur vaste silence,' counsels the French poet, but no sense of religious awe, however pagan, appears to have prompted the faery faith. How, then, explain its singular vitality? For it is alive to-day; nearly everybody in Ireland must at one time or another have spoken with persons to whom marvellous things have happened, have heard stories, at first or second hand, pointing to the existence of a race of beings in close relationship with yet sharply divided from the human race. Moreover, such persons—when they are not poets like Yeats or A.E.—seldom strike us as being particularly imaginative. They are farmers who in an unlucky hour have cut down an ancient thorn-tree on some part of their land, or simple peasant women who are not in the least eager to make a convert. The statements are matter-of-fact, because the element of wonder is absent from the mind of the informant: the existence of the supernatural is an axiom, a commonplace taken for granted: that these 'others' exist is accepted without question.

They, these 'others', are the Sidhe, the faery people, 'thick as the sands of the sea', fallen angels perhaps, yet not essentially evil, still retaining a hope of salvation, and sometimes busy with such thoughts, so that they have been known to send back an 'old spent man' whom they had taken long ago, in order that he might make his peace with God and receive absolution before he died. But this faery people is divided into two races, one gay and handsome, the other ugly and malicious. They are not visible to everybody; they can take any shape they will; they pass us in the storm; they dwell in old grass-grown forts and lisses, and gather about ancient thorn-trees. Yet, though they can do marvellous things (building up a house in the twinkling of an eye), their powers seem to be limited—seem in many cases dependent upon human aid, so that human children are stolen, as well as young men and young girls, always the strongest and handsomest; while it is said that all children born in their kingdom must have one human parent.

Little is known, however, either of their kingdom, or of themselves. Those who return are reticent or forgetful. This we may note, nevertheless, that all who have been taken are anxious to come back. That ardent yet shadowy life, so full of laughter and gaiety, of dancing and card-playing and feasting, seems to bring no happiness with it; there is an eagerness to escape from it; and many who have been captured do indeed escape. Others, while still in thrall, have power—it may be through some great love—to return at intervals in a form more or less ghostly. Thus we learn of a son returning to his mother, but more frequently it is a mother who returns to her child. Only those who have eaten the faery food pass entirely under the malign power; while this is still untasted there is hope.

And the benefits 'they' are able to confer upon their favourites are not numerous. Chief among them appears to be the gift of healing. It was from 'them' that Biddy Early, a famous wise-woman of the West, derived her gift. Yet Biddy Early was not in the accepted sense of the word a witch: neither in Lady Gregory's book, nor elsewhere, as Yeats points out, is there any hint of a compact with the devil. In all this world, indeed, there is no suggestion of Black Magic, nor of any of those subtle forms of damnation so dear to the medieval and monkish mind. The priests, as a rule, were antagonistic to Biddy Early, but the grounds of their disapproval remain vague, and the priests also, according to tradition, can and do perform miraculous 'cures', some of them suspiciously like those accomplished by Biddy herself. Many instances are given of wonders they have worked, not always in connection with human patients. But a penalty is exacted. Father Rivers dies 'within two years' of his first dabbling in such matters, and 'they never live long', we are told, 'when they do these cures, because that they say prayers that they ought not to say'.

On this point, however, opinions differ: the evil may not always react upon the healer, though a penalty must be paid by somebody. Even Biddy Early 'had to cast the sickness on some other thing—it might be a dog or a goat or a bird'; and one is reminded irresistibly of the story of the Gadarene swine. It is safer, then, not to meddle in such matters: it is wiser even to leave untouched the treasure 'they' may offer. 'And whenever he'd want money, for a fair or the like, he'd find it laid on the table in the morning. . . . But after that going on for a time he lost his son.' The gold, too, is often in itself elusive, faery gold, gold that turns to trash, to dry dung or a heap of withered leaves.

Does there, in truth, behind all this—behind these warnings and apparitions, the crying of the banshee, the vision of the death-coach, the wasting away of those who have been 'touched'—lie anything but the grey fog of superstition? I remember reading in a daily paper, years ago, an account of an old woman who had been done to death by her neighbours. It happened in the south of Ireland, and was as unpleasant as any story of American lynching. Here, at all events, a belief in witchcraft of the more orthodox kind must have existed. The whole thing has its dangerous side. Fear is the begetter of violence, and there have been cases tried in modern criminal courts where what has been punished as abominable cruelty was in reality only a super-stitious following of the wisdom of the seer. The change-ling, for example, can be driven away by fire; but what if he should happen *not* to be a changeling! Lady Gregory mentions the 'cure' of a little boy by one Father Callaghan:

' "Go out and bring me in a bundle of sally rods that will be as thin as rushes, and divide them into six small parts," he said, "and twist every one of the six parts together." And when that was done, he took the little bundle of rods, and he beat the child on the head with them one after another till they were in flitters and the child roaring. Then he laid the child in the father's arms, and no sooner there than it fell asleep, and Father Callaghan said to the father: "What you have now is your own, but it wasn't your own that was in it before."'

What, then, are we to make of Lady Gregory's two volumes of recorded experiences? Taken down with skill and patience from the lips of living men and women, they form certainly a valuable contribution to folk-lore, but is that all? Not quite, perhaps, since they are indigenous, and, if on nothing else, throw a peculiar light on the psychology of the Irish people. Those who would seek something more will find encouragement for such speculations in the characteristic notes and essays contributed by Yeats.

1920.

THE LETTERS OF
KATHERINE MANSFIELD[1]

It has, I am afraid, been the experience of most of us, and on more than one occasion, to have felt, on reading the private correspondence of a writer whose work we admire, a bewildering and chilling sense of disappointment—a disappointment sharp enough perhaps to rob even that work itself, when we have gone back to it, of something of its virtue; but no such disillusionment awaits the reader of Katherine Mansfield's letters: the living woman who emerges from them has all the charm and lovableness the stories had led us to expect; the writer and her work are one.

What, then, is the dominant impression we receive? I think it is this, that Katherine Mansfield was absolutely, uncompromisingly *true*. Not a note of insincerity, of exaggeration, is sounded anywhere in these two volumes; in her life, as in her art, truth was what she sought for—fearlessly, passionately—and if her criticism of some of her contemporaries is at times severe, she is always an even more exacting critic of herself. Her stories were successful; they obtained immediate recognition; they were praised lavishly; she became, one might almost say, a fashionable writer; yet while she enjoyed the recognition she was never blinded by

[1] *The Letters of Katherine Mansfield.* Edited by J. Middleton Murry. 2 vols. 1928.

the praise; she knew exactly what it was she had tried to do and whether she had done it or not; the letters bring home to us again and again the integrity of her vision and of her art.

The earlier letters—those written before her fatal disease had declared itself—have a delightful gaiety. She is writing from her room in Paris, at the open window, on a May morning in 1915:

'And now there comes a little handcart with three babies in it and a quantity of newspapers. It is dragged by two other infants—men of about eight or nine. They stopped outside here, let down a kind of false leg which steadied the cart and strolled over to the lavatory, talking, unbuttoning their breeches and shouting to the babies to keep tranquille. But alas! no sooner had they disappeared than the infants with screams of rage began throwing the papers into the wet gutter. Back rushed their lords, and now they are picking up the muddy papers and the culprits hang their heads over the side of the wagon like people about to be guillotined . . . terribly chastened.'

Humour, indeed, she possessed to the end; but the later letters, written when she was fighting against the consumption that eventually killed her, are tinged with a tragic 'awareness' of the uneven struggle, and this tragedy becomes all the more moving because, in her passionate love of life, she never gives up hope, no suffering or weakness of the body can quench her indomitable spirit. Here is the beginning of another letter, written at night, four years later:

'I am at present being stared at by (1) a very old winged beetle who is evidently looking to see if this is his club or not and whether there is an octogenarian or two to have a chat with; (2) three white moths with their little moth's noses pressed as flat as flat can be; (3) an Unknown, with six legs and the appearance of a diminutive lobster; (4) one very large grey moth, apparently in a shawl, who appears by her anxiety to be endeavouring to see if there really is a large barrel of butter hidden behind the counter for regular customers only or not. All these are on the outside of my windy pane, drawn to the light because I have not closed the shutters. It's a black night, calm, and with a great sweeping sound of sea.'

It is hard to choose among so many things one would like to quote, and only quotation can show how good these letters really are. Their descriptive passages are marked by the delicate impressionism she brought to perfection in her stories; her personal encounters with all varieties and classes of people are here; and so is (to me most interesting of all) the history of her development as an artist—for she had come by the time that last extract was written to reject her earlier work, while towards the end we find her dissatisfied even with the work of her second period. The idea of writing on in the same way, of standing still, as it were, instead of reaching out to ever wider and wider fields of life, was abhorrent to her; we watch her growing, growing continuously, until, in 1923, death cut short that brave beautiful career, leaving us with a strange sense of loss and of a question unanswered. For she had quite ceased during the last few months to write fiction. Not that she had given up the idea of writing it: on the contrary, she looked forward eagerly to beginning again after she had found something— something her spirit was seeking. But to what ultimate flowering her genius would have attained—that, alas! we shall now never know.

Let me give two more brief passages, written in 1921, and chosen because in them we seem to see her actually at work:

'It's a very queer thing how *craft* comes into writing. I mean down to details. Par exemple. In *Miss Brill* I choose not only the length of every sentence, but even the sound of every sentence. I choose the rise and fall of every paragraph to fit her, and to fit her on that day at that very moment. After I'd written it I read it aloud—numbers of times— just as one would *play over* a musical composition—trying to get it nearer and nearer to the expression of Miss Brill— until it fitted her.'

And again:

'I must stop this letter and get on with my new story. It's called *At the Bay* and it's (I hope) full of sand and seaweed, bathing dresses hanging over verandas, and sandshoes on window-sills, and little pink "sea" convolvulus, and rather gritty sandwiches and the tide coming in. And it smells (oh, I *do* hope it smells) a little bit fishy.'

1928.

RICHARD GARNETT[1]

 Why, until this re-issue of it reached me the other day, had I never read *The Twilight of the Gods*? It was first published as long ago as 1888—which probably, indeed, is the reason. For 1888 was too early for me, and the book, meeting with no success, was allowed to drop into an obscurity where it has remained ever since. Dr. Garnett himself accepted the rebuff as final, and made no second attempt to gain a hearing.

 Yet since then the public has welcomed *Jurgen*, and, except its vulgarity, there is nothing in *Jurgen* that was not in *The Twilight of the Gods*. Instead of vulgarity and a monotonous and puerile indecency Dr. Garnett supplies wit, learning, and good taste. These qualities do not in themselves make a story-teller, but they should not constitute a drawback when the gift of the story-teller is there also, as in his case it obviously is. On the contrary, the charm of erudition combined with imagination is a rare and precious thing, though possibly one that appeals most to a bookish type of mind. In Peacock erudition outweighed imagination, but in Richard Garnett, as in Anatole France, the two qualities are evenly balanced. Hence the perpetual liveliness of these

---

[1] *The Twilight of the Gods*. With an Introduction by T. E. Lawrence, and illustrations by Henry Keen. 1925.

stories, the wealth of colour, the varied and surprising incidents.

Not that by bringing in Anatole France I wish to exaggerate their importance. They remain pastiches, however brilliant, and an enormous gulf divides them from such a masterpiece as *La Rôtisserie de la Reine Pédauque*, with its breadth of humanity, and truth to life. Dr. Garnett belongs definitely to the 'little masters', and a more fitting comparison would be with Beckford, who after all, in *Vathek* and its *Episodes*, was the first to write this kind of story. Like Beckford, he places his tales in a world of his and their own, which cannot ever, in any age, have been the real world; like Beckford, he has a taste for the occult and fantastic, while, even more than Beckford's, his humour is ironical, and its seeming callousness a part of the fun. 'On the point of scholarship,' says Mr. T. E. Lawrence in his preface, 'let us give the book a first-class. Ditto in magic, in alchemy, in toxicology; ditto in wit and humour.' In magic in particular, or at least in the peculiar vocabulary of magicians, Dr. Garnett is deeply versed. He knows as much about it as did Ben Jonson, and Ben knew everything.

' "I have need of thy art," said the bishop, coming to business. "I am exceedingly bothered—flabbergasted were not too strong an expression—by this confounded bell. All my best exorcists have been trying all they know with it, to no purpose."

' "It will be a tough business," observed the sorcerer, surveying the bell with the eye of a connoisseur. "It will require fumigations."

' "Yes," said the bishop, "and suffumigations."

' "Aloes and mastic," advised the sorcerer.

' "Aye," assented the bishop, "and red sanders."

' "We must call in Primeumaton," said the warlock.

' "Clearly," said the bishop, "and Amioram."

' "Triangles," said the sorcerer.

' "Pentacles," said the bishop.

' "In the hour of Methon," said the sorcerer.

' "I should have thought Tafrac," suggested the bishop, "but I defer to your better judgement."

' "I can have the blood of a goat?" queried the wizard.

' "Yes," said the bishop, "and of a monkey also."

' "Does your Lordship think that one might venture to go as far as a little unweaned child?"

' "If absolutely necessary," said the bishop.

' "I am delighted to find such liberality of sentiment on your Lordship's part," said the sorcerer. "Your Lordship is evidently of the profession."

' "These are things which stuck by me when I was an inquisitor," explained the bishop, with some little embarrassment.'

Medievalism, the medieval world with its saints and sinners, plays, in spite of its title, a much larger part in *The Twilight of the Gods* than paganism. The treatment is gaily irreverent, but the details, the feeling and the colour and the atmosphere of the past, are evoked with extraordinary vividness.

'Screaming with agitation, the aged sorcerer laid a scroll engrossed with fairly written characters before the youth, stabbed the latter's arm with a stylus that at once evoked and collected the crimson stream, thrust this into his hand, and strove to guide it to the parchment, chanting at the same time litanies to the infernal powers. The crystal flagons rang like one great harmonica with a shrill but spirit-stirring music; volumes of vaporous perfumes diffused themselves through the apartment, and an endless procession of treasure-laden figures defiled before the bewildered youth.

. . . But every drop of blood seemed frozen in his frame as he beheld an enormous claw thrust through the roof, member, as it seemed, of some being too gigantic to be contained in the chamber of the tower itself. Cold, poignant, glittering as steel, it rested upon a socket of the repulsive hue of jaundiced ivory, with no vestige of a foot or anything to relieve its naked horror as, rigid and lifeless, yet plainly with a mighty force behind it, it pointed at the magician's heart.'

In many of the stories the devil is a principal character. He is never very far off, he is the 'fiend hid in a cloud', waiting till the cup of evil is filled, and then snatching his prey. And as Dr. Garnett presents him he is a quite credible, and, in comparison with some of his dupes, a not wholly unattractive person. He is cruel and wicked and subtle, but he is distinguished, and has a sardonic sense of humour; and he keeps his word. The religions of the East are not forgotten, nor is philosophy. There is a pleasing story of Plotinus and his City of Philosophers, and there is a still better one about the miracles of Ananda, the Buddhist. Dr. Garnett's mind is sceptical. He is not persuaded that man is a rational animal, still less that he is a virtuous one. Consider the pious Bonze of *The Potion*, who for reasons of his own is anxious to discover certain adherents to the unfashionable sect of Lao-tsze. These unfortunate persons are believed to have taken refuge in a cave, which is also the home of a tiger who protects them.

'The Bonze dressed himself up as much like a votary of Lao-tsze as possible, provided himself with a bodyguard of bona-fide disciples, and, accompanied by a small army of huntsmen and warriors as well, marched in quest of the den of the tiger. It was discovered about nightfall, and having tethered a small boy near the entrance, that his screams when being devoured might give notice of the tiger's issue from or return to his habitation, the Bonze and his myrmidons took up a flank position and awaited the dawn.'

That is the note, and it sounds perpetually throughout the book. 'Are there no means,' asks a youth of inquiring mind, eager to be initiated into the sacred teachings of the Buddhists—'Are there no means by which the course of study may be accelerated?' And he is told that it may be accelerated by the practice of religious austerities.

'The king of the country most graciously came to his assistance by causing him to be fastened to a tree, with his uplifted arm secured by iron bands above his head, a fan being put in his other hand to protect him against the molestations of gnats and mosquitoes. By this means, and with the assistance of the monks who continually recited and expounded the Buddhist scriptures in his ears, some time even before his arm had stiffened for ever, the doctrine of the misery of existence had become perfectly clear to him.'

But it is not the only note. Some of the stories carry us into the sinister and eerie regions of witchcraft, and to me these are the most fascinating. Dr. Garnett evokes the right atmosphere, the right setting, for such things; he makes them disturbingly real. For a sense of humour often co-exists with an equally strong sense of the macabre, as several of the Ingoldsby Legends prove; and the learned Doctor seems to have pondered pretty deeply over many a quaint and curious volume of forgotten lore. Through such unholy scenes there strikes an odd kind of gaiety, which plays lightly with murder and torture and all the ghastly rites of necromancy. But in spite of this gaiety the thrill remains, is somehow even intensified by it. In the tale of *Ananda, the Miracle Worker* the incantation scene in the cemetery has a grotesque horror which it would be difficult to surpass.

These, then, as stories, are good stories, quite apart from their philosophical content. Dr. Garnett's vast reading, his scholarship, his humour, his imagination, have all here found equal play. He writes only of what interests him, and in the manner most agreeable to him. He tells the legend of the Virgin Mary who takes the place of the errant nun, but the Virgin in his story becomes Apollo, and the nun a young priest of Apollo. It is not one of the best stories, but it shows plainly enough—as plainly as *The Poet of Panopolis*, which *is* one of the best—on what side Garnett may be counted. He is on the side of reason, candour, and humanity, but any form of mysticism probably was distasteful to him, and he is suspicious of whatever shuns the open light of day. His belief seems to be that man will get exactly the God of whom he is worthy; in other words, that he creates his own God. As for the visions and ecstasies of saints and hermits—concerning his view of these he leaves us in no doubt at all. It is not a sympathetic view, nor is it calculated to promote faith in such phenomena; but it is extremely amusing.

1925.

ARTHUR LYON RAILE

It would be easy to do less than justice to Raile's poetry, so difficult in manner, so unusual in content. On the face of it, anything less likely to be popular would be hard to imagine, and yet fifty-two of the ninety-five pieces printed in this final edition of *The Wild Rose*, published shortly before his death, had already appeared in 1903 under the title of *Itamos*, eighty-six in 1909 under the title of *The Wild Rose*; which means, I suppose, even if the editions were very small, that the poems had found a certain number of appreciators. What, then, is their character; to what impulse or inspiration do they owe their existence; and have they any literary value?

I think their chief merit lies in a remarkable constancy of spirit and of faith. The mood may vary in different poems, but never the underlying faith. For faith it is, though not a faith in Christianity, and the only god evoked is pagan. It is a faith in three or four human qualities—courage, fortitude, loyalty, faith itself:

> This wall is patience, and that, fortitude.
> The third is knowledge, and the fourth, restraint,
> Wherein a door, but in the door the rood.

The crabbedness of form in much of Raile's work dis-

171

guises its peculiar intimacy: the language is too often obscure
—sometimes, it would seem, wilfully obscure. Nor is this
poetry remarkable for richness of imagery, for music, or for
any verbal felicity. At times we are inclined to question if it
is poetry at all. In certain passages I think it is; but largely
because of the sincerity that vibrates through it, the emotion
held in austere control; never because it possesses any
natural singing quality, any particular beauty of phrase,
for there is neither. With the exception of a few pieces the
entire collection really forms one single poem—an *apologia
pro vita sua*, a confession, a creed. There is neither complaint nor self-pity, yet beneath the stoical reserve one
becomes conscious of an undertone of pain. There may be
here and there, happiness, hope, pride, but the fundamental
note is the realization of exile, of captivity, of loneliness.
Therefore the poet turns backward to an antique, legendary
land, in which he can imagine his dreams coming true; the
spirit of the book is pagan, though not completely pagan—
how can it be, when it finds it necessary to explain itself,
to defend its choice, to make a choice at all?

> Dead heathen god, that fillest all my brain,
> whose perfect counsel maketh sorrow plain,
> whose sovereign word alone hath power
> to save each hour.
>
> .   .   .   .   .
>
> With healing in thy wings re-risen to bless
> thou comest in Hellenic nakedness,
> spurning each terror-stricken soul
> that shuns thee whole;
>
> and I perceive thee, as a monk distraught,
> or philosophic sage inured to thought,

may see beyond the book or prayer
his dream in air;

and I believe thee, as a vision sent
to mourner in perpetual banishment
from his own ruined hearth and home
in Greece or Rome; . . .

This is part of a hymn to Eros, and here is the last stanza
of another:

All paths can end but at his holy seat,
nor is there any labour, any praise,
no service meet,
that lays not down its burden by his chair—
an old man's loneliness, a saint's despair,
his works, *his* ways.

The Eros here hymned is no playful wanton Cupid, but
the 'implacable Eros' of an older tradition. His modern
shrine is built in an alien, antagonistic land; now and then
it is illumined by a momentary light, but when the light
passes, it leaves the surrounding darkness deeper. And in the
end—what? Patience, fortitude, knowledge. Not, at any
rate, despair.

Grasp man's delight. Reach out thy hand anew
for pleasure. Slake thy thirst upon the streams.
Cast forth thy humour in the hot sun's beams.
Mount with thine eye, and revel in the blue.

No chase is ended while the huntsman lives;
no hope is hopeless while desire still burns;
no spirit quenched which, reckoning not returns,
giving with bountiful content, yet gives.

But even this 'pride of life' is based on a full knowledge of life's inadequacy, of its inevitable failure to make the dream reality. 'Love shalt thou know, and, loveless, walk'—in that lies the tragedy. To accept the lower for the higher, however, would be more tragic still, and the whole teaching of these poems rejects such an acquiescence, such 'tarnished consolation'.

> Love flieth out to thee over the sea,
> sheering the misty spray;
> keen and light with fasting fare
> and the ache at the heart that is always there,
> hungry and eager as bird of prey
> stretching beak perpetually
> Love flieth out to thee.
>
> Strong from the travel far and fleet,
> fresh from the airy quest,
> bright from windy shiverings,
> soon shall he gather thee under his breast,
> soon shall he bury thee under his wings,
> draw thee to him with arms and feet,
> cover thee with his heat.

I am perfectly aware that these poems are full of faults. There are lines of sheer doggerel, there is often a pedantic pretentiousness of diction; and the tyranny of rhyme sometimes has had disastrous results. But a book of lyrics describing the birth and growth and decline of a spiritual or emotional experience is not common. Inevitably the imagination of the reader tries to create out of hints and half-lights a more logical and explicit story than is actually presented. Hence the different interpretations of Shakespeare's *Sonnets*. True, these happen to be great poetry, and *The Wild Rose* is not great poetry, is not always even very readable verse. What seems certain is that it does spring directly out of such a spiritual and emotional experience, and that once this had been expressed the desire to write ceased, the creative impulse was exhausted. The earliest poems are dated 1882, the latest 1910; but, throughout, the gaze of the poet is fastened on his own soul, the very landscapes are subjective. What he gives us, nevertheless, is no sentimental reverie. Much more frequently there is a harshness of note, and always an impatience with weakness, self-pity, above all with the consolations of a fool's paradise. And the experience itself? That in one sense is individual, and in another, it may be, universal. It is the desire for that complete union with another being in which the very idea of self is lost and found. Out of this desire the mythopoeic imagination of boyhood creates a dream image, a breathing shape, the soulmate who never was and never can be. The years of youth are haunted by the pursuit of this beloved phantom: for a moment perhaps it seems almost grasped, but next moment it is gone; what is flesh cannot become spirit, nor can the spirit become flesh. The momentary illusion is all that remains: upon it is founded a hope that somehow, somewhere, the reality exists. Only, time is passing, old age is approaching, and with it a vision of the end—the end of struggle, the final surrender, and after that rest.

> A song of weariness. The day is long;
> the way is slow;
> I have no wish to go
> one forward step, but fain would lie,
> watched over by the godhead to whom I
> belong.

> 1928.

SEUMAS O'KELLY

I never met Seumas O'Kelly. In March 1917 he wrote to
me from Naas, suggesting that we should exchange books,
and I sent him everything I had published up till that date,
while in return he sent me his own crop. We talked then of
arranging a meeting, but, as I say, this never took place,
because in the following year he died suddenly—dropped
dead in the street.

The letters that passed between us had been concerned
only with writing, but they had been very friendly; there
was a sympathy, a point of view, I know not what, that we
shared. He had produced a novel of great beauty, and three
or four short stories that seemed to me beautiful—these
among other things I either did not know or had found
less striking. He was at work, as he told me, on a long short
story to be called *The Weaver's Grave*, and there was a considerable quantity of earlier stuff (published after his death)
which still awaited his final revision. His talent was not precocious—was, indeed, of a kind that develops slowly—and
the untimely breaking-off of a career so brilliantly promising
was a genuine loss to Irish literature. *The Lady of Deerpark*
(1917) was, I thought, the best novel that had yet come out
of modern Ireland—not flawless, but a work of genius. The
writing was sometimes incorrect; on the other hand it was

often beautiful, and there was never a cliché, never a ready-made phrase. His dramatic experiments interested me less. The conventions of the stage seemed to hamper him; it was only in fiction that he found a medium in which he could express fully a talent that was extraordinarily poetic and individual. What ultimately he might have accomplished is impossible to surmise. In his latest work, *The Weaver's Grave* (and *it* is unrevised), we can see that he was creating a new technique. Therefore his second novel probably would have been quite unlike his first. I am assuming that the posthumous *Wet Clay*, published in 1922, was *not* his second novel: to me it bears all the signs of being an earlier tale that he had found unsatisfactory and laid aside.

The Lady of Deerpark should have brought O'Kelly more than the esteem of a few fellow-writers; it should have brought him popularity. Quite apart from its humour and charm and masterly construction, it is what the novel-reader calls 'a good story'. I have his own assurance, however, that it attracted little attention in Ireland and none at all elsewhere. True, it is not a startling, not a revolutionary book; O'Kelly accepted in it the formal tradition of English fiction; yet none the less it reveals him as an original and in some respects a great artist in prose. Perhaps the manner of it was too quiet for the general public; perhaps the whole conception was too delicate. Otherwise I cannot see why it should have failed. For the story, as it develops, becomes most dramatic, holds us as few novels have the power to hold us; and it is told with such admirable restraint that when at last the underlying emotion *is* allowed to break through, the effect is proportionately intensified. Nevertheless, it is a quiet book. And when I say this I do not merely mean that it is free from violence; I mean that a strange and haunting atmosphere of stillness deliberately has been created, through which we watch Miss Heffernan, the ill-fated lady of Deerpark. Tone and drama, scene and character, are exquisitely harmonized, and the result is beauty. Miss Heffernan is a woman of extreme refinement, no longer young, leading a life that is almost the life of a recluse, that is lonely and sheltered as some secret pool hidden in a hollow of the mountains—until suddenly all this is changed by a deep and tragic passion she conceives for the young agent who looks after her property. She realizes that it can come to nothing. He is so boyish, so respectful, so aware that his family has always been in the service of her family, and that she herself belongs to an older generation. And then, for a brief moment, a tremulous hope is born—and instantly all the strings are set vibrating, like the strings of Miss Heffernan's harp, and a wild melodious music swells out and fills the air.

The last chapters, it is true, are not quite on this level. The inspiration may have failed, or possibly the desire to provide a strong climax proved too tempting. The climax certainly is there, but it is obtained by the sacrifice of what we value most in O'Kelly's writing—a quality of imaginative suggestiveness that I can best describe, perhaps, by saying that the effect of his finest stories is infinitely richer than the sum of their recorded happenings. Over *The White Goat*, for example—a tragedy of animal suffering—there broods a shadow of universal tragedy; behind the grotesque, fantastic comedy of *The Weaver's Grave* there looms a vision of human mortality.

O'Kelly was a realist; the cheap, the sentimental, the insincere, were utterly abhorrent to him. But he was not a materialist. He looked at life simply and directly, and there was nothing significant in life from which he turned away; nevertheless, his work is conceived always in the spirit of poetry. Even when he writes of what is ugly, a spiritual beauty creeps in through the manner of the presentment. Several of the stories in *The Golden Barque* might have been sordid enough. The actual details are sordid. But because they have passed through O'Kelly's imagination they stretch out roots and branches into a world far beyond the world of immediate perception. Nothing is glossed over, nothing withheld, yet the impression of beauty triumphs. What, for instance, is the subject of the longest of the short stories? The squabble of three doddering old men about the exact locality of a grave—the weaver's grave. O'Kelly treats it in the spirit of comedy: only, it is a comedy through which, from beginning to end, we hear the rattle of spades and coffins. Behind the cracked, high-pitched, ancient voices, the flickering movements and flickering senile passions; behind the lonely ruin of the disused burial-ground, we see a tall, white, waiting figure—standing in shadow, motionless, and with lifted scythe.

That O'Kelly had the objective imagination and rich inventiveness of the born story-teller is proved by the variety of his tales. The stories connected with the Golden Barque bear little resemblance to *The Weaver's Grave* or *The White Goat*, and less to *The Lady of Deerpark*; while those in *The Leprechaun of Kilmeen* break up completely new ground. This Golden Barque, despite its romantic name, is a very ordinary and ungilded river barge, its crew as tough as may be, the chronicle of its voyages a chronicle of just such everyday incidents as must come into the lives of just such men. Yet, as we journey on those trips up and down the river, with Michael and Hike and Calcutta and the Boss, we somehow *are* in a world of romance. The introductory story, *Michael and Mary*, is pure romance, pure poetry. And how slight the material out of which it has been fashioned! A girl standing on the canal bank watches a barge passing, drawn by an old horse who is being led by a small, bent, muttering figure; and watches a young man at the tiller. A few days later, though only for the short stretch between one lock and another, she stands by this young man's side, while he steers the boat through the rain. A few days later still she learns from his companions that he has 'gone voyaging', gone in a three-masted ship, nobody knows whither, 'for he had the blood in him for the wide ocean, the wild blood of the rover'. That is all, yet the thing is profound. Told with the utmost simplicity, it is steeped in all the sadness of youth and of a first dream of love. Equally successful, in its so different way, is that chapter which merely describes a group of carters and boatmen drinking in a public-house. How, we may ask, do such things become stories at all? That was O'Kelly's secret, as it was the secret of Tourguéneff when he wrote *A Sportsman's Sketches*.

But he worked in many veins, sometimes simple, sometimes subtle; and was constantly experimenting in new forms and with new subjects. In *Billy the Clown*, an admirable study of a small boy, the story is plain enough; in the *Leprechaun* book the stories become yarns, with all the earthy raciness of folk-tales. I do not know for whom O'Kelly wrote these particular tales (whether for children or grown-ups), but it is marvellous how inventions so fantastic and broadly comic should yet keep so close to life. Therein lies their originality. This book of the *Leprechaun*, besides being a history of his pranks and humours, is a rich and vivid evocation of the whole parish of Kilmeen, with its smells and sights and sounds, its cats and dogs and hens and human inhabitants, all as realistically alive as in one of the professedly realistic fictions. The yarns are spun under a haycock in Ned Darmody's field by 'oul' Tom Kelleher', to a circle of barefooted small boys, 'the eyes of them lookin' over the country with the wonder of the world in them. You could see well in them that they all expected to come across a Leprechaun in no time, up in an oul' ditch or the like, an' that they were makin' up their minds how they'd handle him when they'd nail him.'

The Leprechaun of Kilmeen was published two years after O'Kelly's death, and unfortunately, as in his other posthumous books, the text bristles with misprints, misreadings, misspellings, and grammatical solecisms a schoolboy could have corrected. He himself was no purist; if an infinitive could be split he never hesitated to split it; but he had the artist's pride in his work, and this slovenly or incompetent reading of the proofs was a poor tribute to his memory. His genius remains. I use the word deliberately, for his best stories have a poetic substance, a beauty of light and of atmosphere, a beauty of tenderness and of understanding, that imply something more than talent. And there is always the lonely natural beauty, rising dream-like through them, of the most beautiful country upon earth.

1920.

MISCELLANEOUS ESSAYS

A GARDEN BY THE SEA

To-day, after a period of many years, I revisited the place by the merest chance. I had passed it frequently, but knowing that its former tenants, the people I had cared for, were long since dead and gone, I had never felt any desire to intrude upon their old home. This afternoon, however, perceiving that the green door in the garden wall was slightly ajar, I got off my bicycle and entered. It was scarcely a garden now, scarcely even the ghost of a garden, but a wilderness of weeds, among which only the coarser plants and shrubs had survived. The house, too, wore that forsaken melancholy expression common to houses that have long been empty. The dark bare windows were like sightless eyes in a dead face; a broken urn that had once held a flowering shrub lay in the long grass beside the doorstep. Questioning one of the men working there, I learned that a new tenant was expected in the autumn. It was for him they were building a motor-shed; house-painters, plumbers and carpenters, would be busy next week; everything was to be put in thorough repair. I came away with those words sounding ominously in my ears. 'Thorough repair' was certainly needed: on the other hand, not all the repair in the world could bring back the place I had once known, and late in the evening I felt a sudden desire to look again on what remained of it—a desire to catch some last floating shadow of the past before it should be quite irrecoverable—one of those purely sentimental impulses that usually lead to disappointment and regret.

The door, of course, was now locked, for the men had ceased work for several hours, so I scrambled over the stone wall and dropped down among the nettles on the other side. Miss Caroline's rustic bench at any rate was still in its old position, and there, upon the half-rotten branches through which ivy and convolvulus now pushed, I sat down to smoke a meditative pipe. Darkness had brought back something of its bygone beauty to the place. I could almost imagine that the house was still inhabited, its occupants asleep—just as, for that matter, they would have been in the days when I had known them, at this ungodly hour of half-past ten. And the sound of the waves breaking on the beach below filled the night with music. . . .

Quite by accident, when I was a small boy, I had come here first. A butterfly, an 'azure blue', which in my too great eagerness I had failed to net, had flitted over the wall, and boldly I had pushed open the green door, and followed it. In those days I was an incorrigible trespasser, nevertheless I felt a certain embarrassment when—hatless, breathless, with net in hand and one stocking sagging down over my ankle—I found myself immediately confronting an elderly lady, who was walking slowly towards me, a gardening-basket and a large pair of scissors in her hands. My first impulse was to take to my heels; but seeing that she smiled at me, I hesitated. 'If you are coming in, shut the door behind you, like a good boy. I don't want dogs: they scratch up the flower beds. You're quite sure you haven't a dog?'

I blushed and begged her pardon and told her I hadn't a dog. I dare say I stared at her, for she was a very nice old lady, dressed in black, and with black lace mittens on her wrists in spite of the gardening-basket. Her thin hair, the colour of old silver, was parted in the middle and smoothed closely down on either side of her forehead. She wore a cap of soft white lace with a lilac ribbon in it.

When I had stammered out an explanation of my intrusion, she laughed, and waved her scissors at me. Then she asked me if I would like some gooseberries. But she would not allow me to catch butterflies, which was disappointing, because the garden seemed a veritable paradise of them. A striped purring cat, with tail erect, followed her along the box-lined paths, and when she sat down on a bench jumped into her lap. As for me, I was already busy among the gooseberry-bushes. A scent of flowers floated upon the air— roses and mignonette, carnations and sweet-peas. The July sun was hot; bees swung in the foxgloves; and down below, the slow listless splash of the sea made me plan to have a second bathe in the afternoon. A haunted sea—blue, deep blue, with a narrow line of white foam where the waves curled over on the yellow sand.

When I thought it would be 'rude' to eat any more gooseberries, I emerged from the bushes and was conducted to the house, where, in a dim cool parlour, I partook of cake and raspberry wine—rather a greedy little boy, it now strikes me. And here I was introduced to Miss Caroline's sister, and to her brother, an odd-looking old gentleman with a red face and white hair and the queerest of clothes. (Later I learned that he was a retired sea-captain, whose hobby it was to be his own tailor.) The parlour was full of curiosities brought from distant lands, and while I examined these, and talked to the Captain and Miss Caroline, the elder sister sat in a deep chair, with her thin delicate hands folded. She was old—much older even, I thought, than the Captain and Miss Caroline. And she was so frail and so quiet that I should hardly have believed her to be alive at all if every now and again a word or two had not dropped from her lips. Once only she spoke to me directly, and then her voice was so low and toneless that it seemed to come from far away—like a whisper from a star.

That was my first visit, but I paid many others before the ending of the summer holidays took me back to my own home in town. I knew, of course, that for some reason my elderly friends liked me—liked me to be there, within sight or call, even when we were all occupied with our private concerns. They were not clever, I imagine, and my conversation, of which they must have heard plenty, never seemed to bore them. The Captain, smoking interminably, stooping every now and again to pull up a weed, would tell me strange and involved tales that, as I dimly recall them now, can hardly have been more than 'founded upon fact'. His ships appeared to have put in at every port in the world, to have weathered countless storms and to have come through infinitely perilous adventures, but they must have sailed up the rivers of wonderland too. He played the flute, and Miss Caroline played his accompaniments on the piano, with stiff fingers and a questionable mastery of the bass notes. When visitors called, which was very rarely, I amused myself in the garden till they were gone. The hours passed lightly as a dream.

Both sisters probably were readers, for the house was full of books, and the Captain, I know, preferred doing things, making things, to reading. On wet afternoons, and sometimes even on fine afternoons, curled up in the window-seat, or lying on my stomach in the garden, I pored over the back volumes of *Temple Bar*, devouring the romances of Rhoda Broughton, with an obliviousness to all else that no book could produce in me to-day. On several occasions I met Miss Caroline and the Captain beyond the precincts of their little world: I have a dim recollection, too, that Miss Caroline and my mother exchanged visits (in fact, I had made this almost inevitable), but I don't think it can have gone much beyond a formal call and its return. I also saw them in church on Sundays, when they seemed to me to be altered in some mysterious way by their changed surroundings. For me they belonged to this particular house and garden where I had first discovered them: anywhere else they were not in their right setting. Even in those days they must have been old-fashioned. . . .

The moon had come out from behind the clouds as I sat smoking a second and a third pipe, listening to these echoes from the past. A cat glided stealthily through the grass, disappearing in the shadow of the wall. The moonlight grew brighter and the shadows blacker. The place, the hour, my own state of mind—all were singularly appropriate to ghosts, but no ghosts came. The Captain, Miss Caroline— and with them everything they represented of leisure and graciousness and quiet—had retreated too far to return, and even my memory of them was tinged with legend. Yet long ago beauty lingered here—lingered like the grey moths now hovering among the tangled currant-bushes—lingered for a space before taking flight.

1914.

STEPHEN GOODEN:
AN ICONOGRAPHICAL NOTE

Since the eighteen-sixties there have been perhaps no illustrations produced by an English artist more charming and interesting than the line-engravings of Mr. Stephen Gooden, and in the following paper my aim has been to give a brief account of all the plates he has made up till the date of writing—July 1930. There may be one or two unimportant omissions, but I have the artist's own assurance that there are none, and also that of my friend Mr. J. N. Hart, who has collected Gooden's work from the beginning.

Stephen Gooden was born in London in 1892. There was the tradition of art in his family. His father, who had been in the employment of Messrs. Agnew, started a picture-dealing business of his own in Pall Mall about 1888, which later developed into the firm of Gooden and Fox; his great-grandfather, Henry Linton, had been an engraver; and Henry Linton's half-brother was W. J. Linton, the artist and wood-engraver. As a child, Stephen was frequently in his father's galleries; the best pictures that passed through the firm's hands were shown to him; and also on many occasions he was taken to Christie's. He was educated at Rugby, but was not particularly fond of his books, or at any rate of his lesson-books. His chief interest was in drawing, and he wanted to be an artist. One evening, during his holidays from school, the well-known connoisseur, Sir Hugh Lane, happened to call at the house. Possibly there had already been some earlier discussion about the boy's future career, for Lane asked to see his drawings, looked over them, and recommended that he should be sent to the Slade School. This advice was followed; Stephen Gooden in 1909 joined the Slade School, where he remained during the next four years. We have a specimen of his work at this period, a large etching entitled *The Ark*. Of the first state, in pure line, of this delightful and amusing composition only two or three impressions exist, and only two, I think, of the second state (aquatint), one of which is in the Fitzwilliam Museum, Cambridge, and the other in the possession of Mr. Hart, whose unique collection of Gooden proofs contains everything the artist has done. The ark is depicted in the hour of its completion. As yet no rain has fallen, but the faithful Noah is already welcoming his guests, who are crossing a bridge in sedate pairs, though not without one or two private misunderstandings. It is a fine show, and must have afforded at least temporary solace to the doomed inhabitants of that row of suburban villas, which, with their back gardens, compose the chief feature of the landscape.

The Ark belongs to 1912 or 1913, but in 1914, on the outbreak of the Great War, Stephen Gooden joined the army as a private soldier, and for the next three years served in France. One memento at least he brought home with him: the beautiful design on the title-page of *The Brook Kerith* is a memory of the war. It is based on Dürer's *Ecce Homo*, but actually it is a portrait. Somewhere in the region of the Somme Gooden saw this man, his Good Shepherd, a peasant seated at the gate of a field, and the impression he received was so vivid that he jotted it down on the back of an envelope.

When peace was declared Stephen Gooden came back to London and started once more on his career as an artist. But he had to begin all over again, in altered conditions, and moreover, it seemed to him that in the interval he had forgotten or half forgotten how to draw. His choice of line-engraving as a medium was, in fact, to some extent a disciplinary measure. It pleased him; its possibilities were further and further revealed with each experiment he made; and he has been faithful to it ever since.

The first engraved plate (it was exhibited at Zürich), the *Absalom* of 1923, is distinctly experimental. Its effects of chiaroscuro are more those we look for in a painting than in a line-engraving. Its *naïveté* is not deliberate—it is the *naïveté* we find in Uccello, and spiritually it belongs to that younger world. It was this design which earned him his first commission, a book-plate for Mr. Hart, who from now on took the keenest interest in the young artist's progress. The book-plate was a success (it is indeed, as a book-plate, among the best he has ever done) and in its turn led to a second commission, this time from the Nonesuch Press.

For the Nonesuch *Anacreon* (1923) Gooden designed four full-page plates, a title-page, a head-piece, and a tail-piece. In these he shows himself already a master of his medium, and some of the youthful nudes are as lovely, or nearly as lovely, as any he has done since. My own favourite is *Cupid, the Cunning Beggar*. The attitude of this little naked boy, who has come through the rain and the night to knock at the old poet's door, is beautifully natural and expressive. He stands at the edge of the portico, suddenly revealed in the candle-light, with one hand raised against his breast, the other pressing against the pillar behind him, bold yet half-timid, doubtful of his welcome, eager to come in out of the cold, but ready to dart away should the disturbed sleeper in dressing-gown and night-cap show the slightest sign of anger. Of course the subject is there in the poem, but Gooden has made it his own, the thing is intensely characteristic in its quaint humour and charm, and if I had to pick out half a dozen plates by which to illustrate the artist's individuality, his peculiar temperament and vision, this surely would be among them. The *Anacreon* is a book to be treasured, for it possesses the special interest and freshness which the first manifestations of an unfolding and original talent always must have for us. There is, to begin with, the thrill of novelty, the pleasure of discovery; also there is the singularly fascinating mixture of promise and achievement. Stephen Gooden can draw better now than when he made these drawings—his technique is firmer, and even the very next plate he made, *The Rider on the Lion*, shows a marked development in his sense of design—but the *Anacreon* will always remain among my own favourites, and particularly this drawing of *Cupid*, and the beautiful head-piece in which we see our small Eros again, singing to a lute, his plump hand plucking at the strings, his mouth rounded to an O; and the tail-piece, in which he carries a smoking torch.

The other and minor engravings of 1923 consist of designs for a pair of silver buckles and a brooch (Solomon, the Queen of Sheba, a Musician with a lute and a swan), and a book-plate for Mr. Leigh D. Brownlee. This last was done immediately after Mr. Hart's book-plate, but is much less successful, the artist having been obliged to work strictly according to instructions. It remains, however, a curious example of Gooden's ingenuity, for, in spite of the instructions, what it actually suggests is an illustration for some tale by Edgar Poe.

In the following year he designed the Nonesuch Press imprint, and a little later one for the Walden Bookshop in

N   193

America. But a really important plate of 1924 is *The Rider on the Lion*—an independent composition, not an illustration, and a very fine example of his work. There are two states— one without, and one with the landscape—both beautiful, though I prefer the former.

The *Nonesuch Bible*, in five volumes, each with an engraved title-page, head-piece, and tail-piece, was begun in this year, and the first volume, containing the Apocrypha, issued. The second and third volumes appeared in 1925, the fourth in 1926, and the fifth, containing the New Testament, in 1927. It was a work entirely suited to Gooden. His temperamental affinity with the early Italian masters here could find complete expression. His Tobit, his David, are as guilelessly and frankly pagan as Botticini's or Verrocchio's. He accepts the ancient tales as simply as a child accepts a fairy-story, and as unconsciously finds in them his own imaginative visions. His *Creation of Adam* is a joy, with its two donkeys rubbing noses in the background, and his *Adam and Eve* under their apple-tree is more fascinating still. These things have been remoulded nearer—very much nearer—to the heart's desire—are in the highest degree individual. Susanna, seated innocently in her bath, is not a bit angry with those two old men who are looking at her; they may not realize it, but there is not the least necessity for them to skulk behind the garden bushes. And the David, standing dreamily, half sadly, over the fallen Goliath, is most beautiful of all—a lovely thing, breathing all the bright, stilled poetry of youth.

The tail-pieces to the third and fourth volumes—*Praise Ye the Lord*, and *The End of the Prophets*—are, I think, the most exquisite examples Gooden has given us of his decorative work, while the prophets themselves, those fierce old fanatics, have been admirably imagined. There is in truth only one of Gooden's inventions at which I feel inclined to cavil, and it occurs in that otherwise so successful title-page to Genesis. We have at the top the delicious *Adam and Eve*, beneath them an impressive *Abraham and Moses*, then two angels holding up a rainbow. But who is this kneeling figure below? Between pillars we see the ark aground on Mount Ararat; the waters are subsiding; a couple of unicorns, followed by two lions, have already found their way ashore; the kneeling figure raises his hands in thanksgiving to heaven. . . . Only, there is no use telling me he is Noah, for he is Will Shakespeare to the life.

Before leaving the Bible I must mention an interesting plate the artist made and did not use. It shows the Virgin seated on a heap of corn outside the manger, nursing her Child. Joseph, a dark figure against the evening sky, has been drawing water, and returns, carrying a pail; the three Kings are approaching on horseback. It is a fine thing, but Gooden thought it too different in style to be included with the other pictures, and it *is* different. So he designed the *Flight into Egypt* to take its place, while the rejected design was used as a Christmas card.

In the meantime the Nonesuch Press published in 1925 *Songs of the Gardens*, with a delicate Watteauesque design of a lady and a gallant posturing on a toy bridge in a conventional landscape. This was originally an engraving on copper, but in the book was reproduced by lithography. In 1926 appeared George Moore's *Ulick and Soracha*, with a symbolic frontispiece illustrating the elaborate dedication to Lady Cunard. The dedication itself is the very purplest of patches, but Gooden has done what he can with it in his not very characteristic picture of a formal garden, with a fountain rising under the moon. Much more satisfying is the return to paganism we naturally get in the tiny designs for *The*

Pythian Odes of Pindar (Nonesuch Press, 1928)—particularly the head-piece of an athlete running, and the tail-piece of a chariot driver—both exquisite as old Greek coins. *The Latin Portrait*, a somewhat similar book issued from the same press in the following year, is also charming.

In 1929 appeared George Moore's *The Brook Kerith* (Heinemann) with twelve admirable plates, nine of which are full-page.[1] These reveal a dramatic power that his earlier work had hardly led us to expect. Everyone will have his own favourites, but for my part I should pick out the title-page, the head-piece, and among the full-page plates, *Master and Pupil*, *Banu*, *Father and Son*, *The Little Ram*, and *Jesus Meets Paul*. Note the lovely quality in the shadows and in the rendering of wood and stone in this last design; and, differing from George Moore, who complained that it was like an advertisement for toffee, I am especially fond of the *Master and Pupil*. The drawing is, at all events, brimming over with life and movement. That small boy really *is* talking as he hurries his ancient friend along (rather too quickly for comfort); the picture is filled with his chatter, and is yet another proof of the artist's appreciation of youth—an appreciation, it seems to me, to which we owe the most attractive examples of his work.

Before passing to the miscellaneous pieces it might be better to mention another major work upon which Gooden is now engaged, since very likely it will be published sooner than this article. La Fontaine's *Fables* (Heinemann) is to contain twenty-six plates, twelve of them full-page engravings, and these latter are already completed. As we know, the majority of the characters in the fables are birds and beasts; still, there are a good many in which human beings

---

[1] Mr. Hart has a dry-point proof of a plate begun but never finished—*The Casting out of Devils*.

play a part, and it is to these that Gooden has gone for his subjects. The first is a fine illustration for *Death and the Woodman*. The evening light streams down through the trees, illuminating the expression of mingled terror and protest on the face of the old man, who stands aghast, while the attenuated figure of Death, all too rashly summoned, towers above him. A rather strange drawing of a nude female figure illustrates *The Lion in Love*. The treacherous woman leans in lassitude against a tree, her arms resting on the lower branches, while the lion contemplates her faintly depraved beauty with an expression of sensual adoration in his eyes. For the fable of *The Hag and the Slavies* we get an interior. The cruel task-mistress stands at the door holding up a lamp, a cock perched on the banister crows viciously, and the two maids lie in deep sleep on the bed, the soft curves of their bodies delicately revealed beneath the light coverlet. These are admirable things, but to my mind the most striking plate of all is *The Acorn and the Pumpkin*—one of Gooden's happiest inspirations. The beautiful drawing of the oak-tree under which the satyr-like peasant reclines, the drawing of the hands and of the loose clothing, in fact of every detail, and the bold simplicity of the pattern, place this picture among his best.

At the beginning of my paper, which is addressed primarily to collectors, I mentioned Gooden's two early book-plates. I now give a list of the others:

G. F. and A. E. Waley (1924).

Joseph Hugh Leycester (1924). This plate was cancelled and only two or three proofs exist.

Katharine Cromer (1925).

S. L. Courtauld (1925).

Mary Thynne (1926).

Dorothy Moulton Mayer (1926).

Geoffrey Keynes (1926).

Mona Gooden (1926).

Antoinette Brett (1928).

Edward and Cicely Hutchinson (1928).

Bertine Entwisle Sutton (1928).

Margaret Griselda Wedderburn (1928).

The Courtauld, Sutton, Brett, and Hutchinson plates are my own favourites. They are little gems, though perhaps two of them are more in the nature of pictures than of book-plates proper. A book-plate executed for Mr. Harold Hartley in 1927 hardly counts, since the artist was commissioned to re-draw a design of Simeon Solomon's. Mr. Hartley certainly is faithful to the 'sixties.

A few things still remained unchronicled. Four head-pieces engraved in 1924, but not used. A Christmas card of Eros and Aphrodite (1925). A portrait of the artist's wife in fancy dress (1926). The design made by Gooden for his own notepaper (1926). A frontispiece of a soldier on horse-back lighting a pipe, made for the Prince of Wales's edition of *The Legion Book* (1929).

Lastly, there is Stephen Gooden's only wood-engraving, *The Translation of Habakkuk*, made for the Cresset Press in 1929. It is an illustration for the tale of Bel and the Dragon, and is so successful that one regrets the artist is not attracted by this medium. The *Habakkuk* is a white-line engraving, the method employed by Bewick, but not by the artists of the 'sixties. The design is broad and powerful, and if one did not know that this was a prophet to whom the angel of the Lord has just appeared one might take him for a magician with his familiar. According to the story, Habakkuk was carrying the reapers' dinner out into the fields when the angel commanded him to take it to Daniel, then in the lions' den in Babylon. 'I never saw Babylon,' the indignant prophet cries, 'neither do I know where the den is. Then the angel of the Lord took him by the crown, and bare him by the hair of his head, and through the vehemency of his spirit set him in Babylon over the den.'

It is the very moment before they take flight that Gooden illustrates. The dark-skinned lusty young angel already has his hands in the prophet's hair. His wings are unfolded—white against a black sky. His long waving hair is parted down the middle, his features are bold and sensual, with full lips, large heavy-lidded eyes and arched brows: his loin-cloth flutters in the wind, his muscular limbs are bare. And below the hill on which they are is a little town in an arid landscape, with one or two small trees here and there, and at their feet a sparse growth of cactus.

1930.

BRUGES

I write of Bruges as it was, as it still is indeed;[1] but this European war has only just begun, and before it is ended everything may be changed. A few shells, a few bombs, and all those ancient buildings would collapse like a house of cards, the most perfect survival from medieval Europe be no more than a memory.

On entering Bruges one seems to lose the sense of time, though in no other city is one so constantly reminded of the passing of time. For all day long the carillon, which is the voice of Bruges, marking off the hours, the half-hours, and the quarter-hours, breaks through the stillness of the city; and if one wakens in the night one hears it. A strange, sweet, soon very familiar music, with now and then an odd jangling in the tune that never becomes unmelodious. It sounds far and faint, curiously ethereal, when you are wandering along the outer canals; loud, but not too loud, when you sit in the afternoon at a café in the great Belfry Square; almost deafening if you ascend the many steps of the tower, where two fantastic little men, like gnomes out of a fairy-tale, pass their days in looking after the bells.

The carillon accents the quiet of Bruges—that quiet

which is one of its greatest charms. The clear notes spread out upon the air in circling waves of sound which gradually diminish and die into a silence that is but the deeper for this brief disturbance of it. Almost immediately, certainly within an hour of my first arrival, which took place on an afternoon of mingled rain and sunshine, I became conscious of the beauty of this quietness, but it is not until the sights are seen, the churches, the galleries, visited, that it begins to produce its peculiar effect, which is, as I have said, like a gradual blotting out of the sense of time.

Bruges is a small city: every place is just round the corner from everywhere else. You may easily see all that the guide-books mention in a very few hours: yet, if you wait over the second day, you will probably, as I did, stay on and on, in the mood of Tennyson's Lotos-Eaters. Then it is that day follows day and you never quite know whether it is Tuesday or Friday. There is nothing to tell you, because there is nothing to do; each morning, each afternoon, is an exact counterpart of the last.

I have never been in Bruges in winter, but I have been there in the spring and in the summer and in the autumn, and though each season has its own appropriate beauty, the dominant impression left upon my mind is of an endless autumn. The colouring of the city itself is autumnal—rich and sombre, the grey stone-work mellowed, warmed, and stained by age, the brickwork and woodwork all reds and browns and deep blending shades of green and yellow. Yet the aspect is constantly changing. It alters, like one of our Irish lakes, with each change in the sky above it, is extra-ordinarily responsive to the different lights of morning, of afternoon, of dusk. I have seen Bruges on a cloudless June day when the heavy sunlight, baking old crumbling bricks and stones and casting a trail of liquid fire on the water of the canals, brought out its immense antiquity by revealing each crack and cranny, as a strong light reveals the lines in an aged human countenance; and I have seen it under a mist of rain, when everything was grey and delicate and, as it were, spiritualized, the whole city seeming hardly more solid than the mist itself.

Bruges has been called—probably by the guide-books—the Venice of the North, but no town could be less like Venice. It is true that it is threaded by canals, but they are unused—are silent and dark and sluggish, in autumn strewn with dead leaves; while the white swans that now and then float down them, drift by like ghosts. Beside these canals are roughly-cobbled streets. On a wet day, with the rain pattering on your umbrella and running in streams along the gutters, you may see Bruges almost at its best. For its charm is of an exquisite melancholy, which even in the most dismal weather never becomes depressing. From that it is saved by beauty—a beauty so rare and admirable that it gives much of the pleasure of a work of art.

At night Bruges becomes wonderful. At night it is transformed, and seems to waken to a new and mysterious life. The strange, insidious, narcotic influence that all day long rises from the nearly stagnant waters, and seems to touch you almost palpably, has now lost its power. After ten o'clock, if you wander out into the dark streets you will find them deserted. A flickering lamp-flame at each corner gives only the minimum of illumination, but flings abroad fantastic shadows, and the whole city becomes a creation of magic. One might be back in the Middle Ages. The moonlight, white and cold, touches the figures of a Madonna and Child set in some high niche in a wall: by the Lac d'Amour the frogs cry shrilly. Then one may feel—or at any rate I felt—that behind all this there is an enchantment—and I mean literally an enchantment—the spell of witchcraft. Is this most religious city given over at night to the powers of sorcery? I could believe it, for the religion, too, is medieval. The shadows, as I watched them, seemed to grow more and more equivocal; I became as suspicious, as credulous, as the hero of *The Golden Ass*; tales of the grotesque and arabesque floated up in memory; a silhouette behind a blind, in the solitary lighted window of a dark narrow street, had a strange and sinister suggestiveness.

But all day long the pervading spirit is infinitely peaceful, and only gradually one becomes aware of something in the atmosphere subtly and persistently enervating. It is not the peacefulness of Nature, the peacefulness one finds in the open country or by the sea. It promotes neither physical nor mental activity, but a state of dreaming. I had imagined that Bruges would be an ideal place to work in, yet I found that what I actually did was to ponder over the work I would begin to-morrow. True, I planned a story that in feeling, colour, and tone was to reflect this peculiar atmosphere, but I did not write my story, *An Ending*, till I had left Bruges behind me. I carried a notebook and pencil, but rarely used them. Instead, I lay on the grass under the elms in the Béguinage, and watched the demure Sisters moving quietly to and fro on their business there, utterly incurious as to my identity, going into and coming out from the Church of Saint Elizabeth, usually escorted by a vivacious little dog who attended all the religious services, and gave me, in passing, just a flash of recognition.

In Bruges not only the churches and gate-houses and public buildings, but many of the ordinary dwelling-houses, are beautiful. They rise up directly from the canals, whose dark green water washes their basements. Creepers drop from hidden gardens, spreading out their delicate green tendrils over grey stone or red brick. From the quays and from old stone bridges one gets marvellous pictures; though there are many things that can only be seen from the water. On my first visit no boats were to be found on the inner canals. I made inquiries, but was told there weren't any, and I had given up hope when one day, happening to pass a yard whose door stood open, I saw inside a rough, home-made canoe. With difficulty I persuaded the incredulous owner to hire it out to me, and thus found myself sharing with the swans the whole of that watery world.

When I returned a year or two later, however, an absurd Italian had appeared on the scene, with an equally absurd gondola. Clothed in picturesque costume, he looked as if he had stepped out of the chorus of a comic opera, and on the narrow canals his gondola looked gigantic as a battleship. I do not think he did much business, but on the few occasions when he managed to pick up a load of tourists he furnished a delightful pastime for the small boys of the city, who rushed from bridge to bridge, and with remarkable accuracy spat down on the heads of the sight-seers. Last year a motor-boat had supplanted the gondola, and I trust proved equally unlucrative. This, like the train which runs through the Grande Place, is a vandalism so stupid that one might have thought even a City Council would have rejected it. But the authorities in Bruges have become progressive, and in a report recently published express their determination to make their town more popular. What dire threats lurk behind that ominous phrase I cannot think. Even during the Exhibition of the Toison d'Or the city lost much of its peculiar character, just as it does on the days of a religious festival.

As a matter of fact the poverty of Bruges has been its salvation. I have been told that two-thirds of the population are paupers, and without money it is difficult to do much harm. At the first hint of financial prosperity what lovely things would be swept away! A prosperous Bruges would simply be another Ghent—a third-rate commercial town with a few interesting buildings and pictures. As it is now, it is a city of religious houses and charitable asylums.

Only on Saturday mornings is there any stir of business activity. Then, the great open square in front of the Belfry is turned into a temporary market. The ground is covered with stalls, and the effect is of some huge but far from gorgeous bazaar, where all sorts of cheap goods, new and second-hand, are displayed. Buyers and sellers for the most part speak Flemish, though some have a smattering of French. And now and then, on a summer evening, the same people gather in the same place to listen to a band playing. The bandstand is erected in the middle of the square, and everyone walks round and round it in a slowly revolving circle, or sits at one of the three or four cafés, which produce, for the occasion, an unsuspected quantity of chairs and tables that sprawl out over the side-paths.

The art treasures of Bruges are not to be found in the churches. There is a statue of the Madonna and Child by Michelangelo in Notre Dame, and a charming Madonna of the Della Robbia school in the church of Saint Jacques, but nearly all the pictures are valueless. The precious Van Eycks and Davids and Memlincs are to be found either in the Academy or in the Hospital of Saint John. Jan van Eyck and Hans Memlinc are the two great masters of Bruges; and though I am inclined to think that the only authentic work of the former is the superb altar-piece in the Academy (certainly the most beautiful picture the city possesses), Memlinc can be studied here as nowhere else in the world. Among his works I would single out a small square picture hanging in the Hospital of Saint John, the portrait of Martin Newenhoven, painted, as the inscription tells us, when the sitter was twenty-three years old. Only the head and torso are given—set against an open lattice window, through which one sees a pleasant green landscape, divided by a stream whose blue water winds away among distant meadows. The face, Flemish in type, has a grave charm, at once strong and delicate. The lips are slightly parted, and the brown hair waves to the shoulders, falling obliquely on either side of the russet-coloured cheeks. The light comes through the grey window, making visible the faint shadow of down on the upper lip, except for which the face is smooth as a boy's. The hands are folded; an open book, with jewelled clasps, rests before him. The thing would be perfect if it were not for a panel in the window showing a knight on horseback. The blue and red and white of this panel—doubtless introduced by special command—are out of tone with the colour-scheme of the rest of the picture, which nevertheless is among the best of Memlinc's portraits, and gives us an idea of what the people were who once trod these streets.

1915.

KENNETH

Kenneth has been writing now for more than a year, yet his works are still very little known. They appear for the most part in *Kenneth's Magazine* (illustrated), a journal in which, if you happen to be friends with the editor, you may read his shorter pieces, and at the same time follow some six or seven of his serials. These last, it must be confessed, pursue a rather erratic course, dropping out and reappearing with a sort of Jack-in-the-box-like inconsequence. This is due less to bad editorship than to the annoying trick manuscripts have of disappearing at the very moment when a new number is in preparation. There are other reasons too. How many precious chapters of *The Devil's Kin*, of *Pearl Island*, of *Captain Salisbury*, must have found their way to the dust-bin through the carelessness of Minnie, the housemaid, who seems to regard everything that has reached the floor— often quite accidentally—as rejected! Perhaps there is a lack of system, for even I, only a few minutes ago, was on the point of lighting a pipe with a page of *Life's Need*, a romance of whose very existence I had been until then in ignorance. It was this, indeed, that suggested the idea of attempting some brief account of the author's works, for though I do not profess to have read every line he has written, I fancy most of those I have not read have been read to me.

The works consist entirely of novels, short stories, dramatic sketches, and poems—*John Milton: A Critical Study* having been abandoned almost at once, owing to the surprising and unsuspected dullness of *Paradise Lost*. The novels and short stories are the main thing, and though dashed off at an amazing speed, are by no means to be sneezed at. I know few that contain less padding and a greater variety of incident. The fat is in the fire with the first words, and the reader need fear no subsequent disappointment. From the start, the heroes act heroically and the villains villainously, the lovers really love, and the comic characters are as steeped in buffoonery as the criminals in crime. The pirates are no soft-hearted rogues, after the fashion of the degenerate pirates of Marryat or Ballantyne. Captain Aaron Salisbury tosses off a bumper of human blood at the conclusion of each engagement, and at the height of his career returns to his native town for the sole purpose of murdering his old Sunday-school teacher. Never a pang of remorse does *he* suffer while his victims walk the plank and drop into a sea boiling with sharks. He fears neither man nor devil, and has not a spark of sentiment even when it comes to the women and children.

A striking feature, in fact, of all these romances, is their singular *un*likeness to the Sunday-school books. Not one of them—not even *The Young Viking*, not even *The Hero of Sheldon College*—would be published by the S.P.C.K., while what that society would make of such a thing as *Split, the Burglar* may be left to imagination. Yet it would be unfair to accuse Kenneth actually of siding with Split and Aaron Salisbury; he is too detached a writer for that: on the other hand, he never condemns them, and certainly sheds no tears over their dupes. His attitude is completely unsentimental; for me it is too unsentimental. I prefer my rogues to have some redeeming qualities, but in his very choice of names Kenneth is inexorable. Split McAlinty—could he be anything but a crook of the baser sort? Occasionally, I think, a disillusioned view of human nature is pushed over-far. Captain Black, for instance, the swashbuckling hero of *A Rebel's Love*, is too callous for the part he has to play in a tale that was at least conceived romantically. We are invited, in the beginning, to sympathize with him, but he is not a lovable person. True, he 'stifles' most of his oaths, but he is always stifling them, and when we have filled in the blanks for ourselves (which I for one never can resist doing) the result is deplorable. Kenneth belongs to Ulster, and his foul-spoken hero plays an active part in the Irish Rebellion; still, I think that is no excuse for making him act as he does in the face of a fallen foe. Captain Black is leading (I admit with reckless bravery) a company of rebels, when the Ulster Captain—obviously with pacific intentions—rides up at the head of *his* band. ' "Stop all communication——" he began, but the sentence was never finished: he fell backward and about fifteen men on top of him. "I'm afraid it's a case of fifteen men on the dead man's chest!" ' is Captain Black's sole comment.

But perhaps I am dwelling overmuch on a single aspect of the novels, for they have their lighter side, particularly the school stories, though here also the notes most frequently struck are those of lawlessness and violence. Curiously enough, the short stories dealing with the exploits of Evan Forster, a private detective, are among the least sensational. Perhaps it is because they consist so largely of conversations on the telephone, and naturally we get only one side of these. 'Hello! Forster speaking,' is the usual opening; and Forster, you may be sure, is ringing up Scotland Yard to put them right about some case they have bungled. It seems an unnecessarily difficult technique.

The pathetic is what most rarely is attempted. At the moment I can remember only a solitary instance of it—the death of Doctor Titterington in *My Martyrdom*—and the failure here seems to me absolute. The Doctor has fainted; a physician (or as the text has it, a 'pycain') is hurriedly summoned; and upon his advice the patient is repeatedly plunged in and out of a very hot bath. The treatment may be scientifically correct, I have not inquired, yet it *seems* odd, and I confess I was not surprised when, after a good many immersions, the Doctor 'fell back into the pycain's arms a corpse'. The scene certainly is vivid; one can positively hear the grunts and the splashes; what it lacks is tenderness. But at least we are convinced of the Doctor's death, therefore our bewilderment is the greater when, a few chapters further on, we are told that 'he had only been in a trance'. This 'trance' is difficult to swallow; clearly it was an afterthought; we had even seen the Doctor shrouded and coffined. Nor do I feel that it is made more plausible by the abrupt substitution of verse for prose:

> From the land of death and sorrow
>   The Doctor rose again;
> Like a rabbit from his burrow—
>   *But totally insane!*

The last line is grim, and the italics make it grimmer. To tell the truth, we wish the Doctor safely back in his winding-sheet, when we think of the pranks he will now be made to play, of the gruesome farce which we are pretty sure our author has in preparation.

It is such things that make me doubt whether Kenneth's work is really destined to be popular. Women will not like the very subordinate place allotted to them in the tales. The first chapter of *A Love Romance* (all that so far has been written) opens, for example, with this extremely frank description of the heroine: 'She was not beautiful. No, far from it!' Then, true to his method, the author plunges us bang off into the midst of a 'situation'. Oscar Eslington has come to ask the unlovely Laura to be his wife, but for some not yet explained reason she refuses him, tells him she *can't* marry him, though she loves him—leaving us to suspect all sorts of sinister complications in the background. He takes her into the garden, and a discussion follows on the particular charms of various fruits, while, in the intervals, the painfully nervous Oscar continues to urge his suit. Laura leads him on, so that presently we begin to wonder if she is not at heart merely an unscrupulous 'vamp' with a highly original technique. Even when speculating as to the possible ripeness of still green apples, she speaks 'in a manner for which love is the word'. At the same time she remains obdurate on the nuptial question, and poor Oscar cannot conceal his discomfiture:

'His long opened gaw fell. It opened again shortly afterwards as he muttered a solemn "good night".

'"Good night," she said, and they departed.'

Yes; and there we are; and it may be weeks before we get the next instalment! I must say that this habit of writing ten or twelve novels at once has, for the reader at all events, its disadvantages.

Turning from the prose to the poems one finds a difference so marked as almost to suggest another hand. To begin with, they are extremely personal, and usually rather sad. In the less successful, indeed, this sadness appears to be deliberate, and our response is proportionately feeble. Why, we ask, compose an *Ode on an Infant Leper who Died as soon as Born*? 'What a distemper of the eye of the mind! What an almost bodily distemper there is in that!' Possibly: yet I, who have read the Ode, could almost swear that it was written with a dry eye. I shall not quote it, but here is the *Fireside Memories*, written, as I think one could almost guess, towards bedtime.

> I love to sit on a dark winter's night
> By the lovely blazing fire;
> To see its heart so bright!
> I wonder, yes I wonder, and I wonder by the fire
> If my heart's as bright.
> Yes, I wonder, I wonder,
> While I'm all in delight.
> I close my eyes very tight,
> And I think of old, old memories,
> Some sad—some happy too:
> I open my eyes which are dim
> With the tears I have shed,
> And I look up at the ceiling
> Far above my head,
> And see the fire casting its far-off shadows there.

1918.

Note.—This paper was written twenty-two years ago, when the subject of it, Kenneth Hamilton, then a small boy (gay, responsive, affectionate, and with the merriest laugh I have ever heard), was my constant companion. He became a sailor, but after two or three voyages forsook the sea. He wrote to me regularly, and I know he was planning a visit to the South Sea Islands; but the last news of him, received from strangers, was that he had ridden out alone one day into the Australian Bush. From that ride he did not return, and no trace of what had happened was ever discovered.

1940.

TALES

THE SPECIAL MESSENGER

When she had washed up the tea-things and got the sticks ready for the morning fire and cleaned the boots, she sat down in the kitchen to rest. At last the long day's work was over, and she had now nothing to do except answer an occasional ring at the door. At ten she would carry in the supper, and a little later she would go to bed, taking up with her the cheap noisy alarm-clock set for half-past six.

It had been washing day, and she was tired. The mistress, too, had been cross. The mistress, for some reason, was always cross on washing day, yet Annie half wished now that she would come in and scold her again, she felt so lonely. It must be the spring that was affecting her. The lengthening evenings, the starlings chirping in the eaves above her bedroom window in the early morning, the sunshine, the budding trees, reminded her of so many things. She spread out an old number of the *Christian Herald* on the scoured deal table before her, but she had never been a reader, and the paper had no power now to come between her and her thoughts. . . .

Her thoughts were of her home; they gave her no rest; and presently she went to a small cupboard beside the range, where she kept a few things for her own private use. She brought out an ink-splashed blotter, a pen, and a little bottle of ink; then she sat down to write. But if she was no reader she was still less a writer. She wrote with difficulty, her head bowed over her task, her face flushed, her lips moving as if spelling out each laborious word as she scratched it on the cheap glazed paper.

DEAR MOTHER,

This comes hoping to find you all well as it leaves me at present. How is your roomitism? How is father? Tell William I thought I saw him one day but it wasn't. With fondest love to all,

Your loving daughter,
ANNIE.

She thought of adding a postscript: 'Tell John——' but this she did not do. Her letter finished, she sat there very quietly, her hands folded. The cat jumped into her lap with a small ingratiating mew, and she began to stroke him. . . .

She had been in service here for nearly six months now—in service in town. It was her second place. Her first had been in the country, near home, but she had been tempted by the offer of higher wages, and had come up to town to better herself. . . . She hated it. Every day her longing for the country seemed to increase, yet it never occurred to her to give notice. She stayed on, with a sort of simple un-questioning patience—the patience of a domestic animal that has no share in the moulding of its fate. The streets be-wildered her; the noise, the traffic, the unknown faces. On her evenings out she very often remained indoors—an un-usual state of affairs her mistress was quick to appreciate—and when she did go out she was always glad to get back again. Everything about her was alien from her—strange without being attractive—even the little brown dusty sparrows seemed to belong to a different world from that of the sparrows at home. . . .

Next morning, when she came downstairs, she opened the hall-door and went out into the April sunshine. She did the steps, and swept the porch. She was just finishing when she heard the sounds of a rattling can and of a boy whistling. . . . She watched him as he came on down the empty street, a brown, snub-nosed, merry-faced boy, with quick, dark, bright eyes, and a spray of green hawthorn, plucked from some hedge, stuck in his cap like a feather. She did not know him, but she could not help watching him. She felt suddenly quite happy and different.

She expected him to pass on, but when he reached the gate of the small dusty garden he stopped, opened it, and came inside, holding out his can of milk to her. She took it from him in silence. His dark alert eyes dazzled her. They looked at her with that clear bright soullessness which one sees in the eyes of a bird, and quite automatically she carried the milk into the pantry and poured it into a basin. It was only as she was returning him the empty can that she remembered that he was not their milk-boy at all, and thought that perhaps he had made a mistake.

'Where's Jimmy?' she asked.

'He's in the next street. I'm helpin' him.'

She looked at him half wistfully. 'You're not a town boy—are you?'

'Ay; but I'm from the country. . . . So's these. Will you have them?' From the pocket of his ragged jacket he took out a big bunch of primroses.

She accepted them in a kind of dream. She did not even thank him. She seemed to have forgotten he was there till his voice awakened her.

'What are you goin' to give me for them?'

His bright dark eyes glinted oddly. She began to answer 'Nothing'. Somebody, in fact, must have spoken the word, for she heard it quite distinctly as she stooped a little and kissed him. . . .

A great light rushed out on all sides, as if the sky were opening. She caught her breath and her head for a moment swam dizzily. Where was the street? Where were the houses? Where was the milk-boy? She was in a green lane whose banks were gay with clumps of primroses. The trees were over her, swaying against a blue spring sky. She knew this old disused road, with its ruts worn deep by carts that no longer passed down it, its mossy stones and mossy banks. A lark sang rapturously above her—high, high up, a brown speck in the bright air. She walked as far as the low stile, and stood there waiting. She stood by the field path and remembered their past meeting there, and the little quarrel which had somehow grown out of nothing and had yet spoiled everything. She had started it in fun; she had wanted to see if she could make him jealous—he had so often said she couldn't. And then—and then—somehow it had all at once become cold and bitter earnest. . . .

She drew her hand across her eyes as the gate clanged. The milk-boy was moving down the street, whistling, a green hawthorn branch stuck in his cap like a feather. For how long had the kiss lasted? It seemed to her that it must have lasted a long time, yet it could not have, for the blind on the window opposite, which, as she stooped, had begun to be drawn up, had not yet reached the top.

She went indoors. All day, as she worked, she saw the green primrose lane; all day she smelt the scent of primroses and heard the singing of the lark. What matter if the air was thick with the dust of swept stair-carpets? What matter about the shrill scolding that followed the breaking of a dish? In the afternoon, when the rattle of the milk-carts began again to sound, she listened eagerly for the ringing of the door bell. It came at last, and she hurried to answer it. But it was only Jimmy, and she stared at him in disappointment, heedless of the can he offered her and of the 'Good evening' he muttered, 'Where's the other?' she asked in spite of herself, and Jimmy stared at her in his turn.

'What other?' he said stolidly.

'The boy who came this morning.'

'Oh, him! How would I know where he is?'

'Who is he?'

'Just a fella I met. He offered to leave in the milk for you while I was doin' the other street. He said he knew you.' But something seemed to strike him now for the first time and he scratched his head. 'I don't know why I give it to him,' he confessed, puzzled. 'But he brought back the can all right.'

She returned to the kitchen. There was no use questioning Jimmy, he was too stupid: the other boy was gone and would not come back. It was as if she had been dreaming and had now awakened. And in the evening, when she had time to sit still, she sat turning it over in her mind, not very sure of anything, though the primroses were there, a proof that it had all really happened. She rose and set them on the table. She bent down over them. They had darkened slightly in colour; they were no longer so fresh as when she had first got them; but their cool faint fragrance still made the air sweet, and as she breathed it she felt something of the same feeling she had felt that morning when she had kissed the m lk-boy. Only it was not so strong. She was still in the kitchen, though its walls were dim and shadowy, and through them she could make out other walls, and the outlines of trees, and a door and a window. She knew the house at the end of the field path; she recognized it as one recognizes a blurred and indistinct photograph. She looked through the window, and everything gradually grew clearer. He was there—reading a letter. In a sudden, dying, flickering brightness she seemed to recognize the letter and to see him kiss it; then the whole vision faded out.

She sat on with folded hands and lifted face. . . . He must have asked her mother for the letter, or perhaps William, who was always good-natured, had got it for him. . . . She would send him one for himself—just a line or two—asking him to write. . . . Later in the evening she dropped it into the pillar-box at the street corner.

DEAR JOHN,

I am very lonely here. Will you write to me? With kind thoughts,

ANNIE.

She waited, but he did not write. On the third day, however, he came himself.

1918.

THE ACCOMPLICE

As the boy came in she pointed to a small square package wrapped in a piece of newspaper and lying on the window-ledge. 'There's your lunch; and mind you're home in time for dinner. Father wants you to give him a hand up at the strawberry-beds.'

'All right, mother.'

She regarded him with a kindly humorous eye that had a light of pride in it. 'And now you can give me a kiss and be off.'

'All right, mother.'

She was a stout, plain, ruddy-faced woman, and she was standing in her kitchen—the kitchen of the gardener's lodge —with a big apron covering the front of her striped cotton dress, and her sleeves rolled back from bare strong arms which, like her rough hands, were flaked with flour, for she was baking. The boy did not resemble her. He was slender, while she was stout; he was fine, while she was coarse; he seemed subtle, while she was simple; and there was an enigmatic expression in his dark, narrow, wide-set eyes— something half-mocking, half-ironic—which now and then made her feel vaguely uneasy. Subtle—and with little of that air of engaging innocence one expects of rustic youth. Brown-skinned, attractive, yet not quite agreeable. Her only child probably, her only son at all events—that could be gathered from the way she looked at him as she bent down to kiss him with a certain superficial roughness.

They lived—she and the boy and the boy's father—in the front lodge of the demesne, within sight and sound of the sea—and she came to the gate to see him off, watching his slender figure on the white, dusty, sunlit road as long as it remained in sight. At the curve of the road he looked back and waved his hand. He never forgot to do that; he knew it pleased her; and for that matter he never forgot anything. She waved too, but she returned to her baking with a sigh. She couldn't have told you why she sighed, except that she wished she knew a little more about him; and there was no-body—least of all his taciturn unnoticing father—to whom she could express what she felt. She could not clearly express it to herself. She sometimes wondered if he would be a successful man, but more frequently, and with vague mis-givings she was ashamed of, she hoped he would be a good one. For he *was* a good boy—always considerate and—and discreet. That was a very queer word to use. She did not like it, and did not know why she had used it. In any case, he would not be a gardener like his father, for he was clever. Mr. Connell had said that he ought to go to college, and that with scholarships it might be managed. He was now nearly fifteen and still at the village school. But in her day-dreams she already saw him, after a brilliant University career, returning home, stiffly garbed in black, assistant and successor to the present minister.

Meanwhile the minister in embryo, who was perfectly aware of his mother's views and never discouraged them, reached the small red-brick school. Here his first quick glance was directed at Mr. Connell, whom he had been study-ing now for nearly a week, though there was little alteration to be noted from day to day, except that on each day the schoolmaster looked perhaps slightly more moody and ill than on the day before. Mr. Connell had always taken a kindly interest in him, but now for the first time he was taking an interest in Mr. Connell. This morning the schoolmaster's face had an unhealthy yellow pallor; his eyes were bright, and wandered here and there with a feverish restlessness; his manner was odd; and there were brief intervals when he seemed to lose consciousness of what was going on around him. Sometimes, on glancing up, the boy found those restless eyes fixed on him, yet not looking at him; and at such moments they had a curious, haunted expression, which perplexed him, but nevertheless could easily be worked into his theory. He did not communicate these impressions to his companions; partly because his companions would have been incapable of attaching any meaning to them; and partly because he rarely communicated anything. But when school was over he waited for Mr. Connell at the painted iron gate.

They frequently walked home together—that is, as far as the lodge, for Mr. Connell's house was about a mile further on. This afternoon, however, the boy passed his own gate, and was still pacing side by side with his friend when the schoolmaster's house came into view. At that instant the grey little man unexpectedly sat down on a low wall of loosely-piled stones by the roadside, and bowed his face between his hands. Why he should choose to sit here when he was so near home the boy could not guess: at least he only half guessed. He said nothing. His detachment was exquisite. Almost from the beginning their walk had been a silent one, and now he simply stood there, a kind of angelic sweetness and serenity upon his face, as he watched his companion bend forward—helpless, crushed, and broken.

He knew that the schoolmaster had forgotten about him, and he was not at all sure that when he looked up and saw him the surprise would be a pleasant one. Dinner, too, would be waiting (not that this mattered, except that his father had said he wanted him and would demand an explanation). But an explanation could be invented, and since his curiosity was very strong, and Mr. Connell looked as if he might sit there for ever, he presently proposed that they should continue their way to the house. The words, though spoken very quietly, had a startling effect upon the man on the wall. Mr. Connell sprang to his feet, pale and shaking, and also very angry. In a sharp unnatural voice he asked his pupil what he was doing there, and told him to run on home at once. Then, pitifully, he seemed to grasp at a sign of friendliness in the boy's having come so far out of his way, and apologized. He tried to smile, murmured a few inaudible words, and hurried on alone.

These things gave the boy plenty to think about while he helped his father with the strawberries, and he thought of them again after he had gone up to bed. Not a syllable had he breathed at home of the odd behaviour Mr. Connell had been indulging in of late, which he had found so interesting. He had begun to notice it on the very day after Mrs. Connell had left home to go to nurse a sick aunt who lived in Scotland. Mrs. Connell had gone in a hurry, and without saying good-bye to anybody; which was not particularly surprising, for she was far from popular, and he had heard several people—his own mother amongst them—declaring that they wouldn't mind if she never came back again.

Slowly he began to undress. He hung his jacket over the back of a chair and then paused. He took off his socks. With his trousers half off he paused again, sitting down on the low narrow bed and staring at the door, a slight frown on his face. He next turned to the window. He had not drawn down the blind and he could see a full moon shining. He could hear the waves breaking on the shore. He had sat up late over his work, and his father and mother by this time probably had been asleep for a couple of hours. The strange, dark, alert face became absolutely still, as if carved in bronze. Then, noiselessly and swiftly, he re-dressed himself and opened his bedroom door. The door of the other bedroom was slightly ajar, too, for the night was close. With the lithe effortless movements of a young panther he crossed the landing and descended the only flight of stairs. He got his shoes from the kitchen, and very carefully let himself out before putting them on. The lodge gates were locked at night, but there was a stream which flowed out of the estate beneath a bridge that formed part of the wall, and in dry weather this stream shrank, leaving on either side a narrow path of stones along which one could pass dry-shod. He chose this way now, startling some rats, who startled him, so that he nearly slipped into the water. Climbing out on the farther side of the bridge, he reached the sea road and had no more difficulties.

He descended the hill and turned to the right, following the line of the coast. At this hour not a soul was abroad. He walked on swiftly until he reached the spot where he had left Mr. Connell in the afternoon. Then he slackened his pace, and finally stood still; for the schoolmaster might be in bed and asleep, but also he might not, and it was upon the latter contingency that he had counted. He had thought of it in his bedroom and had acted on the thought. But what to do next? He got into the field beside the lonely house, with its narrow garden sloping down to the road. He sat down on a flat stone in the bank under the hedge.

From his present position he had an oblique view of the front and one side of the house, but there was no light in any of the windows. He obliterated himself in the shadow and waited. Twenty minutes, half an hour, must have passed, and he was even beginning to think of going home, when he heard a faint click as of a latch slipping. Almost immediately after, a white face appeared in the bright moonlight beyond the hall-door. The schoolmaster emerged from the shadow and walked down the garden path to the little gate, whence he looked up and down the stretch of bare road. The boy gave no sign. He was perfectly hidden where he was, and a strange feeling of elation took possession of him, just as it had on one or two similar occasions—when he had watched the movements of the man who had burned Wilson's ricks, for instance. That, of course, had been exciting chiefly because of the element of personal risk involved. Afterwards there had come the sense of power, and his own delighted, ironical assistance in the mystification of the police.

Mr. Connell had begun to make a tour of the garden, and the boy dropped down silently, lying at full length in the narrow ditch on the other side of the hedge. The schoolmaster passed without detecting him, yet so close that the boy by stretching out a hand could have touched him. He raised his head cautiously above the side of the ditch and watched Mr. Connell go back into the house. 'Does he do this every night?' he wondered. In his own nature there was a steel-cold determination which danger only stimulated; but he did not despise other people for being afraid; he was interested, that was all.

A very dim light appeared in one of the lower windows, and the boy, swiftly and noiselessly entering the garden, crept close and peeped through a chink in the blind. The schoolmaster was seated at a table upon which a solitary candle burned. He was not reading; he may have been thinking; but it struck the boy, as he watched the white face and strained bloodshot eyes, that more than anything else he was waiting and listening. His gaze seemed fixed on the handle of the door, as if in terror of seeing it turned by somebody on the other side. His hands were spread out upon the tablecloth, and a bottle and an empty tumbler stood by his elbow. Once his head jerked up with a sudden start, as if he had heard a footstep on the upper floor. Then he gave a little moan that the boy's quick ears divined rather than caught, and his hands worked feebly, fighting against something—perhaps merely his own weakness, or fear, or indetermination. The boy watching him had in that hour a passionate sense of living, of rejoicing in the strength of all his faculties, mental and physical. He saw the schoolmaster rise unsteadily and cross the room, only to stand hesitating by the door. Next moment he turned the handle, and the boy outside disappeared like a ghost.

He had plenty of time to get back into hiding before the schoolmaster came out again, this time with a spade. Mr. Connell walked down the garden path, crossed the road, and proceeded to the extreme edge of a patch of cultivated land beyond, where he grew potatoes and other vegetables. From here the cliff dropped down to the rocks fifty feet below. The boy in the hedge crept after him. He, too, crossed the road, almost on his stomach, and glided between the furze-bushes till he was within ten yards of the schoolmaster, who had already begun to dig, shovelling out the loose soil with an amazing rapidity. Every now and again he raised his head and cast a hurried glance all round. 'He's frightened,' the boy said inwardly—'too frightened to be any good.' Then he thought, 'I'd like to help him. But if I came out now it would nearly kill him. There,' he added, as with a little sob

Mr. Connell stopped digging; 'he's too scared to go on: he'll make that do.'

And at the same moment Mr. Connell indeed laid down his spade, and returned, almost running, to the house. But the boy, blotted in the shadow of his furze-bush, did not trouble to follow him, for he knew he would come back. Presently he heard him. And this time he was making quite a lot of noise, staggering and stumbling under a large heavy burden tied up in sacking. The boy was genuinely thrilled, though not surprised, for he knew well enough what the sacking contained. He even knew how it had all happened. By this time he knew everything—including the mistakes that would be made, and had already been made. It was a poor job—very. To begin with, the hole was not nearly deep enough. And to leave it like this—half done! The dark narrow eyes grew thoughtful and dreamy; in the moonlight the young face had a curious, haunting beauty. For he had half emerged from his hiding-place, moved by a repressed desire to take the situation in hand. But it *was* repressed; he knew he could not trust a weak fool like that. The white road, which ran straight for a couple of hundred yards, left an open field for keeping watch. Unfortunately, the night was clear, far too clear for this rather grisly business. The sky was a deep bluish black, and the full moon still floated high above the distant golf-links. When he moved, Mr. Connell's shadow danced fantastically and as if in mockery.

And why in the name of goodness did he delay now? Why did he stand there, spade in hand, as clearly outlined in the moonlight as a figure on a screen? For a man to be so mastered by terror when his life depended on his keeping his nerve, irritated the boy as nothing else could have. Then he too, abruptly turning, saw the approaching gleam of the bicycle lamp. Even so, the danger was slight, the man must be a stranger and would pass harmlessly on his way. Next moment, however, he saw that the cyclist had stopped, and that Mr. Connell was staring at him across the sinister bundle lying beside the shallow grave. The man leaned his bicycle against the low wall and advanced towards them. Yes, he was a stranger, and moreover quite young. 'Don't be a fool—don't do anything,' the boy hissed savagely, in spite of himself. 'He only wants to ask his way.'

'I suppose you couldn't tell me how far——' But the sentence never was completed, for Mr. Connell had him by the throat. And the boy, no longer hidden, watched them swaying and rocking together on the cliff's edge. The whole thing was finished before he had time to do more than shout a warning. For perhaps three or four seconds he saw the two figures writhing and struggling in a silent embrace; then they disappeared. The boy ran to the edge of the cliff and peered over, but he could see nothing, he could hear nothing—nothing except the murmur of the waves, which seemed strangely remote and peaceful. He lay there looking down into the darkness, and out of the darkness there suddenly arose a vision of his own bedroom at home, of his mother stooping over him and telling him he had slept too long and would be late for school, of the morning sunlight, of the birds singing. But that was only a momentary lapse, a brief return to childhood; the scene he had just witnessed swept back upon him. Should he do anything? They must be dead. At any rate he could not possibly climb down, and he had a strong desire to get away from this place. Nobody could survive such a fall; they must have been killed—or very nearly killed—instantaneously; and at least it was important that *he* should not be mixed up in the affair. He rose to his feet, casting a sidelong and far from amiable look at the dead woman tied up in her sack. Then he remembered having read in some tale, of a bushranger who had gone out to execution 'with a cigar between his teeth'. This action had appealed to his imagination; it had struck him as particularly fine. In the desire to emulate it he stood still and fumbled in the pockets of his jacket till he found a packet of cheap cigarettes. And one of these he lit with grave deliberation as he walked—neither faster nor slower than usual— down the road towards his home.

1913.

BREEZE

Everybody knows the way things have of turning up in the
most improbable places, and I don't think I was particularly surprised to get a letter from Morenni telling me that
he had discovered a Giorgione in the museum at Larne.
What he wanted me to do was to get the picture photo-
graphed, an arrangement he had not had time to make himself. I felt ashamed that I had been ignorant even of the fact
that Larne possessed a museum, but I had no difficulty in
finding it—a couple of dingy rooms on the ground floor of
an ordinary dwelling-house. What I failed to find was the
Giorgione. Morenni had said that it was in the museum, yet
a single tour of the rooms revealed that they contained no
pictures of any kind: the walls were bare; and except for
the usual cases of stuffed birds and flint arrow-heads the
place was empty.

There seemed to be nothing for it but to consult the
curator, a melancholy little man with a black beard, who
had bowed to me politely on my entrance.

He now regarded me with a trace of suspicion. 'What
makes you think we have a Giorgione?' he asked, but it
struck me he was careful not to say that they hadn't one.

'Morenni,' I replied. 'I had a letter from him yesterday.
He says he saw it.'

' And Morenni—who is Morenni?'

'He is the greatest connoisseur in Europe—the greatest authority on the old Italian Schools at any rate.'

At these words my melancholy friend suddenly brightened up. 'But this is most important!' he cried. 'We shall be able to star it, to double star it, to triple star it, in our new catalogue. It will attract crowds, it will attract Americans—they are always the most intelligent. It must have been taken to the new building. All the pictures were taken there last month. The gallery hasn't actually been opened yet—to the public—but if you care to come with me now——'

Of course I accepted his offer, and shutting and locking the door behind us, he led me along the main street, and down a narrow alley, at the end of which the new building came into view. Surrounded by smooth lawns, itself circular in shape, with its slender fluted columns and broad flight of marble steps, it looked a fitting abode for the picture we were seeking. I regarded it with admiration, and I wondered, though I did not ask, who on earth could have designed it, for it suggested the work of a magician rather than an architect. At all events, whoever he might be, he was a genius.

Unluckily, on entering the alley we must have attracted attention, for while my companion was unlocking the door I became aware that we had been followed by at least a score of interested persons, who, as I drew back, pressed on ahead in a compact flock. The ambition of the little curator had been fulfilled, I reflected, and with no loss of time: he was already 'personally conducting' a group of eager sight-seers athirst for information.

The great hall into which we all passed was as charming as the exterior had promised, but it bore no resemblance to a picture gallery. It was more like a conservatory, except that its spaciousness left plenty of room for visitors to wander where they pleased. The floor was of delicate mosaic work; there were tall green plants growing in tubs; and in the centre, under a glass dome, a fountain rose nearly to the lofty roof before dropping back with a soft musical splash into a sunken pool. The apricot tint of the walls was the natural colour of the marble, and all round the hall were narrow leaded windows through which the sunlight streamed. Opposite the main door, at the top of another flight of steps, hung dark straight curtains concealing the entrance to a second room.

It was in this farther room, our guide informed us, that the Giorgione must be, and with an air of importance he led the way thither, followed by his docile flock, so that next minute I found myself alone.

I dislike conducted tours, I dislike guides, and I prefer to look at pictures in my own way, unhurried and uninstructed. So I began to make a leisurely circuit of the hall, threading my way between the plants, and marvelling at their beauty and profusion. Presently I came upon an easel, which supported a large picture in an old, massive, and elaborate gilt frame. But the picture itself was not old; not older, I decided, than the 'seventies or 'eighties of the last century, for clearly it was of the French impressionist school—though with a difference: it definitely was not French. It was a landscape, painted broadly and loosely, yet with considerable detail too. And suddenly I knew that I was looking at a masterpiece. The longer I gazed the more convinced I was of this, and I had forgotten all about the Giorgione when at last I drew up a chair and sat down to enjoy my discovery. The naturalism of the thing was astonishing. I could see the branches of the trees waving, actually waving, as they were blown about by what must have been quite a strong wind. The tall grass in the meadow was all ready for mowing, and the two little girls who now walked out from the side of the heavy, ornamental frame, one behind the other, were knee-deep in it in a moment. They wore no hats, and their dark hair was plaited into pigtails. They smiled when they saw me looking at them, but very shyly, and their smiles deepened at the same time as the colour in their cheeks when I spoke.

'How on earth did you get in there?' was what I said.

'It was Breeze who showed us,' the older of the little girls answered, speaking very precisely, though in so small a voice that I could hardly hear her.

'Breeze?'

'He knows how: he showed us how. . . . There he is.'

I looked quickly to the other side of the picture, and there indeed he was—a small boy of nine or ten, in a rather crumpled sailor-suit, and with a broad-brimmed straw hat such as, at his age, I used to wear myself. Not at all a beautiful little boy—in fact, distinctly plain—but jolly, rosy-cheeked, and bright-eyed. He carried a bow and arrow in his hands, which he promptly raised and aimed at me.

'He reminds me of somebody,' I said, puzzled. 'Or something. . . . I wonder——'

'The sun,' answered the little girl, in the same low shy voice.

'The sun?' I repeated, not understanding what she meant.

'Not the round sun in the sky: the sun in the room.'

I stared. For it *was* that. I saw it at once. But how extraordinary! I mean, how could anybody be like the sun, like what was just a glow, a brightness, a pleasantness?

I got no further in these questionings, for with one bound he had jumped clean out of the picture and landed on my knees. There, himself kneeling, with his short arms gripping my neck, and his nose about ten inches from my own, he began to laugh. 'I can show you the way in. Don't you want me to show you? I know you do.'

'In where?' I asked.

'There—there.' He pointed to the field of waving grass, and the little girls chimed in chorus, 'Breeze will show you; Breeze will show you.'

'Come round to the side,' said Breeze, slipping down off my knee and giving my hand a tug. 'Quick—before he comes.'

But I had already heard the voice of the curator, who, missing me from his flock, had now returned. 'The Giorgione,' he called out in a querulous, complaining tone. 'Don't you want to see the Giorgione?'

'Yes, yes—presently.'

'Don't let him come near—don't, don't,' Breeze whispered from somewhere behind my chair.

'The Giorgione,' the curator repeated.

There was something intensely irritating in the way he stood there bleating that one word. 'I don't care a fig about the Giorgione,' I answered impatiently.

He seemed hurt. 'But I thought you came on purpose to see it. I thought Morenni——'

'I don't care a fig about Morenni either.'

He mumbled to himself, gazing at me with an injured expression, but at last he shrugged his shoulders and turned away. I thought he had gone, and looked round for Breeze, when the now odious voice again was raised, this time almost tearfully. 'I think you asked to see the Giorgione. It is in the next room; but we really can't keep the gallery open for you all day.'

'Go away. Go away,' I shouted angrily—the more angrily because I felt the struggle to get rid of him was spoiling everything, was dragging me back, back to something of which I was already dimly conscious as another world, a less attractive world, a world I knew only too well and did not want.

'Quick—quick—he's coming. Oh, come quickly or it will be too late.'

It was the voice of Breeze I still heard, but it had grown faint and far, as if Breeze himself were receding. The picture too was receding, was spreading out—out from its frame— was growing darker and darker, colder and colder.

'The Giorgione——'

1927.

This extremely ingenuous little tale appeared in the *Saturday Review* without apology. Yet I felt that it needed one—rather badly. The truth is, it was wafted to me through the Ivory Gate, and I scribbled it down merely to prolong and 'fix' a pleasant impression. At the time, I was working diligently on a book about the wood engravings of the 'sixties, but I cannot tell why, out of the many thousand drawings I had examined, this one—a *Punch* picture by Charles Keene —should have been chosen by the dream-fabricator for the nucleus of his story. True, he has altered the drawing very cunningly—coloured it, and expanded it to the dimensions of an oil painting; nevertheless it is still perfectly recognizable—the landscape, the small boy and his bow and arrows, the sunlight, the happiness, all signed with a large unmistakable C.K. For his Morenni and Giorgione he had to delve deeper. *They* go back to a period when, under the influence of Berenson and Morelli, I was pursuing Old Masters in Italy and elsewhere. But why change Morelli's name? Why introduce him at all if I was never to get a glimpse of the Giorgione? As for the art gallery where the pictures, few in number, were placed on easels instead of being hung on walls—that is the fabricator's own invention, and it was like him to build it in the wildly improbable seaside town of Larne. I admit that for a week or two I *did* work at my 'sixties book when I was staying near Larne, but if it comes to that, I worked for a couple of months at least in the British Museum.

COURAGE

When the children came to stay with their grandfather, Michael, walking with the others from the station to the rectory, noticed the high stone wall that lined one side of the long country lane, and wondered what lay beyond it. Over the top of the wall trees stretched green arms that beckoned to him, and threw black shadows on the white dusty road. His brothers and sisters, stepping demurely beside a tall aunt, left him, as usual, lagging behind, and when a white bird fluttered out for a moment into the sunlight they did not even see it. Michael called to them, and four pairs of eyes turned straightway to the trees but were too late. 'A pigeon,' Michael said to nobody, and trotted on to take his place among the rest.

'Does anybody live there?' he asked, but the aunt shook her head: the house, of whose chimneys he presently caught a glimpse between the trees, had been empty for years; there was not even a caretaker in the lodge.

Michael, a rather persistent little boy, learned more than this, however, from Rebecca, the rectory cook, who told him that the house was empty because it was haunted. Big boys at the right time of the year would climb the wall and strip the apple-trees, but they took care to do so in broad daylight. The ghost had been seen of course—that was a silly question—how else could people have known about it? It was the ghost of a lady who had lived there once and been very wicked; and probably unhappy too, since she couldn't rest in her grave. Then Rebecca added, more prophetically than explicitly (though Michael understood her perfectly), that there were boards up, with 'Trespassers will be Prosecuted' on them, and that his grandfather would be very angry. . . .

It was on an afternoon, when a game of croquet was becoming increasingly acrimonious, that Michael slipped away unnoticed, and set out to explore the stream running past the foot of the rectory garden. He would follow it, he planned, wherever it led him; follow it just as his father, far away in wild places, had followed mighty rivers into the heart of unexplored forests. His father was a traveller, and had written a book, with lots of photographs in it. Michael had never been able to finish the book, or for that matter even the first chapter of it, but he had looked at the pictures, and now, by an easy process of imagination, he was a traveller too.

The long, sweet grass brushed against his legs, and a white cow, with a rejected buttercup hanging from the corner of her mouth, gazed at him in mild curiosity as he passed. He kept to the meadow side, and on the opposite bank the leaning trees formed little magic caves tapestried with green. Black flies darted restlessly about, and every now and again he heard splashes—the splash of a water-hen, of a rat, of what might have been a fish, though this was un-likely—and then, behind him, the heavy, floundering splash of the cow herself, plunging into the stream up to her knees. He watched her plough laboriously through the sword-shaped leaves of a bed of irises on the farther side, while the rich black mud oozed up between patches of bright green weed. A score of birds made a quaint chorus of trills and peeps, chuckles and whistlings; a wren, like a small winged mouse, flitted about the ivy-covered bole of a hollow tree. But a few yards further on he came disappointingly to the end of his journey, for a rusty iron gate was swung here right across the stream, and on either side of it, as far as he could see, stretched a high grey stone wall.

He paused. The gate was padlocked, and its spiked bars were set so closely together that it would not be easy to climb. While he gazed, a white bird rose out of the burning green and gold of the trees, and for a moment in the sunlight was the whitest thing in the world. Then the bird flew back again into the mysterious shadow, and Michael stood breathless.

He had realized where he was, and that this wall must be a continuation of the wall in the lane. The stooping trees leaned down as if to catch him in their arms. He looked more closely at the padlock, and saw that the spring was half eaten away by rust. He took off his shoes and stockings. Stringing them round his neck, he waded through the water, and with a stone struck the padlock once, twice—twice only—for at the second blow the lock dropped into the stream. Michael tugged at the rusty bolt and in a minute or two the gate was open. Passing through, he clambered up the bank on the other side, and it was while he was pulling on his stockings and his shoes that he saw the gate swing slowly back into its old position.

That was all, yet it slightly startled him, gave him an uneasy feeling that his movements had been watched and that he had been shut in deliberately. Of course the gate must have moved of its own weight, he told himself; nevertheless he had abruptly ceased to be an explorer in remote, untrodden forests, and Rebecca's quite different kind of story had taken the uppermost place in his mind.

Before him was a dark moss-grown path, roofed by trees, whose overarching branches shut out any gleam of sunlight. The path seemed to lead on and on through a listening, watching stillness, and Michael hovered at the entrance to it, doubtful, gazing into its equivocal shadow, not very eager to proceed further.

A nice explorer he would make! His lips pouted and he frowned. Then he made up his mind, and though still frowning, walked on determinedly, while the noise of the stream died away behind him, like a last warning murmur from the friendly world outside.

Quite unexpectedly, for the path turned at an abrupt angle, he came upon the house. It lay beyond what must once have been a lawn, but now the unmown grass, coarse and matted, grew right up to the doorsteps. And to Michael the house itself had a daunting, forbidding look. Lines of dark moss and lichen had crept over the red bricks: the shutters looked as if they had been closed never to be opened again; yet next moment his heart gave a violent jump, for one of them, with a loud and most dismal rattle, flapped back from a window on the ground floor.

He stood motionless while he might have counted fifty. He was on the verge of flight, but fought down the impulse, and there was no further alarm. Moreover, even from his present distance he could see that the window was broken and most of the glass missing—the work, no doubt, of the apple-raiders. A puff of wind had blown back the shutter, that was all. In the reassuring sunlight the spirit of adventure revived and he advanced to make a closer inspection. With his hands on the low window-sill, he peered into a large room. Next, kneeling on the sill, he unlatched the window and pushed it up. The other boys had not dared to enter, he thought, for if they had he was sure they would not have troubled to re-latch the window. Then he clambered across the sill.

Instantly, and most cheeringly, all sense of fear vanished. He could *feel* that the house was empty, that not even the ghost of a ghost lingered here. And with this certainty everything dropped comfortably, if half disappointingly, back into the commonplace. He opened the shutters, letting the rich afternoon light pour in. Though the house had been empty for so long, it still smelt sweet and fresh, and not a speck of dust was visible anywhere. This was surprising, but though Michael drew an experimental finger over the top of one of the little tables, his finger remained clean; the table might have been polished that morning. He also touched the faded upholsteries and curtains, and sniffed at the dried rose-leaves in a china jar. Above the wide chimney-piece hung a picture —the portrait of a lady, still quite young. She was seated in a chair, and beside her, with one hand resting on the back of the chair, stood a boy of about Michael's own age. It was easy to see that they were mother and son, and Michael's thoughts immediately turned to *his* mother, and they were rather strange thoughts, and rather sad, so that presently he wished he had not looked at the picture at all. He drew from his pocket a letter he had received that morning. She was better, she said, and would soon be quite well again. Yesterday she had gone out for a drive, but to-day she felt a little tired, which was why her letter must be so short. But he was to enjoy himself, and be a good boy, and give her love to the others. . . .

He went out into the hall and unbarred and flung wide the front door before ascending to the upper storeys. There he found a lot of interesting things, and in one room discovered a whole store of toys—soldiers, picture-books, a bow and arrows, a model yacht, and a musical box with a small silver key lying beside it. He wound up the box, and a simple melody tinkled out, faint and fragile, losing itself in the empty silence of the house, like the light of a taper in a cave.

He opened the door of another room, a bedroom, and sitting down near the window, began to turn the pages of an old illuminated volume he found there, full of pictures of saints and martyrs, all glowing in gold and bright colours, yet somehow vaguely disquieting. It was with a start that, on glancing up from his book, he noticed how dark it had grown. The pattern had faded out of the chintz bed-curtains and he could no longer see clearly into the further corners of the room. It was from these corners that the darkness seemed to be stealing out, like a thin smoke, spreading slowly over everything. Surely he had not fallen asleep! yet he did not see how else the time could have passed so quickly without his noticing it. It was so dark now that the bed-curtains were like pale drooping wings, and outside, over the trees, the moon was growing brighter. He must go home at once. . . .

He sat motionless, trying to realize what had happened— and listening, listening—for it was as if the secret hidden heart of the house had begun very faintly to beat. Faintly at first, a mere stirring of the vacant atmosphere, but as the minutes passed it gathered strength, and with this consciousness of awakening life a fear came also. He listened in the darkness, and though he could hear nothing, he had a vivid sense that he was no longer alone. Whatever had dwelt here before had come back, as a beast returns to his lair, and was even now, perhaps, creeping up the stairs. A paralysing dread held him weak and inert—though only for a few seconds. It had not—whatever it was—come for him, he told himself. It could not know about him, and perhaps he could get downstairs without meeting it. He glided swiftly across the room and opened the door.

Out on the landing, he had before him the great yawning well of the staircase, that was like a pit of blackness. His heart thumped as he stood against the wall. With shut eyes, lest he should see what he had no desire to see, he took two steps forward and gripped the banister. Then, with eyes still tightly shut, he ran quickly down, unconscious instinct guiding his feet in safety.

At the turn of the stairs the open hall-door showed as a dim silver-grey square, and once he had reached this his panic left him. Fear remained, but it was no longer blind and senseless. He even halted on the threshold, and while he stood there a voice from far away seemed to reach him— yet not a voice, really, so much as a soundless message. He waited, and the message became clear. The way of escape lay there in front of him, but there was something he must do before he took it, and if he left this undone, then he would have failed.

He looked up at the dark, dreadful staircase. Nothing had pursued him, and he knew now that nothing would. Whatever was there was not there with that purpose, and if he were to see it, to face it, he must go in search of it. And if he left it? Nothing would happen; he would be quite safe. Only he knew this, that he would be leaving something else as well, for the message most surely, though he did not know how nor why, had come from his mother. It was her spirit that was close to him at this moment, as if holding his hand, holding him there upon the step. But why?—why? She wanted him to stay, but she did not or could not tell him why. He was free; the choice was his. Yes; but if he were a coward she would know, he would have to tell her, he could not hide it from her. She would accept it, she would forgive him, but that would be wretched, he did not want her to have to forgive him. He steadied himself against the side of the porch. The cold moonlight washed through the hall, and died out in a faint greyness half-way up the first flight of stairs. With sobbing breath and wide eyes he retraced his steps, but at the foot of the stairs he stopped once more, dreading the impenetrable blackness of those awful upper storeys. He put his foot on the lowest stair, and slowly, step by step, he mounted, clutching the banisters. He did not pause on the first landing, but continued straight on into the darkness, which seemed to close about his slender figure like the gates of a monstrous tomb.

Groping his way, he opened the door of the room with the toys. It was bathed in moonlight, and he prayed, 'Let it come now,' for he felt he could not bear the strain of waiting. But nothing came; the room was empty. And he knew, perhaps had known all along, that this was not the right room. Yes, he had known, and with the blood drumming in his ears he now made his final effort. He opened the other door, and was at first conscious only of a sudden, an immense relief, for this room, too, seemed blessedly empty. Then, close by the window, in the pallid twilight, he saw something. At first hardly more than a shadow, a thickening of the darkness, and then, drawing inward and gradually defining itself, a human form. It made no movement towards him, and so long as it remained thus, with head mercifully lowered, he felt that he could bear it. Yet the suspense tortured him, and a faint moan of anguish rose in his throat. With that, the grey marred face he dreaded to see was lifted. He tried to close his eyes, but could not. He felt an increasing weakness and clutched at the doorpost for support. But in the stillness, as he waited, the strange realization slowly came to him that it, too—this shadow—was afraid, and that what it feared was his fear. He saw in the dim, sad eyes the doubt and despair that could find no utterance, and as he did so another and more generous emotion began to stir within him. Why was she like this?—so different from the picture downstairs—and where was the boy who had stood so close to her, who had seemed so close to her? Michael made no effort to retreat though now she was approaching him—timidly, uncertainly. He looked at her steadily; he wasn't going to run away. He was quite sure now, and was no longer afraid. She wanted him, so he came to meet her, and when she held out her arms he came nearer still and held up his face to hers. But as her arms went round him it was as if he were wrapped in an icy mist, through which he had a last brief vision of a radiant happiness shining down on him —and then he was alone. . . .

Alone in a moonlit house that no longer held any terror for him. Alone, but with a strange glow of happiness that seemed not only within, but all around him. He must certainly go home, and yet now he felt loath to do so. Only, they would wonder what had happened to him, must have begun to wonder long ago; and he was very hungry. He pulled back the curtains as far as possible to let more moonlight in, and on the window-ledge a box of matches was revealed. This was lucky, for now he could light the two tall candles on the chimney-piece. And it was while he was doing so that he became more vividly aware of what he had felt subconsciously during the past few minutes. A subtle change had come about in the surrounding atmosphere, though in what it consisted he could not tell. It was as if the earlier stillness were no longer empty, had become, rather,

a hush in the air, like that which accompanies the falling of
snow. But how could there be snow in midsummer?—and,
moreover, this was within the house, not outside. He lifted
one of the candlesticks and saw that a delicate powder of
dust had gathered upon it. He looked down at his own
clothes—they, too, were covered with that same thin
powder. Then he knew what was happening. The dust of
years had begun to fall—silently, slowly, like a soft and
continuous caress, laying everything in the house to sleep.

Dawn was breaking when, with a candle in either hand,
he descended the broad whitening staircase. As he passed
out into the garden he saw lanterns approaching. It was a
search party, he guessed; and guessed that, after many
hours, Rebecca must have remembered an early conversation. Yet, to his surprise, nobody scolded him, nobody asked
questions. Nor was it till the next day that he learned of the
telegram which had come in his absence.

1914.

THE WHITE KITTEN

White rose in red rose-garden
Is not so white.
—Swinburne.

All day the heat had been insufferable—a heat that was a weariness as much to the spirit as to the body. The coolest place, we repeatedly assured one another, was the hotel; yet after dinner not a few of us had wandered out. I might have gone myself, possibly even to the 'pictures', which I detest, had I not expected the Bostocks to ask me to cut in at bridge. 'Cooler indoors than anywhere else this weather,' General Bostock remarked as he tapped the barometer. 'Shouldn't be surprised if we had thunder to-night.' And I followed him on into the lounge. I trust I am not a snob, but I do like to know the right people, and the Bostocks had been extremely gracious—Mrs. Bostock having even commissioned me to go to a local library and choose a novel for her.

The lounge was a long, narrow room, furnished with the usual arm-chairs and little glass-topped tables, and larger tables on which were *Punch*, the *Sketch*, magazines advertising motor-cars, and bound volumes of *Country Life*. I took up a Dunlop book, only to discover that the map I had intended to remove was already gone. A justifiable wave of indignation passed through me. The map, I *knew*, had been there that morning, for I had been within an ace of securing it when Mrs. Bostock had come sailing into the room with the affable remark that she had just learned that I was a writer, and if I *should* happen to be passing a library, etc.. I felt inclined to discuss the matter—the matter of the pur-loined map—with a furtive-looking little man who had arrived after lunch, accompanied by a melancholy wife; but in the end only remarked that it was cooler to-night in-doors than anywhere else.

It wasn't really cooler: it was exactly the same. The only thing that appeared to be cool was the palm-tree growing in a tub in the centre of the floor. I felt exhausted, bored, and stale; and glancing round the room, saw boredom and stale-ness stamped upon every face there. Even exceptionally hot weather seemed scarcely to account for it. Perhaps we had eaten too much; but, since we had come here largely be-cause the food was good, surely it would have been foolish to have starved! A horrible question occurred to me: were we always like this? Once we had arrived anywhere, had haggled over our rooms and our tables in the dining-room, did we straightway relapse into this condition of semi-coma? There were no attempts at conversation; only broken and apathetic murmurs. We felt not the least interest in one another, for I cannot pretend that my sympathy with the Bostocks was of a nature to blind me to their dullness. No; our parts in life were played. Left stranded by the marriage of our children, we had reached a stage when the important things were an open or a closed window, tea of exactly the right flavour, the crowing of cocks in the morning, or the barking of dogs at night.

General Bostock, his wife, and the two friends who had dined with them, calmly took possession of the only visible card-table. I could see that this selfishness was resented, though nobody cared enough to inquire if there were other tables. What I really needed was a pretty stiff whiskey-and-soda. General Bostock's rapid glance at the clock, however, and subsequent silence, told me that the hour for whiskies-and-sodas had not yet arrived. A huge man, whose purple-veined face I am convinced attracted the flies in from the garden, was fanning himself with the *Financial Times*, while his wife read aloud passages from a letter—probably from their married daughter, since the ailments of children were minutely dwelt upon. And near them, with glassy blue eyes fixed on empty space, and lips parted in a strange little smile, sat a powdered, lip-sticked, overdressed woman to whom no one ever spoke, and who appeared to have nobody belonging to her.

Each minute drawing us nearer to bedtime seemed to add an appreciable weight to the heaviness of the atmosphere. It was strange, it was more than strange, to think how we created this nightmare simply by sitting together, simply by our collective presence. It was as if we each had to bear not merely the burden of his own existence, but that of all the others as well. We were a single comprehensive consciousness: I not only heard, but felt in my throat, the whistling breath of the purple-faced man; I realized the suppressed irritation behind General Bostock's laugh when his partner went three no-trumps and made five tricks; I was bored by the novel over which the lady in tortoise-shell spectacles was stifling yawns. It was at this moment that the white kitten entered.

The door, you see, was open, to give us more air, and the white kitten came straight in, with tail erect, not pausing indeterminately on the threshold after the usual manner of his kind, but entering as if he had known he should find us there, and could give us just these few minutes. He was an extraordinarily beautiful creature—slender, lithe, white as snow and light as thistle-down. Cat-like, he paid no atten-

tion to the 'puss—puss' which made General Bostock look
up from his cards. He bounded lightly on to the back of the
purple-faced man's chair and patted his ear; then he sprang
to the tub in the centre of the room, raced up the palm-tree
and raced down again. He pranced across the floor sideways,
with arched back, to the novel-reading lady; he leapt on to
the card-table; he crouched with quivering body in the
middle of the room before darting at whatever new object
happened to catch his fancy; for everybody now was calling
him, waving things for him, trying to attract his attention.
And suddenly everybody was alive, the dullness had vanished, the air was filled with laughter and animation.
General Bostock (usually a timid bidder) called five spades
when the white kitten jumped on to his shoulder.

But what had happened? Why were we all now as gay as
children at a Christmas party? And this unwonted feeling of
friendliness—whence had it arisen? For half an hour, perhaps, the white kitten stayed with us: then he departed as
suddenly as he had come. But he left us transformed. There
was a murmur of plans for to-morrow: General Bostock
told a rather pointless story of a cat out in India, at which,
since his eyes were fixed upon me, I laughed heartily: the
conversation became genial, reminiscent, almost intimate.
Was the whole thing accidental, or was it some master-
stroke on the part of the management? Why should the
sight of a white kitten have so enlivened us? What secret,
passionate sympathy with youth was here revealed?

I do not know, but later in the night, really late in fact,
coming down for my book which I had forgotten, I switched
on the light and discovered the white kitten lying asleep in
the General's chair. So he had come back again when we
were gone! He looked as if a puff of wind might have blown
him away. The small, bright, hard cat-soul, wandering in a

feline dreamland, had left the slender, delicate body like a closed white flower. I glanced out into the hotel gardens— soft and shadowy in the moonlight. Then, though I knew that quite probably I should be making trouble for one of the servants in the morning, I opened a window, so that the white kitten, when he awakened, might go out into his own world.

1924.

AN ENDING

There are memories which seem to live of themselves, detached from and independent of the mind that gives them shelter; things seen from a distance and yet amazingly vivid, clear as the visions of an abnormal sleep, as the visions of delirium. There are things that may happen—quite easily happen to anybody, he told himself—things one can understand one's self, but which it is foolish to expect anybody else to understand. Brief lapses from a perfect sanity, yieldings to a sudden temptation, actions regretted instantly, but never forgotten by one's fellow-men, without whose esteem, trust and good-will, life becomes hardly possible. To have paid the legal penalty makes no difference; a public sentence is always a life sentence; when one 'gets out' one has to begin all over again, to build up a new life in new surroundings and among strangers, and often with very little of the desire for life remaining.

This he knew, but with the passing of years the thought had lost something of its first bitterness. He could regard it now impersonally, sometimes with a calm that approached indifference. It was as if in losing his identity for others, he had lost in the end much of it for himself. His place in the world was little more real than that of a ghost; his real life, his past life, seemed as remote as something he had read about and half forgotten.

Was it this that had held him here for so long in Bruges—a town of ghosts and memories? He had wandered through Europe, lingering by choice in those cities from which the tide of active competitive life had ebbed. He had lingered in Arles, he had lingered in Siena, but it was in Bruges that he had found peace. Here he could wander through silent streets and by decaying waterways with only the echo of his own footsteps for company, and there were days when he was almost surprised that he should awaken even so slight a sound as this.

Time at last stood still—morning and evening blended in a perpetual twilight. It had been like this ever since the illness from which he had not desired to recover, but from which, nevertheless, he *had* recovered, though with a gradually relaxing hold on material things, so that he had passed long hours in a kind of half-conscious lethargy, that only for brief and broken periods deepened into sleep.

His days were monotonous and placid. An illusory convalescence had thrown a strange pallor about them, had drawn, as it were, an effacing sponge across them, renewing a lost innocence of childhood. He got up late in the mornings; he went to bed early at night. In the afternoons he took slow loitering walks through the ancient city, pausing by silent canals, leaning over crumbling bridges, or entering some church, to sit there for an hour, and at last issue forth into the dusk of dark streets and faintly glimmering windows.

About five o'clock he would return to his rooms, or to a little café in the Grande Place. Here sometimes he would sit, looking across the great paved square, with the belfry straight before him, towering up against the sky. He would listen to the carillon, never very long silent, and watch the birds fly out from the tower with the first sound of the bells, to wheel about it in the evening light. And insensibly the fascination of Bruges had wound its way into his life. It was not that he took any joy in the beautiful decaying town, but that it had begun to seem a necessary part of his existence. He could not imagine himself living anywhere else. He was here like a vessel in a quiet harbour, a vessel that had been withdrawn finally from the storms and perils of the high seas, to lie safely at anchor in calm waters, with each to-morrow exactly like its yesterday. . . .

As the autumn advanced, and the evenings grew longer, he would take his walk sometimes on a grey misty after-noon that was soft as a caress. When it rained he could be seen walking slowly, with umbrella raised and bent head, by the silent waterways, over rough pavements and cobble-stones. The water grew paler under the rain; the outlines of things became blurred and dim; and solid buildings seemed to dissolve into a mist. The old houses, the old streets, the old bridges and canals, came to have a human appeal. They were sad with the same sadness he felt in his own soul; they appeared to sympathize, almost to under-stand; and unconsciously he began to love them. They dulled in some measure the faculty of memory; they helped to throw a veil of dreaming about his life; and there were moments when his sense of loss became hardly distinguish-able from the melancholy of Bruges itself, looking backward at the faint light of a vanished glory.

From the beginning he had gone much to the churches, had felt the morbid attraction of that religion which had found its perfect expression in the art of Roger van der Weyden. In the mornings he went to the little chapel of Saint Basil. It was the oldest of all, belonging to the twelfth century, and was without ornament of any kind. The roof was supported by pillars of rough freestone, and the floor was rudely paved. Here he would mingle with the kneeling peasants. Many candles filled the air with a smell of burning wax, and threw a pale light on worn, unlovely faces. Sometimes he went to the church of Saint Jacques, or to Saint Sauveur, and sometimes to the chapel of Our Lady of the Pottery. As he knelt alone, or with some kneeling penitent by his side, a mystic emotion would gain possession of him, but never to bring him happiness, or strength to escape from the shadows. For the religion of Bruges was wholly medieval. It was a religion of sorrow, of the sorrowing Mother of God and of the wounded Christ. That pale tortured figure, crowned with thorns and in the agony of the Crucifixion, hung everywhere above dim altars. The blood from the pierced hands and feet and side flowed in a perpetual twilight heavy with the burden and mystery of sin and death; and in the quietude and lassitude of a diminishing vitality he found a vague relief in yielding himself to its power. Then, in the darkness of his spirit, he sometimes saw a faint far light that had once shone clear, but was now diminished to a remote gleam, flickering ever more feebly in an immense blackness. . . .

To-day something in the mildness of the air tempted him abroad earlier than usual. The soundless mellow afternoon into which he emerged was full of sunlight. Leaning on his stick he walked slowly in the direction of the Béguinage, by old red-brick houses of the fifteenth and sixteenth centuries, with quaint bas-reliefs and carvings, and at every street corner, set in a niche in the wall, an image of the Virgin in painted wood or plaster. When he reached his destination he sat down on the dry grass under one of the tall straight trees, sat there in mild enjoyment of the warmth of the sun, his mind almost vacant, alive only to the few simple sights and sounds that composed his immediate surroundings. He could see the tower of the church of Notre Dame rising above the red-tiled roofs of the low houses, clear against a pale blue sky that shaded to yellow as it dropped down to the house-tops. The grass all round him was being cut, and the smell of it was pleasant, and the soft sleepy mowing of the scythes, and the creaking of a cart on three wheels. The scene soothed him—the dark horse who had eaten so much that he could hardly nibble the few mouthfuls he still plucked from time to time, the coloured butterflies, the little girl in a lilac cotton dress. She was raking the loose grass into heaps, and her legs and feet were bare. A man in brown corduroys and a blue shirt was on top of the cart, spreading out and packing the grass.

The leaves of the trees were silver and gilt and bronze. A recluse passed in her black dress and white hood from the chapel to her own house, followed by a small dog barking shrilly. The spirit of late summer was abroad and playing softly on his pipe to the ripening autumn. From time to time a brown leaf fluttered down through the windless air.

Fearing to sit too long upon the grass, he rose to continue his walk, but as he passed out through the porch he saw a crowd gathered on the bank of the Lac d'Amour, a little beyond the sluice-house. Some children ran by him, and he knew enough Flemish to catch the words 'drowned . . . yesterday. . . .' He hesitated, and then an unhealthy curiosity impelled him, as it had impelled so many others, in the direction of the group upon the bank—the dark compact group that he guessed to be formed about a recovered body. On his approach they made way for him, one or two began to explain eagerly, but he did not listen, did not hear any-

R

thing as he gazed fixedly down. It was a boy of twelve or thirteen. The water was still oozing from his stained and ragged clothing, and spreading out in a dark patch on the soil. The hands were clenched: the face was uncovered. The blue eyes were wide open; the corners of the mouth drooped; and there was a frown on the forehead which gave a strange expression of sternness, almost of anger, to the whole countenance. The fixed and sightless eyes stared up at the sky as if with an implacable enmity. A strip of green water-weed was mixed into the dark hair close above the ear.

Every moment the circle of onlookers—eager, loquacious, animated—was joined by fresh arrivals, and to each new-comer was repeated the tale of what had happened. He had been drowned yesterday. He had been playing by the lake with two other boys and had fallen in. His companions had made no attempt to help him, though they now said that they had. On the contrary, they had taken to their heels. Their cowardice had even kept them dumb until an hour or two ago, when one of them had confessed. Little wretches! they were in mortal terror of the police and now both were in hiding. The dead boy's father stood over the body, voluble and excited—gesticulating, weeping, obviously not quite sober. Children made frantic efforts to squeeze their way into the front row in order to get a better view.

Suddenly there was a disturbance in the crowd: the com-pact circle expanded, broke, turned about. A boy, howling at the top of his voice, kicking, biting, struggling, weeping, was being dragged along by a dishevelled, swollen-faced woman, the mother of the dead. Evidently the hiding-place of one of the culprits had been discovered. All eyes were turned on this strange couple as they approached in jerks and spasmodic rushes. Then another mother—that of the screaming, terrified offender—who till now had been hanging back on the outskirts of the crowd, recognized her son and sprang to the rescue. The boy redoubled his cries. . . .

He moved away. He forced a passage through the jostling ring of spectators and turned homeward, walking hurriedly, as if from something he desired to leave behind him as rapidly as possible. But before he had reached his own house a sudden faintness came upon him, and for a moment everything grew dim. By an effort he managed to reach one of the seats beside the Dyver, where he sank down, trembling and exhausted. An utter weariness had come upon him, and he seemed to watch the world grow old before his eyes. The futility and unloveliness of his own life—of all those other lives—was borne in upon him, and his spirit drew back aghast before that meaningless waste. There was nothing he could understand, nothing he could cling to, humanity least of all. A feeling of helplessness swept over him in a heavy, drowning tide, leaving him without power to act, without power to think. He had a sense of a black cold void opening out all round him, of an infinite darkness. He seemed to be standing on a tiny patch of raised ground, while all about him was that enveloping sea of darkness: and the darkness was drawing nearer and nearer as the ground on which he stood crumbled away. For a moment he felt as if he were crying aloud, but no sound was uttered. It was the cold, the awful cold and the loneliness, before which his spirit recoiled. Then, all at once, into the surrounding gloom there floated the pale face of the drowned boy, frowning up at the sky— the face of an outcast, an antagonist, an enemy of mankind. The scene rose up before him again, with all it had revealed of callous, scarcely-repressed enjoyment; and he felt the same horror of life as he had felt at the vision of death. . . .

He was alone. He too was an outcast. . . .

The broad path was strewn with dead leaves, and the three rows of tall lime-trees kept watch over the sleeping waters of the city. In the distance the tower of the belfry stood out against a fading sky. Before him, rising straight from the water, was a garden wall built of grey stone. On the right was the beautiful Quai du Rosaire, on the left a bridge, and above his head the limes, strangely lovely in their tall grave silence. The leaves were yellow, and the ground was covered with those that had already fallen; the setting sun had left a light of gold and silver in the sky; the water of the canal was still green, but very dark, almost black. The carillon began to chime the hour: the sound beat out into the air and died away.

He was alone: and now all his life appeared stretched out behind him like a desert, without a path, without a sign. The evening was nearly over. The carillon chimed half-past six, and two or three labourers clattered behind him, on their way home. Here and there a light showed in a window. Yet still he waited on, while the sky grew paler and paler, the earth darker and darker. Then the old canals seemed to become more silent and melancholy than ever before; the swans dreamed upon the water; and Bruges slipped back farther and farther into the past.

1911.

THE TRUANT

He was nearly fourteen, and never out of trouble: irresponsible, idle, backward as a boy of ten, learning nothing at school, constantly on the verge of expulsion, restless, unpopular with both boys and masters, sometimes acting like a coward, at others doing the most reckless things—a source of constant anxiety to his parents and of mingled curiosity and apprehension to their neighbours—yet withal affectionate and generous, though never self-forgetful and always disobedient.

He came out of the house, a couple of school books and his lunch stuffed in his pockets. His mother watched him from the window as he swung loosely down the street in the bright June sunshine, all his movements awkward and ungainly as those of a young colt, his school cap at the back of his head, his dark eyes glancing from side to side as if on the look-out for enemies in ambush. He knew she was watching him, so while he remained in sight he walked straight on at a steady pace; but the moment he turned the corner the steady pace was abandoned. Outside the window of a confectioner's he hovered uncertainly, his face close to the pane, while he studied the piles of sweets arranged in little glass dishes and covered with a muslin veil to keep off flies. It was the muslin veil that decided him, for he was extremely fastidious. He pushed open the door, and a bell instantly responded with a sharp 'ping'. A woman came into the shop from a back room while he was shuffling his feet and staring round the shelves. The sweets he asked for were in a glass jar immediately behind her, and while her back was turned he lifted a flat package of chocolate from the counter and slipped it under his jacket.

He went out again into the morning sunlight. Already he did not know why he had taken the chocolate. He had simply obeyed an impulse of the moment. There were many things he did in this way, without understanding why he did them —things he did not particularly want to do—things, often, that brought him no pleasure, so that he had not even that excuse. And he felt no pleasure at present. On the contrary, his mind was troubled, though not by this matter of the chocolate. But there was something else—something a great deal more important, since it could not be hidden much longer. To-day was Friday, and he had not been to school for nearly a week.

On the Monday he had played truant of his own will, partly because of the sunlight in the trees, partly because he was sick of detentions and of being sent up to the headmaster. On Tuesday he had played truant to recapture Monday's happiness, and because he might as well defer the inevitable punishment for another day. On Tuesday night he had tried his hand at forging an excuse, but the result had been hopeless, and he had been wise enough to destroy it. Since then he would gladly have been back at school: since then he had played truant out of sheer funk, because he could not face the consequences—the punishment at school, and the thrashing his father would give him afterwards. These things loomed terrifyingly in his mind when he remembered them. But sometimes he forgot them, and he tried to forget them now.

He stood in the shadow of a doorway while he scanned the white dusty length of sunlit road for possible boys. All were enemies, and while rejoicing to see him still skulking about, would take a pleasure in reminding him of the trouble he was making for himself. However, the coast seemed to be clear, so he set off at a clumsy jog-trot, making for the open country and the river.

Presently his pace slackened and he began to nibble at his chocolate. The green summer world was alive with whisperings and hummings. He stopped by a garden gate to watch two very small children playing on the grass inside. He gave them his chocolate and most of the other sweets he had bought, then went on his way. And that too was impulse. He was as greedy as any other boy, but not nearly so provident. He was always giving away things: he would give anything he possessed to anybody who asked for it: but though this idiosyncrasy was well known to his companions, who were quick to profit by it, he himself gained nothing, because shortly afterwards he invariably did something to revive their animosity.

He left the road, crossed a meadow, climbed an ancient stone wall, and dropped down into the long grass on the other side. Through the grass he went, brushing the cuckoo-spittles off against his stockinged legs and bare knees, throwing his cap after a bee that hummed by his cheek. He entered the woods, breaking a path through the dense undergrowth, his feet sinking in a thick matted carpet of dead leaves. Where the trees had been thinned the sun poured down, picking out green pool-like glades that were brimmed with coloured light as a pool is brimmed with water. It was a world of light and shadow into which he passed—green and gold and violet, and filled with music. When he came out upon the bank above the river he flung himself down in the soft grass, lying on his back, gazing up through the shining leaves of a beech-tree at the dark blue sky.

He seemed a part of this world into which he had wandered: he seemed a part of its radiant beauty and freshness. Everything here—the birds, the beetles with their burnished wing-cases shining like precious stones, the delicate plants, the trees, the silent river, the soft deep sky—brought each its own offering of beauty; and he brought his. But he brought something else as well: he brought the imagination in which it all lived and became conscious. Out of his dark eyes the trouble and the sadness passed. He had forgotten; and his spirit had become one with his surroundings. He drank up the beauty of the earth, and it quenched deliciously some hidden thirst in him. He was happy. That faculty for living only in the present which was the source of so many of his troubles could at times also be a boon. He had no thought now for the punishments that awaited him, for the gloomy prognostications so often made as to his future. Forgotten were the troubles at home, the troubles at school, the troubles which always cropped up sooner or later when he was playing with other boys—he had passed, for this brief hour at least, into the heart of Nature.

He felt himself inactive yet free, like a plant growing in the grass. This was the sort of thing he enjoyed—to wander away into the broad world where each day he could begin life anew—unfettered, unknown, ready to make friends and to pass on (for he was good at making friends but very bad at keeping them), yet quite content to be alone. . . .

He lay for a long time very quiet. Then he sat up and began to eat his lunch. It was barely two hours since his breakfast, and he was not really hungry, but he ate more than half his lunch and threw the rest away. This throwing away of what at the moment he did not want was typical. He had always been like that. The future, or any future more remote than a week hence, did not really, perhaps never would, exist for him.

He lit a cigarette and smoked it. The blue smoke curling up lazily through the still air pleased him. But out of his dream he was abruptly wakened by the sound of voices and the noise of oars moving in rowlocks. He hid himself till the boat had passed, for it might just possibly contain somebody he knew. Nor did he come out from his hiding-place till the voices were faint in the distance; then he crept forth and resumed his old position. Once more he stretched himself on his back and gazed up through the dark beech leaves at the sky, but the interruption had disturbed him, a shadow slid back into his mind, and he remembered the punishment he had received when he had last played truant, and his solemn promise then given, that he would never do so again.

It was not really his fault, he told himself. It had not been his fault before. It was the fault of one of the masters who persistently made a butt of him, who burdened him with detentions and impositions. He hated this man. He had tried to speak to his father about him, to explain that he was not fairly treated, that the man disliked him; but his father had only been annoyed, and not with the master. They were all against him, both at home and at school. His own people regarded him as a source of endless trouble, and other people, when they wanted to find an excuse for him, hinted that he was not quite normal. He had heard them, and it was the only excuse he ever *had* heard. He didn't care whether he was normal or not. He was just as normal as he wanted to be, or as they were, a lot of——

But at that moment, through the trees, he caught sight of a hare sitting up watching him. Instantly his mood altered, and he remembered a fairy story he had read, about a hare who was really an old witch. He liked fairy stories, though he kept his taste for them a secret from the other boys, who would have considered it a further proof of his oddity. This, indeed, had been one of his few acts of discretion. But at present, all alone, he had no need to hide his likes or dislikes, and he let his mind slip away into a magical world, and again his troubles vanished. The hot sunshine was lovely; he could feel it even where he was lying in the broken, dappled shadow of the beech: it was like a warm sea in which he floated. He loved it; he loved all the beautiful things around him; he loved the earth, and the river, and the trees, and the sky. . . .

He repeated a poem he had learned at school—about a Lady of Shalott. He half closed his eyes and watched this Lady of Shalott through a green leafy veil. The pictures swam up to him as through a deep green water, then sank away again and were lost. He opened his eyes wider. A bright light lay over everything, and an imaginary scene took the place of the actual scene before him. He saw a countryside rich with green grass and wild flowers. He saw red sleepy poppies and blue cornflowers, and ripe fields of bending barley. He saw the beauty of the earth—of silver streams and green woods —of blue, tree-shaded wells: and somehow he knew that from all these things the strength of his life had been drawn; and he worshipped the spirit of the earth—worshipped with an unconscious adoration and a conscious delight—as he surrendered his mind and soul to the joy of the passing hour.

The imagined picture melted back into a reality more familiar but not less beautiful. He got up and went down to the river's edge. He made a poem about the river, and spoke it aloud as he made it:

THE TRUANT

O river, I love you!
I love your dark water
And the blue sky above you;
And the barge that slowly glides
Through your water;
And the solemn cows who stand
Knee-deep in your water;
And the old grey barge-horse,
And the green grassy bank,
And the green trees that dip
Down to your water;
And the white clouds that sail
Like white ships through your water.
O river, I love you!
O earth, I love you!
I love you! I love you!

With his penknife he cut off a lock of his crisp brown hair and threw it to the river—a gift, or a sacrifice. Hugging his bare knees he sat on the bank watching his brown lock of hair floating on and on, borne by a swift current, in and out, past little islands from which water-rats peeped out with bright eyes, past old grey crumbling bridges, past mossy stones and scarlet-and-blue weirs, past smooth lawns and ripening cornfields, and meadows, and woods—on and on, down and down.

But the river at last widened out into a shallow pool, and in this pool some young girls were bathing; and one of them was a princess and the others were her maidens. The lock of hair reached the pool and was floating away when the princess saw it. She lifted it out of the water and hid it from the others, while they, laughing and calling, continued to splash the bright glittering water to the sky.

The princess hurried to the bank, and ran up the wide marble stairs to the palace, and hurried to her own room. Then, when she had dressed herself, she put the hair in her bosom, and all day long till nightfall it lay upon her warm breast like a bird brooding on its own happiness. But in the night, when she was alone, and not a sound disturbed the stillness, she took the hair from its secret hiding-place, and laid it upon her pillow where the moonlight touched it. And the princess knew that it was a boy's hair. She looked at it as it lay so brown on her white pillow, and from its beauty she created this boy's beauty, and as she kissed it the hair began to sing.

It sang a love song: it called her out into the woods, and she obeyed its call. She took one thread of the hair, and it gave her light, and guided her through the palace. The locked doors opened of themselves when she laid the single thread of hair against them. They swung back noiselessly on their heavy hinges and closed noiselessly behind her. The boat into which she stepped unmoored itself from the bank as she laid the thread of hair upon it, and glided swiftly upstream to the enchanted forest. And he—he watched it all, and was waiting in the moonlight beside the river when the boat drew in to the bank and the princess stepped ashore. He saw her childish beauty and the love in her eyes. He opened his arms and she came to him; and they stood like that, cheek by cheek.

Voices: the sound of oars moving in rowlocks. He sat up. Again the impulse to hide came to him, but it came too late, so he sat on where he was. The boat glided past. Somebody looked up. Others looked up too, but the one who had looked first knew him and waved a hand. She was not his princess—no indeed. She called out, 'Enjoying yourself?'

He watched the boat till it disappeared round the bend.

His face had darkened. The greeting had been more sarcastic than friendly, and he had not replied to it. She had known very well that he must be miching from school, and since she lived in the same avenue, probably would take the opportunity to mention to his mother that she had seen him. He hoped something would happen—that she would slip on the slippery landing-stage and be hauled dripping out of the water amid general derision.

But this was unlikely, and suddenly he smiled; his ill-humour had passed. Perhaps if he went home now he would arrive more or less at the right time and no questions would be asked—unless that girl had been before him. Not that it mattered much, since he was going to tell his mother anyway. He would tell her the moment he arrived, and get it over. He might be punished, but somehow the thought of punishment no longer troubled him. For in his spirit the leaves of the enchanted forest were whispering still, and deep down in his heart he felt that one day it would all come true.

1918.

AN ULSTER FARM

I had stayed at the house several times, putting up there for the night, but this evening when I reached it, and found that the old man had been seriously ill for some weeks, it seemed to me that the best thing I could do would be to push on to the nearest hotel.

He was lying in bed in the big kitchen when I came in, lying in a kind of stupor, and as I looked down at the grey, drawn, uncomely face I saw that death was not far off. Yet I confess my pity was not at all for the sufferer, but for the woman and the boy who stood with me at his bedside. I knew that when the father was gone everything would pass into the hands of the elder son, and I could guess what that would mean for these two. The father had been a hard man all his life—grasping and mean—yet I doubted if he had saved a great deal. The farm had never seemed to me particularly prosperous; it had never *looked* prosperous; and too much money had been spent on whiskey. He had worked the place himself, with the help of his two sons and an ancient serving-man. If it had not been for his wife, who stooped over him now, arranging the pillows and smoothing the sheet, things would have gone to the bad long ago. She had been the saving spirit, and she was a woman for whom I felt a great respect. Much younger than her husband, her married life had not been an enviable one. Indeed, what I had admired about her most of all was just the way in which she had contrived to maintain peace in that ill-assorted household. For the old man had been dour and suspicious, a hard drinker and a fault-finder, and the jealousy between the sons was bitter. In age there was a difference of at least ten years between them. The old man had married twice, and Michael, a boy of twenty, was the child of the second marriage. He took after his mother; was blue-eyed and ruddy-cheeked; and had the same kindly manner, the same frank expression. John, on the contrary, was as surly a boor as I have ever met, sullen when sober and quarrelsome when drunk.

'How long has he been like this?' I asked, as we stood by the bed of the dying man, listening to his hoarse, laboured breathing; and the mother told me he had been gradually getting weaker from day to day. For several nights they had taken it in turn to sit up with him, but this morning he had seemed a little better. It was only towards noon that he had dropped into this strange unnatural sleep, of which even now they did not seem to me to realize the significance.

'John'll surely be back soon,' she added. 'I don't know what's kept him. He should have been here at six. He'll be bringing tea and meal and flour and Maggie McCann with him. Maggie's a good nurse, and offered to come.'

I made a few further inquiries, but I could not ask the question which I felt would have been most to the point—namely, what she and Michael intended to do when the farm came into John's hands. John, as I knew, had been wanting to get married for a year back, and the farm would scarcely support two families.

'Well, I think I'd better be pushing on. I'll just see first if my lamp's all right.'

'Sure, you'll not go out again a dirty night like that!' the mother exclaimed in surprise. 'It's teeming rain and you're wet through already. You needn't think you'll be in the way here. I'd tell you fast enough if you were.'

The boy added something in support of this invitation, and I hesitated. The idea of venturing forth into the November evening was anything but attractive. The nearest town was six or seven miles distant, the rain was coming down as if it never intended to stop, and I had been pushing my bicycle for the last hour against a strong head wind and over roads thick with mud. In the end I allowed myself to be persuaded. I retired with Michael, to borrow his Sunday clothes while my own were hung up to dry; then we all three drew our chairs up to the fire and sat talking in low tones, though the precaution was unnecessary, for no sound we might make was likely to penetrate the deep sleep in which the old man lay.

I asked what the doctor had said about him, and the mother shrugged her shoulders. It was evident that the doctor's skill was not held in high esteem. Much more faith was placed in Maggie McCann; but Michael, who had been staring gloomily into the fire, now looked up. 'Maggie'll har'ly come a night like this,' he said to his mother, and as if in support of his opinion a sudden gust of wind and rain beat furiously against the house, making me mightily glad that I had remained where I was.

'No, she'll har'ly,' the mother agreed, casting an anxious glance at the bed. 'And I can't think what's come on John. I told him to fix up with Maggie first thing; and anyway he should have been back these hours!'

I could tell from her voice that she was more than uneasy, and I knew from my own experience what the cause of her uneasiness was likely to be. The wind moaned dolefully round the chimneys and then sank into silence.

Michael, who had sat up with his father most of the preceding night, began to nod in his chair. But every now and then he would straighten himself with a jerk, blinking sleepy blue eyes, while a slow faint smile spread over his broad face. His mother suggested that he should go to bed, but he would not. Presently she went to prepare my own bed, and the boy turned to me. 'It'll take me to wait and see how John comes home. He'll have been drinking an' forgot all about Maggie.'

'I'll sit up,' I told him. 'I can look after him if he needs it.'

But he shook his head. 'No—no. Mother she's making your bed ready now. You've no call to be bothering. You don't know what he's like either when he's a drop in him. He goes fair mad on it whiles.'

At this moment the mother returned, and Michael's confidences abruptly ceased. We watched her while she laid the table for supper; then, when we had eaten our porridge, we returned to the fire. It was evident that she, too, was going to wait up for John.

Hour after hour passed. We had long since relapsed into silence, and I myself had dropped into a doze, from which I was awakened by the rattle of wheels and the barking of Rory the sheepdog. I started up in my chair, and glancing instinctively at the clock in the corner saw that it was after midnight. I must have slept for nearly two hours. Michael had risen to his feet and was listening intently. We could hear a low scuffling sound, and then suddenly the door was flung wide with a crash, and three men staggered into the room—dirty, bedraggled, soaked to the skin, looking as if they had been rolled in the mud—John, the farm-servant, and a stranger.

They were too drunk even to think of unloading the cart,

and this I helped Michael to do, but all was in a woeful mess. The waterproof cover had come off, and had apparently been dropped somewhere on the road, allowing the rain to pour in on flour and meal, which lay unprotected in a sodden heap at the bottom of the cart. 'See how he's fouled everything, damn him!' the boy muttered, as we got the stuff out and carried it into the kitchen. The servant-man and the stranger had collapsed upon the floor; John had disappeared; and the mother must have gone with him to look after him. The old man in the bed was still asleep.

Michael attended to the horse and cart, while I dragged the flour and meal in front of the fire. Then, not too gently, I pulled the drunk men into a corner out of the way, where they lay like logs, in their dripping clothes. 'What are you going to do with them?' I asked Michael when he came back.

'Throw them out,' he answered savagely, and no doubt he would have done so, but at this moment John, with an unopened bottle of whiskey in his hand, staggered into the room. He was followed by the mother, who had overheard Michael's threat, and now laid a restraining hand on his arm.

'Let them be,' she said. 'You can't be putting them out a night like that.'

'It's *his* fault—drunken swine!' Michael answered; but John, struggling ineffectually to open the whiskey bottle, was too absorbed in his task to take notice of the words, even if he had heard them.

At last he succeeded in drawing the cork. 'Gi'me a glass. Gi'me a glass,' he repeated stupidly.

Michael attempted to take the bottle from him. 'Don't you think you've had enough already?' he asked in a low voice that had something dangerous in it.

'What the hell's that to you?' He shook Michael off and his dull little eyes, glazed with drink, turned to the dresser beside the hearth, where a row of tumblers stood on the top shelf. In an effort to reach up to them he overbalanced himself, and very nearly brought the whole thing down. Yet, through all, he clung with marvellous skill, or luck, to the bottle. Lurching to the supper table he lifted a cup and half filled it with the raw spirit. We had begun to straighten things up, and at any rate what followed was so rapid and unexpected that we could not have prevented it. With incredible swiftness he darted to the bed and hauled his father into a sitting position; then, thrusting back the old man's head, he poured the contents of the cup partly down his throat and partly over his beard and nightshirt. There was a choking sound; the mother rushed to the rescue; and at the same moment Michael hit out at John with his clenched fist. It was a powerful blow, and John sprawled on the floor, the back of his head striking the stone flags with an unpleasant thud. The dying man was seized with a paroxysm of coughing which tore him from head to foot and must have snapped the slender thread of life remaining in him, for a few minutes later, when we lowered him back on his pillows, he lay quite still. The colour had sunk out of his face as water sinks through sand; his eyes remained open in a blank stare; his jaw had dropped; and though we continued our efforts to revive him, I for one knew that they were wasted.

Meanwhile the three men lay on the floor—two of them asleep, while from the mouth of the third a dark mess of blood was slowly oozing out over the tiles. The mother dropped into a chair, and leaned over the supper-table, bowing her face in her hands. She began to cry softly, and the sound of her weeping mingled wretchedly with the drunken snores.

1914.

COSTELLO'S STORY

All day long we had been tramping among the hills, and in the dusk, when we returned to Costello's house, I was very glad to sit down before a comfortable fire, with several dogs sprawling at my feet, and my host seated on the opposite side of the hearth. It was my first visit to him, and I had arrived only the night before. The house stood bare and lonely on the shore of a grey shallow lake. The nearest village was several miles away. The scenery, indeed, was lovely, but it was a loveliness of desolation, with wide tracts of bog-land threaded by narrow mountain roads. In winter, I thought, this desolation must be complete, and Costello, to have made his permanent home in such a spot, must either share Wordsworth's passionate devotion to Nature, or else have friends and resources of which I knew nothing. After all, it was a long time since we had last met.

I was ruminating on these things when he looked up from the gun he had been cleaning and asked me, 'Do you know what day this is?'

The question, following a long silence, was unexpected, and I had to think for a moment before replying. 'Isn't it the thirty-first? Hallowe'en?'

Costello nodded and returned to his task.

I glanced at the thin dark face, which, in spite of the surrounding evidence of dogs and guns and fishing-rods, struck me as more that of an anchorite than of a sportsman. But Costello had always been a mystery to me. He was fond of fishing and shooting, I knew; yet the house was full of books, there were books in every room—they even overflowed on to the landings—and I supposed he read them. We had known each other for many years. He had been a boarder at the northern school where I had been a day-boy, and though even then I had thought him odd and moody, his complete indifference to the laws and conventions of both boys and masters had pleased and amused me, and we had become friends. True, there had been uneasy hours when the friendship had seemed to be chiefly on my side, but I could never be sure. That was the difficulty. After a period of chilling uncommunicativeness his manner would suddenly alter and become responsive and affectionate. In the end I schooled myself to accept these unsympathetic lapses, though I still continued to find them disconcerting, and could never even quite persuade myself that they were involuntary.

'It is also my birthday,' he now added—'Hallowe'en. . . . And the day on which my mother died.'

The last words came after a pause, and did not appear to have been addressed to me, so I made no remark. Then he glanced at me sidelong and I saw that I *had* been intended to hear them. 'I am going to tell you a story', he said, 'that I have never told to anybody else. I dare say you will think it was because it wasn't worth telling, and I know it is capable of a very simple explanation. Still, that is for you to judge. I won't say that my mind is open to conviction, for apparently it is not. I mean, there is very little use telling yourself that two and two make four when immediately afterwards you begin to wonder if they can't possibly make five.'

Again he paused, and I sat waiting, listening to the wind,

and to the sound of diminutive waves breaking on the lake shore.

Costello put down his gun; whereupon one of the dogs instantly rose and laid a head on his knee to be stroked. He stroked it, while he stared into the fire.

'My father, as you know, was a country doctor, and I was an only child. I was badly brought up, for my mother was capricious, thoughtless, and impulsive, and I was her constant companion. This last was natural enough, since otherwise she would have been completely alone. She had married, you see, out of her own class, being a peasant by birth, and even in those days I had a dim suspicion that both she and my father had come to realize that the marriage had been a mistake. *He* certainly had, and, as is not uncommon, my sympathies, which then were given entirely to my mother, have since turned more to him. I now think it was because of the failure of his domestic life that he was usually out during the greater part of the day, and sometimes of the night as well. For he had private means and could easily have afforded to pay an assistant.

'His practice was a very mixed one—large, but not, I should imagine, particularly lucrative—and the houses of his patients being scattered all over the countryside, he had a good deal of driving to do. When I got to be about eight or nine he would sometimes propose to take me with him—an arrangement that would have delighted me—but though I clamoured and protested my mother invariably found an excuse to keep me at home. Her love for me, indeed, was so jealous and exacting that she could hardly bear me to be out of her sight for a moment. She herself taught me to read, and my education, like her own, ended there; yet when on one occasion my father began to talk about a boarding-school, she met the idea with such a storm of tears and indignation

that he walked out of the room in disgust, leaving us together; and he never—in my presence at least—mentioned
the subject again.

'There came, however, a day—it was my eleventh birthday—when my father was summoned to a patient who lived
at a distance, and as a birthday treat he proposed to take
me with him. It was an unusually mild morning for the
time of year—the last day of October—and as I begged very
hard to be allowed to go, my mother in the end consented.
When we returned in the evening she was dead.'

Costello's eyes narrowed slightly, and I guessed that this
was a crucial point in the story.

'She had died of heart-failure; I never heard more than
that. But what seems to me not quite irrelevant, in the light
of after events, is that I found a strange difficulty in believing, or at any rate in realizing, that she *was* dead. Even when,
two days later, I was taken into the room to see her lying in
her coffin, I could not realize it. Those closed eyes, that
white face smoothed into an utterly strange and frozen
stillness, did not suggest my mother to me in any other way
than a faithfully carved image might. I shed no tears, and
both then and during the weeks that followed I must have
earned for myself a reputation for unnatural callousness.

'A not unwelcome change in my life took place almost at
once. I was sent to the village school, and when I was not at
school I was running wild about the countryside. A year
passed thus—a year during which my existence was as different as well could be from what it had been in the past. Why
the boarding-school scheme was not now put into practice
I do not know, but it wasn't. An elderly woman kept house
for us, but she had no control over me, and except at meals
I rarely saw my father. Frequently I miched from school,
and always I was at the bottom of my class. I grew more and

more uncivilized. At school I became inured to punishments, and at home I told lies.

'This was the state of things when one morning, having decided not to go to school, I set out for a ramble among the hills. My progress was erratic and frequently interrupted, but at length I reached the foot of them. The country here was barren and rocky, the only trees being a few twisted thorn-trees, so dry and bleached that their whitened trunks looked as if they had been carved out of stone. In a sheltered nook beside a stream I ate my lunch, and after I had finished, feeling lazy and comfortable, I shut my eyes to drowze for a moment or two. That, at least, was my intention, but when I awakened I felt cold and stiff. I must, in fact, have slept for a long time, because the day was gone, and it was bright moonlight. In all that wild stony landscape I could see no living thing except a white gull with a grey cap on his head, who sat motionless on a withered branch. As I hopped about to warm myself he opened a long, narrow, red bill, gave a harsh cry, and flew away. Then it struck me that he ought to have been in bed and asleep hours ago. Surely there was something strange about him! And I suddenly remembered that this was my birthday, and therefore Hallowe'en, and that on this very day last year my mother had died.

'But I am not easily frightened, nor was I frightened now —even when I saw a small, bent old man coming towards me from the hills. He certainly *looked* old, yet he walked quickly, skipping over the rocks with a goat-like agility. When he was within a few yards he stopped and called out, "Richard Costello, a friend has sent me to bring you to her. She is waiting for you now." He pointed to the hills behind him, and without pausing to see whether I were following or not, turned back in that direction.

'He went indeed so quickly that it was all I could do to

keep up with him, and as we wound about among the boulders it seemed to me that we were taking an unnecessarily crooked path. For perhaps ten minutes he led me on, and then the path, which had become more and more like a cleft leading straight into the hillside, suddenly broadened out into an open grassy space, at the edge of which I saw my mother. I halted abruptly, but still I felt more astonished than afraid. My mother smiled and called to me, "It is all right, Richard; don't be frightened." And when she caught me in her arms and kissed me and laughed, and I felt her warm hands and face pressed against mine, I knew that she was alive and not a ghost.

' "But how did you come here, mother?" I asked her.

' "I have come to live here, Richard," she said. Then she kissed me again. "How rough and untidy your clothes are! And your hair! Why haven't they looked after you better?" She began to smooth my hair and to give little pulls at my clothes, and every now and then, between the pulls, she would take me in her arms.

' "But I saw you lying on the bed, mother," I persisted.

' "No, no," she said, still laughing, though a little impatiently. "That was nothing—only a dead branch left there when I came away. I sent for you, Richard, because I want you to be here too. We are going to be so happy together. But you will see—you will see for yourself."

'With her hand resting on my shoulder, I gazed around me. At a little distance were a number of people—men and women, boys and girls—among them the old man who had been my guide. They were forming into couples, and presently I heard the bright thin sound of a fiddle playing a gay tune, and one by one the couples began to dance. A girl smiled at me and threw me a golden ball, which I caught. But I was too shy to return it. Besides, if it were an invitation to dance with her, I had always hated dancing. So I stood by my mother, looking on. She, however, loved dancing, and as we watched the others I saw her feet beginning to move in sympathy, and next moment she half pushed, half led, me forward, and I tried, very clumsily, to dance with her.

'It was not, on my part, a success, and we soon stopped. And then everybody else stopped, and when they moved aside I saw a feast spread out on the grass—fruit in golden dishes, milk and honey and cakes. And my mother told me to choose whatever I liked best. The others had sat down, but no one had yet begun to eat. "They are waiting for you," my mother whispered. "You are their guest."

'Then I took a bunch of dark grapes from the nearest dish, and as I looked up I saw a circle of alert, watching, smiling faces. I was on the point of putting one of the grapes into my mouth when a sudden notion seized me to say grace. It was a mere whim; nevertheless I bowed my head and began in a low voice. And hardly had the first word passed my lips when the whole of that seated company rose into the air like a thin grey cloud, and melted away before my eyes. From somewhere far above my head I heard my mother's sorrowful cry, and next minute I found myself alone at the foot of the hills, and quite close to the stream, with the moon shining down on me.'

'So it was only a dream,' I said. 'When I was a youngster how annoyed I used to be if a story ended like that! You ought at least to have wakened near the spot to which the old man had led you.' But Costello took no notice of this comment, simply sat there, with his eyes now half shut.

He had heard me, nevertheless, for when he next broke silence it was to agree, though the tone of his voice, I felt, was not quite satisfactory. 'I dare say it was a dream; but you must remember that I was brought up among people who believed in ghosts and fairies. My mother believed firmly in them, and often talked of them; and in nearly every village somebody could be pointed out who had been "away".'

I did not answer. I remembered tales he had told me when we were schoolboys, but I thought he ought to have outgrown such superstitions by this time. I now very much doubted if he had, though in most directions his mind was an extremely practical one. I listened to the wind crying round the chimneys, and was rather relieved, I confess, that when Costello spoke again it was to ask me if I knew of a cure for eczema. One of his dogs was suffering from it, and the ointment recommended by a Dublin vet seemed to be doing him no good.

1914.

AUTUMN

Slowly, one by one,
Through the damp-smelling, misty air of autumn the delicate
    leaves drop down,
Covering the grass like a carpet—
A carpet woven in gold and crimson:—
And the sun,
Shining through the bare black trees,
Turns to a glory of gold these dying woods.

Ah! if any poet
Could stay that brief splendid vision,
Gather these autumn glories into his song,
What joy were his!
Let the winds scatter
The broken scarlet web of autumn wide over the world!
Soft with sleep,
Let the delicate air sigh through the naked branches,
That still preserve their beauty,
Though a barer, a more austere beauty than the green beauty
    of summer.

Now the sap of life runs low:
All that we did in life's springtime and summer seems far
    away.

AUTUMN

Faint as a dream, and quiet, the sports of those days—the
    shouts and the laughter.

Sad enough they seem

Now that we know well how brief and how fragile they
    were.

Gone, gone, is that merriment. Only an echo remains while
    the curtain of night is descending:

But how lovely that echo:—

Lovelier far than the shouts and the laughter, the songs and
    the childish play:—

Lovely as autumn.

1916.